The New Transatlantic Agenda and the Future of EU-US Relations

The New Transatlantic Agenda and the Future of EU-US Relations

Editor

Jörg Monar

KLUWER LAW
INTERNATIONAL
LONDON – THE HAGUE – BOSTON

Published by
Kluwer Law International Ltd
Sterling House
66 Wilton Road
London SW1V 1DE
United Kingdom

Kluwer Law International incorporates
the publishing programmes of
Graham & Trotman Ltd,
Kluwer Law & Taxation Publishers
and Martinus Nijhoff Publishers

Sold and distributed in
the USA and Canada by
Kluwer Law International
675 Massachusetts Avenue
Cambridge MA 02139
USA

In all other countries sold and distributed by
Kluwer Law International
PO Box 322
3300 AH Dordrecht
The Netherlands

ISBN 90 411 9676 5
© Kluwer Law International 1998
First published 1998

British Library Cataloguing in Publication Data
A catalogue record for this book is available from the British Library

Typeset in 11pt/12pt Times by BookEns Ltd, Royston, Herts.
Printed and bound in Great Britain by Antony Rowe Limited, Reading, Berkshire.

Table of Contents

v

List of Contributors

Pedro López Aguirrebengoa, Special Ambassador for Mediterranean Relations of the Kingdom of Spain, Ministry of Foreign Affairs, Madrid (Spain).

David Cullen, Senior Assistant, Department of Political and Administrative Studies, College of Europe, Bruges (Belgium).

Monica den Boer, Senior Lecturer in Justice and Home Affairs, European Institute of Public Administration, Maastricht (The Netherlands).

Kay Hailbronner, Professor of Law, University of Konstanz; Director, Research Centre for International and European Law on Immigration and Asylum (Germany).

Sir David Hannay, Former United Kingdom Ambassador and Permanent Representative to the European Community and the United Nations, London (United Kingdom).

Rolf H. Hasse, Professor of Economics, University of Leipzig (Germany).

Horst G. Krenzler, Former Director-General of DGI of the European Commission, Lecturer at the University of Munich, Munich/Brussels.

Stephen H. Legomsky, Charles F. Nagel Professor of International and Comparative Law, Washington University, St. Louis (USA).

Jörg Monar, Professor of Politics, Director of the Centre for European Politics and Institutions, University of Leicester (United Kingdom).

Wayne Moyer, Professor of Political Science, Director Rosenfield Program in Public Affairs, International Relations and Human Rights, Grinnell College, Iowa (USA).

G. Wyn Rees, Lecturer, Deputy-Director of the Centre for European Politics and Institutions, University of Leicester (United Kingdom).

Earl Anthony Wayne, Principal Deputy Assistant Secretary of State for European and Canadian Affairs, U.S. Department of State, Washington (USA).

Preface

This book originated from an international conference on the "New Transatlantic Agenda" organised in Brussels in July 1996 by the Centre for European Politics and Institutions (CEPI) of the University of Leicester in co-operation with Directorate-General I of the European Commission and Kluwer Law International. While most of its chapters are revised versions of papers presented at the conference, some were commissioned afterwards in order to address several relevant issues which could not be covered adequately within the limited framework of the conference.

The chapters endeavour to provide an analysis both of the innovative elements of the "New Transatlantic Agenda" and of the main challenges EU-US relations have to face at the turn of this century. While the main focus is on the question whether the "New Transatlantic Agenda" constitutes a adequate response to these challenges, this volume also explores the necessary conditions for a successful long-term implementation of the "Agenda" and asks what lessons can be drawn in this respect from previous experiences in transatlantic co-operation. Considerable room has been given to the analysis of justice and home affairs as matters of EU-US co-operation, not only because this is without doubt one of the most innovative areas of the "New Transatlantic Agenda" but also since it is an area in which both are confronted with rapidly increasing challenges.

It is hoped that this volume will make a contribution to the discussion of the future of the transatlantic relationship whose quality is likely to depend on the capability of both sides to respond with new approaches, such as those laid out in the "New Transatlantic Agenda", to inevitable changes in both the bilateral and the global context.

The book project would not have been possible without the generous support given by the European Commission and Kluwer Law International to the original conference. I also would like to express my gratitude to Selma Hoedt from Kluwer Law International for making this publication possible.

Several individuals have provided valuable help in bringing this project to completion. Julie Cornish (CEPI) provided efficient support during the conference project and Gillian Paterson (CEPI) retyped several of the amended manuscripts. Russell Pacey, Editorial Assistant of the European Foreign Affairs Review, deserves special thanks for his help in checking the language and the style of some of the chapters.

Jörg Monar

List of Abbreviations

APEC	Asia-Pacific Economic Co-operation
ASEAN	Association of South-East Asian Nations
BIA	Board of Immigration Appeals
CAP	Common Agricultural Policy
CEEC	Central and Eastern European Countries
CELAD	Comité Européen de Lutte Anti-drogue
CFSP	Common Foreign and Security Policy
CIA	Central Intelligence Agency
CJTF	Combined Joint Task Forces
COREPER	Committee of Permanent Representatives
DEA	(US) Drug Enforcement Agency
DG	Directorate-General
EC	European Community
ECU	European Currency Unit
EDU	Europol Drugs Unit
EEC	European Economic Community
EFTA	European Free Trade Association
EIB	European Investment Bank
EMCDDA	European Monitoring Centre for Drugs and Drug Addiction
EMU	Economic and Monetary Union
EPC	European Political Co-operation
EU	European Union
EUROPOL	European Police Office
EUSE	European Union Special Envoy
FAIR	Federal Agricultural Improvement and Reform Act
FATF	Financial Action Task Force
FBI	Federal Bureau of Investigation
FTAA	Free Trade Area of the Americas
GATT	General Agreement on Tariffs and Trade
GATT 47	GATT concluded in 1947
GATT 94	GATT incorporated into the 1994 Agreement on the WTO
GSP	General System of Preferences
IFOR	Implementation Force
IGC	Intergovernmental Conference
ILEA	International Law Enforcement Academy

IPR	Intellectual Property Rights
IMF	International Monetary Fund
INS	Immigration and Naturalisation Service
ITA	Information Technology Agreement
JHA	Justice and Home Affairs
KEDO	Korean Peninsula Development Organisation
MEPP	Middle East Peace Process
MLAT	Mutual Legal Assistance Treaty
MoU	Memorandum of Understanding
MRA	Mutual Recognition Agreement
NACC	North Atlantic Co-operation Council
NAFTA	North American Free Trade Area
NATO	North Atlantic Treaty Organisation
NGO	Non-governmental Organisation
NIS	New Independent States
NTA	New Transatlantic Agenda
OAU	Organisation of African Unity
OECD	Organisation for Economic Co-operation and Development
OEEC	Organisation for European Economic Co-operation
OJ	Official Journal of the EC
OSCE	Organisation for Security and Co-operation in Europe
OSS	Office of Strategic Studies
PfP	Partnership for Peace
PHARE	Poland and Hungary Action for Restructing of the Economy
PLO	Palestine Liberation Organisation
REDWG	Regional Economic Development Working Group
SFOR	Stabilisation Forces
SLG	Senior Level Group
TABD	Transatlantic Business Dialogue
TAFTA	Transatlantic Free Trade Area
TAIES	Transatlantic Information Exchange Service
TASD	Transatlantic Social Dialogue
TEP	Transatlantic Economic Partnership
TEU	Treaty on European Union
TRIEMA	Trilateral Initiative for Equal Market Access
UN	United Nations
UNDCP	United Nations Drug Control Programme
UNHCR	United Nations High Commissioner for Refugees
UNIDROIT	International Institute for Unification of Private Law
US	United States
WCO	World Customs Organisation
WEU	Western European Union
WHO	World Health Organisation
WTO	World Trade Organisation

PART I

THE POLITICAL AGENDA

Chapter 1

The Potential of the New Transatlantic Partnership: an American Perspective

Earl Anthony Wayne

1. INTRODUCTION

The New Transatlantic Agenda (NTA)[1] highlights many areas in which the United States and the European Union were already working together, but its greater importance lies in its promise, in its potential, in that which is "capable of being". The promise, the potential, of the NTA lies in broadening the focus of EU-US relations from mostly economic and trade consultation to an ambitious and broad-ranging action agenda both visionary in its reach and practical in its approach. It is an effort to meet the challenge and promise of the post-Cold War world and to turn that into a better world not just for Americans and Europeans, but for all the world's citizens. The NTA is a keystone in the post-Cold War European security architecture. The opportunities and the challenges are great, and the US is confident that we can meet them together[2].

The US and the EU still study politics and war. The wars may no longer be within the borders of the US or the EU, but they concern us all. If we stopped studying politics, we would all be out of a job. We now have the luxury, however, to focus also on environmental issues, commerce, and agriculture.

---

[1] See the Appendix *post* where the NTA is set out in full.
[2] One of our founding fathers, John Adams, in a letter to his wife, Abigail, in 1780 wrote: "I must study politics and war, that my sons may have liberty to study ... geography, natural history and naval architecture, navigation, commerce, and agriculture, in order to give their children a right to study painting, poetry, music, architecture, statuary, tapestry, and porcelain".

The US and the EU do not agree very much on agriculture, but we "study" it together. We have made great strides toward improving our world, toward realising a transatlantic world of partners sharing responsibilities, but there is much that remains to be done.

Firstly, consideration shall be directed to the progress made in implementing the NTA during these first months, and then at the *potential* yet to be realised in the EU-US partnership, where we might go and how we might get there.

2. WHERE WE HAVE BEEN AND WHERE WE ARE NOW

The NTA, signed in December 1995, makes a truly significant step forward from the 1990 Declaration on US-EC Relations. The NTA envisions a partnership between the US and the EU that goes beyond the realm of trade and economics, where we have long acted as equal partners. The NTA, for the first time, engages the EU as a political partner as well and foresees the potential for the US and the EU to work as equal political partners on a vast array of foreign policy and diplomatic fronts with shared responsibilities. In addition, the NTA identifies progress we can make in humanitarian and development assistance, in the range of other economic and social areas, and in the exchange of people and ideas.

The NTA testifies to US support for the EU and our continuing, deepening commitment to remain engaged in Europe's security. These first months of the NTA have shown significant progress, as reported to our Presidents at the EU-US Summit in Washington in June 1996.

We have been working together to alleviate the effects of some of the great tragedies of our time. Our combined efforts in the former Yugoslavia have contributed to the civilian implementation of the Dayton Accords. The Bosnia Donors Conference hosted by the EU and the World Bank in April 1996 added US$1.2 billion to existing pledges for reconstruction after the devastation of years of war. We have also worked together on peace and development efforts in the Middle East.

The US and Europe are the largest humanitarian aid donors in the world. We possess tremendous leverage in our joint efforts to assist those in need. In April 1996, USAID Administrator Atwood and European Commissioner Bonino, in the first-ever joint assessment mission, travelled to Rwanda and Burundi to identify what is needed to help resolve the humanitarian crisis in that region. In June 1996, we held our first trilateral consultations with the UN High Commissioner for Refugees. Aware that we must seize today's opportunity to realise a united Europe of stable, democratic and market-oriented economies, we are continuing our co-operation in assistance programmes throughout Central and Eastern Europe and the New Independent States (NIS).

We have made progress in confronting global challenges of crime and disease and environmental degradation. One of the key accomplishments in these first six months of NTA implementation has been the launching of a health task force to work with multilateral organisations and national governments to build a global early warning and response network to combat deadly communicable diseases such as AIDS and the Ebola virus. In our joint fight against crime and drug trafficking, we are nearing the conclusion of a chemical precursors agreement which would prevent illicit shipments of chemicals used in the manufacture of illegal drugs. A top priority in the environmental field is our joint establishment of a network of environmental centres in the Ukraine, Russia, and other NIS. These are but a few of the steps we have already taken to face these global challenges.

In addition to these accomplishments, we have made important progress in our trade relationship, and we have opened new avenues for the exchange of people and ideas. We can be proud of these promising first steps, but we cannot be content with what we have achieved in these first few months. The NTA is a long-range effort, and will take time to realise its goals.

3. WHERE WE COULD BE AND HOW WE CAN GET THERE

As the EU conducts its Intergovernmental Conference (IGC), the US is watching closely to see how the EU will deal with its particular challenges of enlargement, improving Common Foreign and Security Policy, and handling Third Pillar issues.[3] European Monetary Union (EMU), while not officially on the agenda of the 1996-97 IGC, looms large and has our, as well as Europe's attention.

The outcome of the IGC will have a profound effect on the extent to which the promise of the NTA, of the EU as an equal political partner, will be fulfilled. The IGC and its decisions are, of course, EU internal affairs, and the US stands ready to support and work with whatever mechanisms emerge from that process. For the NTA to reach its full potential, the EU, through whatever process it selects, will have to be able to operate efficiently and quickly in the sort of crisis situation which is becoming the hallmark of the post Cold War world.

---

[3]   These are Justice and Home Affairs issues.

3.1 Promoting Peace and Stability, Democracy and Development Around the World

We can already point to numerous examples of efficient and effective EU-US partnership in long-range situations, particularly humanitarian and development assistance. Together, we have shown our political resolve in Bosnia, in the Middle East, in Rwanda and Burundi, and elsewhere. All of these efforts bring greater security to the region and the world.

In a complicated political crisis situation, however, can we point to similar successes? Can the US turn to the EU for a rapid, real-time response ? Until we can confidently answer "yes" to that question, we will not live up to the full promise of NTA and its potential role in European and regional security architecture.

The US supports the EU's efforts to develop its Common Foreign and Security Policy (CFSP). The evolution and development of the CFSP can make the EU a more effective political partner of the US in promoting our common goals of peace and prosperity, democracy and development. It is up to the EU, through its IGC, to decide how this can be accomplished.

For our part, the US needs to consult fully with the EU in areas where joint action is desired. We need to work with the EU to develop joint responses to crises. Through the North Atlantic Treaty Organisation (NATO) we have long worked together efficiently and successfully on military security. In the post-Cold War world, however, where the concept of security includes political and economic as well as military aspects, the US needs to develop a fuller appreciation of how we can work with and complement EU efforts in a range of areas. The EU's ambitious and imaginative Mediterranean Initiative, as one example, offers new approaches and new possibilities which merit our recognition and support. We must remember, however, that this political dimension to the EU-US relationship is a new development. It takes time and experience to develop new ways of working together.

That kind of partnership will become ever more important. A major challenge the US and the EU face over the next five years is to ensure the survival of democratic governments and values throughout Europe and to bring the Central and Eastern European countries (CEECs) progressively into the fold. The progressive enlargement of both NATO and the EU are essential elements in this process. Both processes are essential steps in strengthening the new democracies of Central and Eastern Europe and in building a unified Europe. Although NATO enlargement may be technically easier, it is strategically more difficult. In the EU, however, the situation is reversed. We already know the "who" of EU enlargement, but the process of getting there will be more complicated.

Nonetheless, we can already point to a number of areas where the US and the EU are working effectively together. These include assistance to Russia and the NIS. Regular consultation ensures that our respective programmes complement each other. The EU has taken an active role in the Middle East peace process, especially through the Regional Economic Development Working Group and through its aid to the Palestinians. The US and the EU worked hard together to ensure the success of the Palestinian elections. The US recognises and values EU efforts in Central and Eastern Europe, in the NIS, in the Middle East, the EU's initial support for the Korean Peninsula Energy Development Organisation (KEDO), and the significant contribution of the EU's Mediterranean Initiative. All of these efforts contribute to the safety and security of our world.

In the near future we intend to intensify our co-operation. The US looks forward to greater EU participation in, and support for KEDO. We hope that the EU will approve a significant, annual contribution. KEDO's success would prevent nuclear proliferation in North-East Asia, and enhance regional peace and stability. The forthcoming months also signal a critical period for Middle East peace. We must continue our close political and economic co-operation to advance the process toward a lasting and comprehensive peace.

3.2 Responding to Global Challenges

The "global challenges" set out in the NTA present another area with great, but as yet unfulfilled, potential. The US and the EU have made some progress on environmental issues. Through our efforts in the Organisation for Economic Co-operation and Development (OECD), the use of lead in gasoline, chemicals, and other products may be significantly reduced. We have agreed to co-ordinate our positions in advance of upcoming international conferences such as those on climate change, biodiversity, and chemicals. However, the real value of our co-operation remains to be proven.

We also lack progress on "Third Pillar", or Justice and Home Affairs issues. The US is enthusiastic about building up our co-operative efforts against international crime and drug trafficking, but we have found the EU is institutionally less prepared to move forward. There are internal EU debates with Member States about competence, and there exists the need to establish internal EU practices in this area, which is, after all, a very new area for the EU under the Maastricht Treaty. We have been encouraged by the progress made on the precursor chemical agreement and by our work together in preparation for the recent United Nations Drug Control Programme (UNDCP) workshop on counter-narcotics co-operation in the Caribbean. We have been equally encouraged by the Irish government's decision to make the fight against crime and drugs one of the highest priorities of their presidency in the second half of 1996.

However, we can do more. For example, the US wants to co-operate with the EU in fighting crime in Central and Eastern Europe. As part of this effort, we hope to formalise, in the near future, full EU participation in the Budapest International Law Enforcement Academy (ILEA), which is making a valuable contribution in democratic institution building in Central and Eastern Europe and the NIS. As with the Common Foreign and Security Policy (CFSP), the Third Pillar decision-making structure is a topic of the IGC. The results of those deliberations will affect the extent to which we are able, together, to fulfil the goals of the NTA.

3.3 Contributing to the Expansion of World Trade and Closer Economic Co-operation

In 1776, Thomas Paine, a great American patriot, wrote, "Not a place upon earth might be so happy as America. Her situation is remote from all the wrangling world, and she has nothing to do but to trade with them". Unfortunately, happiness did not last very long. America became involved in the "wrangling world", and the world of trade has joined the "wrangling".

The NTA goal of "Contributing to the Expansion of World Trade and Closer Economic Co-operation" has hit a few bumps recently. Many countries, including the US, have been disappointed with the outcomes of recent trade negotiations in telecommunications, financial and maritime services, areas which remained unresolved after the last General Agreement on Tariffs and Trade (GATT) round. These sectors involve high stakes and strong national interests. Progress comes only with difficulty. At this time, there is simply not a critical mass of high quality, liberalising offers on the table in any of those negotiations.

However, these are areas in which the US and the EU acting together could contribute to the expansion of world trade. That is where success has been found in the past. In the Uruguay Round, it was only when the US and the EU took the lead, when the US and the EU found a meeting of minds, that those difficult negotiations were brought to a satisfactory conclusion. Today, too, this may be where success lies. Jointly, we can influence global trade negotiations to ensure better offers from our global trading partners, resulting in mutually beneficial agreements.

With respect to another kind of trade challenge, the US and the EU agree on the need to reduce both tariff and non-tariff trade barriers, and we have made some progress in this area. We have launched a joint study to identify ways to reduce or eliminate remaining barriers to transatlantic trade.

Steady progress has been made on Mutual Recognition Agreements (MRAs), which would dramatically affect transatlantic trade by allowing products tested, certified, or inspected in one country to be accepted throughout the transatlantic marketplace. We are nearing agreement on a first group of MRAs and continuing our negotiations on others. Although we agree on the goals and objectives, MRAs present a unique set of challenges. They are a tedious and painstaking business. The task is further complicated by differences in our regulatory structures and laws. However slow and painstaking the process may be, both government and industry agree that it is well worth the effort. The business leaders of the Transatlantic Business Dialogue (TABD) have very clearly stated the importance of removing non-tariff barriers, particularly those in the regulatory area. Each day we delay on agreement adds unnecessary costs to businesses and to consumers. These are some of the most significant trade barriers that remain between us. To resolve them would give a new boost to our transatlantic trade.

Our private sectors, on both sides of the Atlantic, have called for the elimination of tariffs in the rapidly changing information technology sector. We have made progress on negotiations leading to an Information Technology Agreement which would eliminate tariffs in this cutting-edge sector. Such an historic agreement would enhance trade and competition for information technology products.

3.4 Building Bridges Across the Atlantic

The final element of the NTA, "Building Bridges Across the Atlantic", has significant successes to show, but also represents an area where we need to exert even greater efforts. Let it be remembered that the US Declaration of Independence states, "Governments are instituted among Men, deriving their just Powers from the Consent of the Governed ... ". In democracies such as ours, it is from our citizens that we receive our mandates, and without their support, the potential of the NTA can never be realised.

The TABD provides a model of the power and promise of the transatlantic people-to-people partnership. The TABD is a forum in which business leaders from both sides of the Atlantic meet to discuss and to give "unfiltered" advice to US and EU officials on how best to improve the climate for trade and investment. Many of the recommendations which came out of their first conference, held in Seville, November 1995, were incorporated into the NTA. The TABD is a success which we hope to see replicated in other sectors. Organised labour recently answered the call. Leading labour unions on both sides of the Atlantic intend to establish a "Labour Dialogue". We expect that this labour counterpart to the TABD will be functioning in the very near future.

At the EU-US Summit in June 1996, we, the US and the EU, pledged to conclude a comprehensive Science and Technology co-operation agreement in 1997[4]. Among the benefits of that will be collaboration on the development of intelligent manufacturing systems and the exchange of ideas and information in the biotechnology area.

Recognising the central role of education in ensuring continuing support for the EU-US relationship, we signed an Agreement on Higher Education and Vocational Training through which we will fund innovative consortia

---

[4] Editor's note: The Agreement was signed on 5 December 1997.

projects to promote transatlantic educational exchange. The first grants, announced at the June Summit, provide funding for projects in areas such as automotive engineering, environmental studies, and health care. The participants represent more than 60 institutions from 12 EU nations and 24 US states. There were some 130 good proposals, but, unfortunately, funding for only eight. This is perhaps the greatest hindrance to the potential of the people-to-people part of the NTA: good will and good ideas are in ample supply. The funding to apply them is not.

In order to obtain support, whether financial, political, or moral, for the goals of the NTA, we need to do a better job of informing the public. Opinion polls and anecdotal evidence indicate, in both the US and Europe, that the public possesses at best, a sketchy knowledge of the EU and its relationship with the US. A recent opinion poll conducted on behalf of the European Commission found that only 20 per cent of the EU citizens surveyed were aware of the 1996/1997 IGC, a conference which is struggling with some of the most basic questions about the shape of Europe's future.

On the American side, there are few, even among well-educated private citizens and senior policy-makers, who know much about the EU. Very little is written about the EU in daily newspapers or magazines published in the US. Very little coverage of the EU appears on American television. This situation, on both sides of the Atlantic, is, in some ways, a Catch-22. Unless this information vacuum is filled, it will be difficult to sustain support for the programmes and activities which, in turn, build that knowledge and support.

At the same time, however, we can point to some progress. The process of negotiating the NTA, for example, included a number of US government officials and agencies never previously involved at the EU level (though perhaps engaged on the bilateral level with member states). Implementation of the NTA will continue to help increase awareness of EU-US relations among US policy-makers.

4. OUTSIDE THE NEW TRANSATLANTIC AGENDA

The NTA is not, of course, the sum total of the US relationship with the EU. Many areas were not included in the NTA. We recognise that some sectors and issues will continue to be too "hot to handle", such as agriculture. We recognise that we have different interests and approaches on several issues, beef hormones, bananas, leghold traps, and eco-labelling, to name some of the most frequently recurring, but mechanisms have been worked out, or are being worked out to help us deal with these issues.

We also recognise that internal political developments and concerns exert their influence on the EU-US relationship. In 1996, the US was inevitably focused on the November elections at the federal, state, and local levels. The EU faces a host of difficult and fundamental decisions over the next couple of years: enlargement; whether and how to restructure its decision-making process; the establishment of a deeper common foreign and security policy; the commitment to and mechanics of a single currency; the development of common policies in Third Pillar areas of crime, narcotics, immigration, and asylum; the creation of jobs and growth. As noted in the NTA, however, "Domestic challenges are not an excuse to turn inward; we can learn from each other's experiences and build new transatlantic bridges".

The US has always supported European integration; it fosters our national interest in seeing a stable, democratic, prosperous, and unified Europe. The fundamental values we share and that we try to advance together, belief in democratic governments, human rights, a strong multilateral trading system, free trade, stability, and security, far outweigh our differences.

5. CONCLUSION

The NTA and the Joint Action Plan[5] offer challenges to keep us busy well beyond the year 2000. They include areas as diverse as helping developing nations toward economic growth and self-sufficiency; exploring ways to limit global emissions of greenhouse gases; increasing coverage of EU-US bilateral commitments on public procurement; and encouraging artistic and cultural co-operation projects.

When, in 1776, the US declared its independence from a European power, it knew not only the negative aspects of European power, but the vitally positive role Europe played in its interests. European nations extended financial support and political and military expertise to our fledgling nation. The ties between the US and Europe have survived radical changes of geographical and political boundaries. The blood of Americans and Europeans have mingled in wars over wide swathes of this continent. The economies and societies of the US and Europe intertwine in a network of thousands of companies, universities, trade organisations, research centres, and exchange programmes. Transatlantic trade and investment are estimated to directly support six million jobs and indirectly support an additional eight million jobs. Tens of thousands of family members and friends cross the Atlantic each year. A few rough spots in a trade negotiation, or over handling a certain foreign policy issue, cannot break the ties that bind us.

The future of the relationship between the US and the EU is bright. We have a strong and vibrant partnership, and the NTA, and the EU-US Action Plan take this to a new level. The NTA is not an end point, but the beginning of a deeper relationship.

We have made progress in the first months of the NTA. Projects set out in the NTA await their turn to be brought to fruition over the next several

---

[5]   See the Appendix *post* where the NTA and the Joint Action Plan are set out in full.

years. This potential must be made to do even more. We must make the potential a reality, notwithstanding the difficult decisions that lie ahead.

We must overcome our differences and pave the way for greater co-operation, so that we can move forward together to our mutual benefit. We can continue to improve our world and do our part to help give to all the world's children, as John Adams would have put it, "a right to study painting, poetry, music, architecture, statuary, tapestry, and porcelain".

Chapter 2

The Potential of the New Transatlantic Partnership: a European Perspective

Horst G. Krenzler

1. INTRODUCTION

The new partnership, which has been growing on both sides of the Atlantic since the end of the Cold War, and which has received new impetus with the signature of the New Transatlantic Agenda (NTA)[1], at the European Union-United States (EU-US) summit in Madrid on December 3, 1995 has great potential and should ideally, over the years to come, develop into a key element on the world political scene.

However, the US and the EU cannot adopt a *laissez-faire* approach *vis-à-vis* their relationship: if the transatlantic limousine is to continue in constant fast forward and if they want the passengers to be satisfied, then they must be sure that not only do they agree on the direction they are going but also that they do not put obstacles in their own way. The Helms-Burton Act and the d'Amato bill of 1996[2] are a case in point. Strong efforts have to be undertaken to eliminate such obstacles of a clearly divisive character.

To illustrate the basic thesis of the important long-term significance of the NTA it is interesting to look back briefly at the beginning of 1995 and compare the analysis of the transatlantic relationship then and the situation in the second half of 1996.

It is also important to outline some of the compelling reasons for continuing

---

[1] See the Appendix *post* where the NTA is set out in full.
[2] US Public Law No 104/114 (Helms-Burton). US Public Law No 104/172 (d'Amato bill).

to build an "ever closer" partnership and to show how in the light of these demands it has been possible to revitalise the relationship. Finally the state of the relationship after six months of NTA implementation will be reviewed.

2. TRANSATLANTIC RELATIONS AT THE BEGINNING OF 1995

At the beginning of 1995, there was talk of stagnation and crisis in the transatlantic relationship. The end of the Cold War was seen as the end of the "*raison d'être*" for this relationship, the absence of the common foe interpreted as the absence of a common purpose. Newspaper articles reflecting public opinion evoked the image of the two continents drifting apart, each immersed in its own interest: the Europeans looking towards the East, the Americans towards the Pacific.

3. HOW THE CRISIS WAS OVERCOME

3.1 The Challenge

If in 1995 EU-US relations were at a cross-roads, there was also the strong political will to take a pro-active approach towards them and adapt them to the needs of the future. In two key speeches leading figures of both administrations, Sir Leon Brittan for the European Commission and Warren Christopher for the US Government, expressed the view that indeed there were many reasons for the EU and the US to work on their relationship and make sure it responded to the challenges of the post-Cold War World.

From a European perspective, what are those challenges? The first is to keep the US engaged in Europe. Bosnia is probably the most striking example of the need for a continued US presence in Europe. As the conflict in former Yugoslavia clearly demonstrates, it is only where the EU and the US have acted in agreement that it has been possible to contain the conflict.

More generally, there is the need to consider together how the processes of the North Atlantic Treaty Organisation (NATO) and EU enlargement can best contribute to the development of a comprehensive structure of security in Europe.

The second is the need for co-operation between the EU and the US to cover the whole international arena. The Middle East, human right abuses in China or the catastrophic situation in Africa's Great Lakes region are cases in point. They all are of a scope that goes beyond any single country's capacities. In the light of the 1994 Congress elections which focused US policies on domestic issues, it was important for the Europeans to receive confirmation of the continued willingness of the US to be globally engaged.

The third is to ensure continued mutual commitment to face up to the other, so-called "new" challenges: environmental degradation, for example, is a global problem and requires co-ordinated responses by the world's leading industrial nations. As they remove obstacles to trade and ease customs controls, improve personal mobility and telecommunications, they are faced with unwanted beneficiaries: terrorists, drug dealers and other criminals take advantage of the improved conditions just as much, and often more, than honest tradesmen. In a century where people are sent to the moon, mankind is still confronted with the scourges of disease and too often defeated by the AIDS virus or malaria. These are just a few examples that again demonstrate that the mere scope of today's problems requires experts and politicians from both sides to sit together and develop joint responses.

Fourth, to refocus US interest on the European market was a key challenge. Trade and investment, have always been the backbone of the EU-US relationship. The figures speak a clear language: the estimated two-way trade flow in goods and services for 1995 amounted to over US$ 450 billion and the stock of transatlantic investment in 1994 stood at around US$ 450 billion, with the EU providing for 51 per cent of all foreign direct investment flows to the US and the US being the source of 42 per cent of all foreign direct investment flows to Europe in that year. Its direct impact on economic growth and the sheer amount of jobs depending on this relationship compel both the EU and the US to work together towards improving the conditions under which their economic operators have to act. Nonetheless, the Europeans were left with the impression that US policy and business were focused on the Americas (North American Free Trade Area (NAFTA), Free Trade Area of the Americas (FTAA)) or the Far East (Asia-Pacific Economic Co-operation (APEC)). This perspective had to be corrected.

3.2 The Response

Neither side, in 1995, stopped short at recognising the challenges. Rather, the EU and the US agreed that something had to be done about it. They also agreed that a pragmatic approach was necessary if they were not to get bogged down in endless institutional difficulties over the negotiation of a transatlantic treaty or potentially fruitless discussions over a transatlantic free trade zone. This is how the idea of the New Transatlantic Agenda (NTA) and the Joint EU-US Action Plan was born: the documents focus on the substance of the relationship regardless of legal constraints, leaving it to either the EU or its Member States to act on specific matters as required. The documents also have an additional advantage over a treaty in that they are both specific and flexible, in other words they commit the partners to take a number of concrete actions now, but they can also be modified and adapted to new challenges as they arise.

The documents were negotiated in a very short time, actual negotiations lasted only three months, and yet it was possible to agree on a remarkable array of actions to be undertaken.

The substance of the documents and the speed with which they were negotiated are probably the most impressive testimony to the quality of the relationships and its future.

Rather than review systematically the context of the Agenda and the Action Plans, which is already known, some particularly striking features should be emphasised in the field of foreign policy.

The breadth and detail of the initiative reflect a degree of the political consensus that is unique and can serve as solid basis for the relationship for years to come. The EU-US political dialogue now covers seven geographical areas (Africa, Asia, Central Europe, Latin America, Middle East, Maghreb and the New Independent States (NIS)) and seven global areas (UN, arms control, consular affairs, human rights, nuclear non-proliferation, the Organisation for Security and Co-operation in Europe (OSCE) and terrorism. The former US Ambassador to the EU Stuart Eizenstat stated that NTA and Action Plan mark "the first time that we (the US) have dealt comprehensively with the European Union not simply as an economic and trade organisation, but rather as a political force able to join the United States as a full equal partner in a whole array of foreign policy initiatives". And there is more to it: for the first time the world's major powers agree to do more than just consult each other: they agree to act together and jointly take responsibility in facing the world's most pressing challenges.

A substantive set of commitments has also been agreed to face the new global challenges, noteworthy are not least those in the field of justice and home affairs on which both partners henceforth intend to co-operate.

In the area of trade and economics, in addition to reaffirming their commitment to consolidating and strengthening the multilateral trading system, the US and EU have also developed an innovative and flexible new concept: the New Transatlantic Marketplace. Under this umbrella they intend to progressively facilitate trade and investment conditions. This exercise is being helped by a Joint Study in which the EU and the US will together look at the remaining trade obstacles and try to develop strategies to overcome them. This study helped to prepare the Transtlantic Economic Partnership (TEP) decided at the London EU-US Summit of 18 May 1998. This study also serves to keep alive the concept of a Transatlantic Free Trade Area (TAFTA), an idea which is not ripe, but one which may merit discussion at a later date. A further element is the Transatlantic Business Dialogue (TABD), through which business leaders have the opportunity better to indicate their priority concerns and to feed concrete proposals into the decision-making processes on both sides of the Atlantic. This dialogue has been proven to be very useful to speed up and to focus the efforts of both administrations.

3.3 Developments During the First Six Months After the Signing of the NTA

An assessment of the first six months of NTA implementation contains both negative and positive elements.

On the negative side there is clearly disappointment at the somewhat limited progress made in the trade and economic field, the most traditional area of EU-US co-operation, where things have been more difficult than expected. In the multilateral area, the US positions both in the telecoms and the maritime transport negotiations have been a disappointment. Bilaterally, despite the strong backing from the business communities on both sides of the Atlantic, negotiations for an Information Technology Agreement (ITA) have encountered problems which delayed the negotiations; and with regard to the envisaged Mutual Recognition Agreement (MRA) on conformity assessment there is still only agreement on some of the sectors envisaged for initial coverage.

Things have of course not been helped by the difficulties with regard to the Helms-Burton legislation and the d'Amato bill with their extraterritorial application. Instead of tackling the underlying issues with the EU in a spirit of co-operation and partnership, the US has taken measures which have a considerable potential to cause serious and unnecessary friction between allies, and could lead to US sanctions against EU firms followed by possible EU retaliation.

On the positive side, the measures have been able to launch many new initiatives that cover areas in which in the past little or nothing was done jointly. From a long list of achievements, two examples are particularly significant. Firstly, important progress has been made towards better co-ordinating of development and humanitarian assistance. Both sides exchanged programming plans, an exercise which should allow the US and the EU, by taking advantage of different fiscal years, better to avoid operational gaps in their response to humanitarian needs. Secondly, in the health sector, an area in which previously there was only a very limited dialogue with the US, a task force has been set up, which has already begun its work of setting up a global early warning system and response network for communicable diseases.

Lastly, but importantly, the transatlantic pastures have been quite successful in laying the foundations for a sustained close relationship and one that will continue to grow by taking steps to improve the people-to-people links across the Atlantic. This is in fact a very important issue, because no matter what the two administrations come up with to improve co-operation between them, the transatlantic relationship and the attempts to improve it need to be first and foremost accepted and supported by the citizens.

It is therefore particularly encouraging that the TABD has been so successful in getting businessmen from both sides of the Atlantic together for an intense and constructive exchange of views on how to improve the policy framework of the transatlantic business relationship.

The successful implementation of the Agreement on Education and Vocational Training has engaged around 70 institutions in the first year of its existence alone in joint research or other academic activity. Work to set up a "Transatlantic Labour Dialogue" is underway and negotiations for a comprehensive Science and Technology Agreement are expected to be finalised successfully in a short period of time. These are first steps only, but making the respected societies aware of the value of the Transatlantic Partnership and showing them how they can directly benefit from this partnership is the best guarantee for its continued vitality and success.

4. CONCLUSION

Clearly, the first months of implementation have not been easy ones. Progress has inevitably been somewhat uneven. It took time for administrations to get used to the new situation and things were not helped by the US gearing up for the Presidential elections, and the Europeans being distracted by mad cows or difficult Intergovernmental Conference (IGC) discussions. Realistically one could not expect that, just because of the NTA, all problems would magically disappear off the table. This, by the way, is not a realistic expectation for the future either: competitive conflicts between the EU and the US will remain. In other words the EU and the US cannot always act in co-operation, co-ordination and harmony and preventive diplomacy will not be able to prevent all conflicts of interest.

Nonetheless, apart from setting a positive agenda for things both sides agree to do together, the NTA is not only there for the sunny days. Rather, it is an all-weather instrument and should help through stormy times as well. This is not least due to the improved structure of the relationship. A group of Senior Level Representatives meets regularly to review the state of the overall relationship and will present progress reports on the implementation of the NTA to the half-yearly EU-US Summits, and these Summits, no longer an isolated *ad hoc* event, will give political guidelines on which issues to focus and which new priorities to develop.

Finally, the NTA is not the last step in the efforts to strengthen transatlantic relations. By encompassing all three pillars of the Treaty on European Union (TEU) it foreshadows the development of a comprehensive legal instrument, the Transatlantic Treaty, in years to come. In the current fragile geopolitical situation, and in the light of the challenges both the EU and the US have to address, there is no alternative to an EU-US partnership. After all, in any major crisis situation, who else would one turn to?

Chapter 3

US-European Security Relations: Surfing or Sinking?

G. Wyn Rees

1. INTRODUCTION

The ending of the Cold War brought enormous changes to the security environment in Europe. These occurred at such speed that it was impossible for states to prepare a blueprint as to how they would respond. The result was a period of confusion as governments attempted to assess the ramifications of events and reconfigure their country's military posture. Nowhere was this change more keenly felt than in the United States military presence on the European continent.

A feeling of crisis was engendered in transatlantic relations with the ending of the Cold War. The underlying question was whether the system that had provided security for the last 40 years would be capable of transformation or whether there be a shift to a new framework. It was clear that a re-balancing of the relationship was necessary but that this would depend both on the path of development that the Europeans chose, as well as the role that the US wished to fulfil. Additional complexity arose from crises that occurred outside of Europe that placed additional strains on US-European relations. A considerable amount of time has been needed to resolve these various factors.

2. A DISINTEGRATING ALLIANCE?

Since the dismantlement of the Berlin Wall and the assumptions that underpinned the security confrontation in Europe, the US has been forced to reassess its role on the continent. The traditional justification for an American presence was undermined with the collapse of the Warsaw Pact. Although there had been periodic debates about the relative burden shared between the US and its allies, nevertheless, there had been clarity about the importance of its mission in Europe. Two administrations, of differing political hues, have been required to reformulate American thinking and argue their case to a domestic audience that expected significant financial savings from the demise of the Cold War. The first factor that the US needed to weigh up was the level of military forces that it would retain in Europe. This had to be calibrated according to both America's wider role in the world as well as to the needs of European security. In the absence of the former threat, the US made major cuts in the combat personnel and the military bases that were dedicated to the North Atlantic Treaty Organisation (NATO)[1]. President Bush decided upon a target of 150,000 US troops, whilst under President Clinton the figure was revised downwards to a ceiling of 100,000 personnel. This raised doubts as to whether the US was committed to remaining a major military power on the continent. For the European countries it raised the question as to how far US troop levels could fall before American leadership in the Western Alliance would be put into question.

The debate about force levels did not occur within a vacuum as there were other tensions in US-European affairs that threw the politico-military uncertainties into sharper relief. Trade was an area where the two sides of the Atlantic had long found themselves in competition, but in the aftermath of the Cold War, renewed attention was focused on the Uruguay Round of the General Agreement on Trade and Tariffs (GATT). This contributed to a perception amongst some critics that the US was switching its attention from foreign policy issues to domestic matters. Neo-isolationist sentiments were apparent in the American Congress and 1993 saw the inauguration of a Democratic President who had campaigned on a platform of domestic economic priorities and decried the preoccupation of the Republican incumbent with foreign affairs.

A second factor was that the *raison d'être* of NATO, the principal post-war vehicle for American leadership in Europe, was unclear. Soviet forces were in the process of being withdrawn from the territories of central European countries and the former state of East Germany had been unified with its western counterpart and integrated into NATO. It was widely recognised

---

[1]   See Sharp, J. *Europe After an American Withdrawal: Economic and Military Issues*, Stockholm International Peace Research Institute, Oxford University Press, 1990.

that the Alliance needed to be adapted to deal with more likely contingencies than an attack upon the territories of its members. Article V tasks, under the 1949 Washington Treaty, would remain the responsibility of NATO but this alone would not guarantee the Alliance's position as the premier security institution. Future challenges could be expected to arise outside the NATO area of responsibility. They were likely to vary in the level of force employed and could therefore demand a broader array of responses, such as peacekeeping, from Alliance members.

In addition, NATO had to confront the issue of what sort of relationship it would develop with former Warsaw Pact states. In 1990, there was optimism about the future role of the Conference on Security and Co-operation in Europe (CSCE, later renamed the Organisation for Security and Co-operation in Europe (OSCE)), that it might serve as a new collective security organisation that would transcend the old alliance structures. But the CSCE proved to be an unwieldy body that did not enjoy the unqualified support of the leading western powers. Violent Soviet actions in the Baltic states in the early part of 1991, followed by the attempted Moscow coup in August, caused alarm bells to ring throughout central Europe. The focus switched to NATO and states previously allied to the USSR began to request entry into the Alliance.

NATO's initial response, in November 1991, was to offer these aspirant states membership of the North Atlantic Co-operation Council (NACC). This was a new consultative forum which facilitated a regular dialogue on security and related political matters between states in central and eastern Europe and the North Atlantic Council. Central European governments were critical of the fact that no distinction was drawn between them and Russia in the inaugural meeting. In the following March, ten newly independent states of the former Soviet Union were permitted to join. As far as countries such as Poland and Hungary were concerned, the NACC was a thinly disguised attempt by NATO to defer the issue of enlargement due to the risk of engendering confrontation with Moscow.

Meeting these challenges would do much to determine the continued relevance of NATO. Yet there was an absence of consensus amongst the members regarding the desirability of achieving these changes. France and Spain, for example, wanted to limit NATO's post-Cold War role to that of collective defence. This reflected an unwillingness to continue reliance on a transatlantic security framework that had imposed superpower priorities on Europe. France believed that the collapse of the eastern bloc offered a unique opportunity to re-structure the western security order and enhance the part played by continental powers. The London and Rome Summits, in 1990 and 1991, focused on the issues of NATO's transformation and the role that could be played by a more active European defence identity.[2] The possibility

---

2   For details see, "The London Declaration a Transformed North Atlantic Alliance", Heads of State and Government of the North Atlantic Council, London, 5-6 July 1990 and "The Alliance's Strategic Concept", Heads of State and Government of the North Atlantic Council, Rome, 7-8 November 1991.

of Europe emerging as a defence actor was given impetus by moves towards political union, led by France and Germany. This raised the prospect of the European Community being invested with newly acquired competencies in the fields of foreign and defence policy. In the Treaty on European Union (TEU), the Western European Union (WEU) was accorded the status of the defence arm of the European Union and declared to be an "integral part of the process of the development of the EU".[3] Subsequent to the signing of the Treaty, France and Germany announced that their joint military brigade, which had been established in 1987, would be expanded and given the title of the "EuroCorps". Other states were invited to join the EuroCorps, which was hailed as the first step towards a European Army.

Washington felt that its leadership position on the continent was threatened by these security initiatives by European states. The perception in the US was that the field of defence was at risk of being used to advance broader political goals. One fear was that the WEU could trespass on traditional areas of NATO responsibility and eventually duplicate its role. This would take some time, as the WEU lacked NATO's integrated military structure and robust capabilities, but if the Alliance was left to wither, then the threat was feasible. Another American fear was that European views would be discussed and agreed outside the forum of the North Atlantic Council and would then be presented as an agreed position. As such, the views of European states could come to represent a caucus within the Organisation.

The problem for the US was that it was unsure how to react to these developments. The result was that it tended to blunder into making heavy-handed statements warning of dangerous consequences if the US was marginalised from decision-making forums. The Bartholomew Letter, sent to European capitals in February 1991 just prior to a WEU Ministerial meeting, was an example of such a response.[4] Drawn up within the State Department, it warned that building up a defence identity within the European Community (EC), rivalling NATO, could force the US to reassess its role. It also reminded the Europeans that the military resources at their disposal were relatively limited. In the following November, a blunt warning was issued from President Bush when he attended the NATO Rome Summit. He cautioned against ill-considered European initiatives in the field of defence that threatened to alienate his country.

A third factor that has raised transatlantic tensions has been the conflict in former Yugoslavia. The significance of this problem was due to four main factors. Firstly, the conflict took place on the borders of the western security zone and was consequently of immediate concern to West European states. Secondly, the severity of the fighting and "ethnic cleansing" ensured that the

---

3   "Declaration on Western European Union" in The Treaty on European Union, Maastricht, 1992.
4   Myers, J. *The Western European Union: Pillar of Nato or Defence Arm of the EC?* London Defence Studies Vol. 16, Published by Brassey's, London, May 1993, p. 38.

repercussions from the conflict, such as the flow of refugees, were felt across the continent. This drew in outside powers who attempted to take steps to alleviate the suffering. Thirdly, Europe's security institutions were paralysed in the face of a complex mixture between an inter-state and a civil war situation. Finally, the US and Europe found themselves advocating different strategies to deal with the crisis.

From the outset of the crisis, the US was opposed to large scale intervention, fearing that it could result in a long and bloody commitment. Washington was eager to endorse the European Community's decision to take the lead in the crisis, which the latter did from a sense of misplaced confidence, based on the progress that had been achieved in European integration. This confidence swiftly turned to frustration as the European states realised their impotence in the face of the warring protagonists. The US found itself dissatisfied with its supportive role: it became dismissive of the efforts of the Europeans and felt insufficiently consulted when a joint EC-UN peace proposal, the Vance-Owen plan, was advanced in 1993. Washington was critical of the plan on the grounds that it rewarded aggression by the Bosnian Serbs. Instead, the US advocated a policy of lifting the arms embargo on the Bosnian Muslims, whilst simultaneously punishing the Bosnian Serbs with air attacks. This brought the Clinton Administration into confrontation with the British and French who already had troops safeguarding the supply of humanitarian aid in Bosnia, serving under the United Nations flag.

As a result of their different approaches to the Balkans conflict, recrimination became a characteristic feature of the transatlantic relationship. In the midst of a major conflict taking place on the mainland of Europe, NATO seemed to be ineffective and plagued with internal disputes. Despite enormous investment in the Alliance over many decades, the US appeared to be witnessing the twilight of its leadership over the military affairs of the continent. It was recognised on both sides of the Atlantic that steps would have to be taken to restore western unity in the face of these numerous challenges.

3. RESOLVING US-EUROPEAN TENSIONS

Against the backcloth outlined above, the resolution of these transatlantic tensions did not occur instantaneously. Nevertheless, there were signs of a reassessment of American priorities in the latter part of 1993 and the first evidence of the implications of this were demonstrated in the January 1994 NATO Brussels Summit. Underlying the US approach was an essentially political calculation: namely, that NATO remained the most effective institution for preserving American interests on the continent. The Clinton Administration re-committed itself to ensuring a central role for the Alliance in all the major security issues facing Europe.

A clear example of this was the launching of the "Partnership for Peace" (PfP) initiative at the Brussels Summit. The US accepted that the issue of enlargement was crucial to the long term viability of the Alliance. PfP offered each of the states in central and eastern Europe an individual agreement which could assist them in the process of gaining accession into NATO.[5] Whereas the NACC had avoided discriminating between the suitability of different states for admission, the PfP programme offered each country the ability to influence the speed at which it could become eligible for membership. During a visit to Poland in the following July, the American President made clear that the enlargement of the Alliance was a question of timing rather than principle and this was followed by a series of studies to investigate the practical questions of the process. In a speech delivered in Detroit in October 1996, Clinton announced a timetable for new members and at the Madrid Summit in July 1997, invitations were issued to Poland, Hungary and the Czech Republic.[6]

Complementing the PfP initiative, the US continued to take the lead in building a close relationship with Russia and supporting the Presidency of Boris Yeltsin. Under the guidance of Deputy Under-Secretary of State Strobe Talbott, the US has kept its former adversary informed on security matters, due to its recognition of Russia's pivotal position on future European security matters. Discussion centred on granting Russia a special associate status with the Alliance. The Kremlin pressed for a more ambitious legal agreement that would make their acquiescence a necessary prerequisite to NATO enlargement.[7] However, the US made it clear that it could not accept a veto by Russia over the enlargement process. There was eventual agreement on a Russia-NATO "Founding Act" which accorded Russia a unique status in relation to the Alliance but was politically and not legally binding.

The upshot of these efforts has been that the position of NATO, as the leading institution in the enlargement debate, has been affirmed. Although the WEU conducted its own programme of developing linkages to the east, offering first a "Forum of Consultation" and then "Associate Partner" status to a group of nine states, the primacy of NATO was unequivocal. The presence of the US within NATO and the limited military capabilities of the WEU ensured that as far as the central and east European countries were concerned, the Alliance would remain the most attractive institution. NATO even succeeded in eclipsing the expansion debate surrounding the EU. It has been accepted that bringing new members into the EU will take longer due to the greater complexity of legal, trading and financial issues that will have to be resolved.

In the case of the Bosnian crisis, a US policy of active engagement took

---

[5]   Holbrooke, R. *America, A European Power*, Foreign Affairs, March, April 1995, p. 43.
[6]   Von Moltke, G. *Accession of New Members to the Alliance: What are the Next Steps?* NATO Review, Vol. 45, No. 4, July-August 1997, pp. 4–9.
[7]   Bremner, C. *Lebed urges NATO to Delay Eastern Expansion*, The Times, 8 October 1996, p. 10.

longer to mature. The US continued to rely on European states to take the lead in the crisis and offered the provision of ground forces only in the event of a peace agreement being reached. American participation in the Contact Group, which was set up in April 1994, was less a reflection of Washington's desire to resolve the crisis than its exasperation with the role that had been played by the UN. American policy towards the conflict was characterised by short term attention and inconsistency of purpose. The over-riding priority was to maintain a semblance of unity between the leading western powers and avoid an open break with Britain and France. This consideration assumed such prominence to the Administration that it prompted Brenner to comment that "... unity itself was accepted as the implicit measure of success".[8]

The decisive change in US policy occurred in the summer of 1995 and reflected a change in circumstances. This took the form of a major offensive by Croatian forces against the Krajina Serbs. The success of this military action destabilised the Bosnian Serbs and gave the US the opportunity to seize the initiative. NATO began a series of punishing air attacks on Serb military and infrastructure assets as part of Operation "Deliberate Force". The US was able to mobilise support from Britain and France who were willing to harden their military stance after the violation of the UN declared "Safe Areas". Washington accompanied the military pressure with energetic diplomacy, spearheaded by Assistant Secretary of State Richard Holbrooke. Pressure continued to be applied on the Milosevic regime in Belgrade as well as the Bosnian Serbs in Pale and they eventually accepted a negotiated settlement to the conflict, the Dayton Peace Accord. In actual fact, the Accord did not differ substantially from what the earlier Vance-Owen plan of 1993 had envisaged. The US proceeded to play a major part in assembling an Implementation Force (IFOR) to police the agreement with a contribution of some 20,000 service personnel out of a total force of 60,000.

The third area was the issue of a European defence identity and from 1994 there was evidence of a more confident American attitude on this matter. This was arguably the most important development of all as it offered a framework for resolving future US-European disagreements. At the Brussels Summit, unequivocal NATO support was declared for European efforts in defence that were expressed through the WEU. This was based upon the assumption that these efforts would be compatible with NATO and dedicated to strengthening the European contribution within the Alliance. The American perception was that, in the light of the weakness of the Common Foreign and Security Policy (CFSP) which was demonstrated in Bosnia, European defence efforts were not a realistic threat to the primacy of NATO. The US had come to the conclusion that early European optimism on this subject had been misplaced.

---

[8]   Brenner, M. *The United States Policy in Yugoslavia*, Ridgway Papers No. 6, Mathew B Ridgway Center for International Security Studies, University of Pittsburgh, p. 14.

At the Summit, the US signalled that, under the "Combined Joint Task Forces" (CJTF) concept, European states could draw on NATO equipment, command and control assets to fulfil tasks that were their unique concern. As operations outside the Atlantic area were unlikely to engage the interests of all states, the Americans were willing to envisage coalitions of European states acting in the absence of the US. The CJTF concept provided American endorsement of "... separable but not separate capabilities which could respond to European requirements ...".[9] The obvious benefit for European states was the avoidance of the need to duplicate defence capabilities that already existed within the American inventory, such as satellite intelligence systems and long-range transport aircraft.

The types of missions that the Europeans might undertake had been agreed in the WEU Petersberg Declaration of June 1992. These included humanitarian and rescue missions, peacekeeping and the role of military forces in crisis-management.[10] The capacity to rescue EU nationals from a conflict zone appeared to be a necessary and sensible precaution when the US might not share the urgency in such a situation. However, it was plain that all of these tasks were at the lower end of the conflict spectrum. States within the WEU had differed on the question of how capable the organisation should become and how ambitiously to define its missions.

Yet the assumption embodied in the CJTF concept was that the Europeans could rely on NATO to provide military equipment and mobile headquarters for them during a crisis. Many of the resources that would be required from NATO for the conduct of a European-led operation would be US national assets. It was therefore an implicit assumption that US-European interests would not diverge in a crisis and that a right of access could be confidently expected. For a country such as Britain, this was not a particularly sensitive issue as they remained committed to the continuation of American military leadership in Europe. However, for a country such as France, that was eager to build up a stronger European defence identity supported by independent military capabilities, the CJTF approach represented a dangerous level of dependency.

Hence, the operationalising of the CJTF concept proved to be fraught with difficulties for more than two years. Paris wanted a WEU-led mission to have a guaranteed right of access to American military resources. It was also suspicious of the right of veto over such a mission that would remain available to the US because of the presence of its officers within a NATO-detached command structure. The French feared that the concept of an European defence identity could be rendered impotent by reliance upon the US. They wished to see spending on military assets such as the Helios satellite intelligence system and a heavy

---

[9]   Declaration of the Heads of State and Government participating in the meeting of the North Atlantic Council, Brussels, 10-11 January 1994, NATO Review, Vol. 42, No. 1, February 1994, pp. 30–33.

[10]   "Petersberg Declaration" of the WEU Council of Ministers, Bonn, 19 June 1992.

lift transport aircraft and wanted greater investment in the EuroCorps, to ensure a European capacity to act independently.

This paralysis in Alliance policy was brought to an end by the decision of France, at the end of 1995, to change its stance both towards the CJTF concept and to the broader issue of its relationship with NATO.[11] The Chirac government's review of defence policy led it to conclude that its self-exclusion from the inner-forums of NATO was harming its interests. The fact that the Alliance was in the process of adapting to new circumstances and had proved itself the only viable vehicle for military action in Bosnia, led the administration to signal its intention to re-integrate into NATO structures. This marked the culmination of a steady process of France drawing closer to the Alliance in practical terms. This formal shift in policy made it possible, at the Berlin North Atlantic Co-operation Council (NACC) meeting in June 1996, for the implementation of the CJTF concept to be approved.

But what was also apparent from the acceptance of the CJTF approach was that the prospects for building up independent European military assets were being abandoned. All the European states were reducing their defence budgets and there appeared to be no political will to find additional resources to grant them power projection capabilities. The countries around which a European defence identity would have to coalesce, France and Germany, were both making heavy cuts in their defence spending. France, at the same time, was announcing the end of compulsory national service and expressing private doubts about the ability of its German neighbour to participate in overseas interventions. For its part, Germany was looking for ways to extricate itself from participation in French satellite programmes and hoping to devote its energies to Economic and Monetary Union[12].

From the American perspective, the Berlin agreement marked the end of the debate about a rival role for WEU *vis-à-vis* NATO. Although presented in public as a way of facilitating independent European military missions, it meant that a US right of approval would exist over an allied action that required additional military assets. Whether the US would be willing to lend its equipment would be highly questionable and would depend on the circumstances. To do so would symbolise the Americans handing over the control of a crisis to the Europeans but it would still risk the US being called upon to help their allies if they became mired in an intractable situation.[13] The Europeans themselves, with the experience of the Balkans behind them, would be extremely wary of undertaking anything except small-scale missions unless the US was accompanying them.

Thus, the military part played by the European powers, independently of the US, is likely to remain limited for the foreseeable future. There has been

[11]   See Millon, C. *France and the renewal of the Atlantic Alliance*, NATO Review, Vol. 44, No. 3, May 1996, pp. 13–16.
[12]   Karacs, I. *Budget cuts shoot down Franco-German satellite*, The Independent, 8 October 1996, p. 8.
[13]   I am indebted to Philip Gordon for this point.

little progress in developing the concept of a European "Common Defence Policy", since it was outlined in Title V of the Treaty on European Union. The 1996-97 EU Intergovernmental Conference (IGC) resulted in no significant changes in the nature of the WEU's relationship with the EU. The European Council's ability to set guidelines for the WEU was not strengthened and the objective of fusing the WEU into the EU remains only a "possibility" for the future,[14] despite the fact that nine of the WEU members support that objective. The only innovative item agreed in the Treaty was the decision to include the Petersberg tasks. This lack of substantial reform means that the CFSP will lack any real military underpinnings. As a result, the US has felt reassured that the Europeans will not seek to exclude American influence from matters of continental security.

4. LOOKING INTO THE FUTURE

It would not seem unreasonable to conclude, therefore, that the tensions that characterised transatlantic relations in the early part of the 1990's have been eradicated. Despite scepticism over the extent to which a European pillar in NATO will prove to be effective, nevertheless the turf battles between the Europeans and the Americans appear to have been resolved. All the European countries, including France,[15] support the role of NATO as the leading defence actor on the continent and as the principle forum for ensuring a transatlantic dialogue. However, such a conclusion risks being premature. There remain clouds on the horizon that could cause tensions within the relationship between the US and its European allies into the future.

The fate of Bosnia is one such issue. The missions performed by IFOR in 1996 and then by the Stabilisation Forces (SFOR) in the first half of 1997, were successful in maintaining the peace in Bosnia. Nevertheless, the extreme sensitivity which preceded the American decision to participate in SFOR demonstrated the high political stakes associated with this issue. The Europeans were fearful of being expected to assume sole responsibility for implementing the Dayton Accords and were desirous of securing an American commitment to remain involved. Not until June 1996 did the US signal the part that they were prepared to play and still insisted that their allies should assume a larger proportion of the burden.[16] At the Bergen meeting of NATO, US representatives announced that they were willing to

---

[14]   Article J.7, Intergovernmental Conference, Amsterdam European Council, 17-18 June 1997.

[15]   France has continued to express unhappiness at what it sees as the inadequate "Europeanisation" of NATO's command positions. This has led it to call into question its intention of drawing closer to the Alliance. See, Evans, M. *Franco-US bickerings sours "historic" Madrid summit*, The Times, 7 August 1997.

[16]   Cornwell, R. *US says troops may have to stay in Bosnia*, The Independent, 13 June 1996, p. 10.

contribute 5,000 personnel to the SFOR mission, to the evident relief of the Europeans.

Yet there is now speculation about what will follow after the expiration of the SFOR mandate in the middle part of 1998. With the previous experience of the difficulties in negotiating a successor to IFOR between the US and European governments, there is uneasiness about the prospects for a successor to SFOR. The lack of progress in bringing the Bosnian Serbs, Croats and Muslims together and the slow pace of the civil reconstruction effort means that the conflict could re-ignite if all western military forces were to be removed. The US has hedged against this possibility by following a simultaneous policy of re-arming the Bosnian Muslims, in spite of the worries of European governments. Any discussion relating to the continuation of the western mission in Bosnia raises the thorny question of the relative burdens to be borne on either side of the Atlantic. As a result, the future of Bosnia remains a potentially volatile issue in US-European relations.

Bosnia is a symptom of a broader question within the transatlantic relationship: whether the US is prepared to maintain its leadership function in Europe? Rather than the often-quoted threat of European defence efforts eclipsing the Alliance, the more realistic problem is that of the Europeans being reluctant to undertake any action without the Americans. The US now talks of a "New Atlantic Community" in which the Europeans represent a more equitable partner,[17] but the US may become disillusioned if the Europeans are unable to do things for themselves. Most European countries have developed a tendency to rely on the US for the management of their security. Their inability to develop a more cohesive foreign policy since Maastricht, as well as the lack of progress towards a common defence policy, underlines this problem. Europe grows more powerful economically but its foreign and defence presence on the world stage remains modest.

However, to continue a policy of dependency on the US is not without its risks. It is no longer realistic to expect an American President to treat the European theatre as his principal area of security concern. The CJTF concept envisages flexible coalitions of countries coming together for specific operations and it signals that the US may not wish to participate in crises where it does not feel its interests are involved.[18] The European countries may be in danger of drawing the wrong conclusion from the experience of the Bosnian crisis; that the US will always come to their rescue if they prove to be inadequate to accomplish a particular task. Yet an alternative interpretation can be placed upon US actions over the Balkans. It was actually the confluence of a number of factors, including a sense of opportunism and the pressure of domestic criticism, that brought America to re-engage over the crisis. It would be complacent to rely upon such circumstances reoccurring in the future.

[17] Christopher, W. *A New Atlantic Community for the 21st Century*, Stuttgart, Germany, Washington File, 7 September 1996.

[18] Sloan, S. *Negotiating a new transatlantic bargain*, NATO Review, Vol. 44, No. 2, March 1996, pp. 19–23.

Neither is the defence of Europe any longer a sufficient basis to ensure the cohesion of the transatlantic relationship. This is not to deny its continuing importance. For example, the relationship with Russia and the issue of institutional enlargement to the east will remain subjects of vital interest to the US. Yet there are a host of other pressing concerns for the US in the world; such as the peace process in the Middle East, the threat of nuclear proliferation and the management of its relationship with a fast emerging China. An American presence in Europe acts as a useful staging post to prepare to counter some of these global concerns, but it is insufficient cause in itself to justify the basing of 100,000 US service personnel. Only if they are capable of sharing more of the burden world-wide and demonstrating their utility as allies, can the Europeans hope to preserve the American role on the continent. The US wants to be confident that its allies are willing to participate in both continental and extra-European responsibilities. According to Gebhard, "If the Western Europeans remain uninterested in security policy beyond their continent, US interest in working with Western Europe will wane to the detriment of European security".[19]

To many in the US, the problem reflects the old adage that their country has a global perspective whilst the Europeans retain a more parochial, regional perspective. What has changed in the aftermath of the Cold War is that the US no longer confronts its former Soviet adversary around the world. This used to provide the justification for the US's taxpayers as to why it was necessary for their country to be involved in all overseas crises. Now the US is more discriminating about its involvement, it seeks to weigh up carefully whether it has vital interests at stake. Hence, the Clinton Administration has placed a heavy premium upon multilateralism and called on its European allies to participate more actively in global problems. Whether the Europeans are capable of acting in this way is open to question but the US will measure their value in these terms.

This is not to suggest that even if the Europeans were more pro-active, it would guarantee a condition of transatlantic harmony. The US and its allies do differ in their attitudes towards numerous issues in the world. For example, there were antagonisms over America's support for the Israeli "Grapes of Wrath" campaign in Lebanon, over US military action against Iraq in September 1996 and over the Helms-Burton legislation in Congress.[20] Similarly, in approaches to the UN and the conduct of peacekeeping, fundamental divergences of view exist between Washington and European capitals. Yet there must be a realistic acceptance of the fact that a shared perspective on all issues cannot be certain. For Europe to have an independent foreign policy may occasionally necessitate defining it in

---

[19]   Gebhard, P. *The United States and European Security*, Adelphi Paper 286, Brassey's for the International Institute for Strategic Studies, February 1994, p. 68.

[20]   The Helms-Burton Act seeks to penalise American and foreign companies that conduct certain types of business deals with Cuba and Iran.

opposition to the US. This should not obscure the fact that European and American interests, in most areas of the world, are fundamentally compatible.

It is necessary for the Americans to perceive that the Europeans will be net contributors to the transatlantic relationship and not just recipients of its benefits. A step towards achieving this objective was the signing of the "New Transatlantic Agenda" in December 1995 by President Clinton and the Presidents of the EU Council of Ministers and the European Commission. This document aimed to put in place a list of items for action, building upon the themes and priorities of the "Transatlantic Declaration" that was signed five years before. It was important in two respects. Firstly, it emphasised global issues in which the two sides of the Atlantic share common goals. For example, the EU offered financial support to the Korean Peninsula Development Organisation (KEDO) in order to alleviate the threat of nuclear weapons proliferation by the North Koreans. This has demonstrated that the Europeans can be persuaded to assist with problems that have previously only been US concerns.[21]

Secondly, the document made an important start in broadening the agenda of transatlantic relations away from its traditional focus on military issues. A wider array of concerns was mapped out in Madrid and included such low-intensity threats as terrorism, international crime and drug trafficking. Although many of these types of problems have long been in existence, the post-Cold War security environment has increased their salience. Critics might argue that the arrival of such issues on the EU-US work plan indicated a desire to avoid matters of greater controversy. Alternatively, it might be seen as an appreciation that transatlantic co-operation needs to be fostered across a broader range of areas. As Warren Christopher stated in September 1996, "The danger posed by these threats is as great as any that we faced during the Cold War".[22]

The Agenda also drew attention to the fact that economic issues must be accorded equal significance alongside military matters. Defence was the glue of the transatlantic relationship in the past but it may no longer be enough to keep the community together in the future. This has led to discussion of new forums for co-operation, designed not to replace, but to supplement existing frameworks. During 1995 there was speculation that a Transatlantic Free Trade Area (TAFTA) might be negotiated in order to ease future frictions between the trading blocs. But the NTA skirted this idea on the grounds that it was premature and needed to overcome major issues such as agricultural subsidies.[23] Instead, it declared the more modest goal of creating a "New Transatlantic Market Place". What has been adopted in the Agenda was the

---

[21]   Krenzler, H. and Schomaker, A. *A New Transatlantic Agenda*, European Foreign Affairs Review, Vol. 1, No. 1, July 1996, p. 21.

[22]   Christopher, W. *A New Atlantic Community for the 21st Century*, Stuttgart, Germany, Washington File, 7 September 1996.

[23]   Peeg, E. *Policy Forum: Transatlantic Free Trade*, The Washington Quarterly, Vol. 19, No. 2, 1996, pp. 105–112.

more modest aim of building up greater US-European dialogue between people in business, education and the respective legislatures. This should put in place important building blocks for constructing a closer relationship in the future.

5. CONCLUSION

As far as the Europeans are concerned, the US remains the key actor for organising and orchestrating the security of the continent. Despite the WEU becoming a more capable organisational instrument, it has been shown to be subordinate to NATO. A more tangible European defence identity may emerge over time to deal with small-scale crises where transatlantic priorities differ, but it is insufficiently compelling to drive the Europeans towards its rapid development. The Europeans want the Americans to continue to provide guarantees against the residual risk presented by Russia and to contribute towards the stability of both Western Europe and the wider continent. They also want to preserve NATO as an instrument that enables them to influence wider US policy. Yet to maintain these objectives, the Europeans will have to be willing to offer more in return. The danger, as the French have recognised, is that the Europeans will continue to depend solely upon the US and Washington will grow to regard this as intolerable.

For the US the familiar tension persists between encouraging the Europeans to do more, yet not wanting their own position of leadership to be undermined. If the US plays a more modest role in the security of the continent, whilst encouraging its allies to share the burdens of global responsibilities, then it must accept the implications. Recourse to unilateral policies must be avoided. Washington must also be prepared to accept negative comment from its allies and not expect them to be uncritical supporters of its policies. Whether the US will ever be willing to treat its allies as equals in extra-European problems will remain a question for the longer term future. The answer will await the emergence of a European foreign and defence actor capable of being treated in such a way.

Surveying the last six years in transatlantic security politics, the enduring lesson remains that constant effort must be invested to prevent the development of tensions. The relationship has been proven to be dynamic with a good deal of inherent strength, but the greatest threat to its survival is neglect and complacency.

Chapter 4

Transatlantic Co-ordination and the Middle East Peace Process

Pedro López Aguirrebengoa

1. INTRODUCTION

Almost everything that happens in the world today is of interest to the European Union and the United States. Both are global players in political and economic terms. Both have a broadly similar set of values, belief in democratic terms, human rights and market economies. Both have a common interest in confronting the same global challenges. They are also unified by close security ties and a common interest in handling effectively a wide variety of political and security issues across the globe. There have been substantial and even serious differences of view throughout this century, but disagreement on particular issues is not a sign of drift in the relationship and they have not undermined its basic strength nor its common purpose.

As the then Secretary of State, Warren Christopher said in an address delivered in the Casa de America, in Madrid, on 2 June 1995:[1]

> For half a century, the transatlantic partnership between the United States and Europe has been the leading force for peace and prosperity, not only in our countries, but around the globe. Together, the Old World and the New World have created a better world .... Together we helped to transform former adversaries into allies, and dictatorships into democracies ....

---

[1] US Department of State, Office of the Spokesman, Madrid, 2 June 1995. The title of the address was *Charting a Transatlantic Agenda for the 21st Century.*

33

He further added, regarding the Middle East:

> ... we must bolster our co-operation in regions where the United States and Europe share common interests and historic ties, for example the Middle East. With EU support the 1991 Madrid Conference launched the most promising opportunity for Arab-Israeli peace in two generations. Now is the time to make that promise real by more effectively co-ordinating our economic assistance and working together to bring into being the Middle East .... We should also expand our co-operation in the Mediterranean, an area of vital interest to the EU and the United States. Spain has played a key role in advancing the EU's initiative on this important region, and we look forward to co-operating with you as the Barcelona Conference approaches ...

Among the major problem areas around the world in which both actors are present, for diversified reasons and historical backgrounds, a key one is the Middle East and its Peace Process (MEPP). Often acting together, on occasions disagreeing, sometimes with parallel but complementing perceptions and policies, they always need to be in close contact to exchange information, views and, where appropriate, to follow an agreed approach.

Links between Europe and this region are not new. There is a long history of interaction and mutual influence in a variety of fields, including of course culture but also politics, a history of complementarity, at times of confrontation, never of indifference.

Since the basic frame of the transatlantic relationship took shape with the North Atlantic Treaty Organisation (NATO) at the end of World War II, the overall political context in the Euro-Mediterranean and Middle East regions has changed fundamentally. To name the two most important factors:

(1) The end of the Cold War fundamentally changed the nature of the situation in the Middle East.
(2) The development of the EU in recent years made it possible for Europe to respond as never before to the challenges in the area and to become the full and equal partner of the US that President Kennedy had sought at the beginning of the 1960's.[2]

The real role aimed at and, so far, accomplished by Europe in the MEPP is thus brought to the forefront. This role has been supported by many but it has also frequently been diminished by some parties, despite the clear need to work together for peace, freedom and development, in order to ensure a climate of stability with benefits for all.

European states have never been indifferent to the MEPP. Some have strong historical links to Palestine and the Holy Places, further developed and embodied in agreements reached with the Ottoman Empire. Others had colonial presence or participated in the Peace Conferences that shaped the new situation in the Middle East after the World War I. Some acquired

---

[2]   Speaking in Philadelphia in 1962 President Kennedy said the US was ready "to discuss with a united Europe the ways and means of forming a concrete Atlantic partnership ... a mutually beneficial partnership" for the US.

specific international responsibilities in the area, as did the British with the Mandate on Palestine. They participated actively in the League of Nations in the debates on the Establishment Mandate and the issue of the Holy Places and Jerusalem. They were also active when the question of the future of Palestine was discussed in the United Nations (UN), leading to Resolution 181 (1947) which was never applied. They have participated in the bilateral or multilateral efforts to bring peace to the Middle East, following the successive wars of 1948, 1967 and 1973.

Certainly, the European political role in the Middle East scenario decreased sharply after the 1956 Suez crisis, and because of the effects of Cold War, while the US took a prevailing one, in the wake of bipolarity. Nevertheless, the European presence and economic and cultural ties remained important. They took a new dimension with the coming of age of the European Community and its Preferential Trade Agreements of the 1960's and the Global Mediterranean Policy of the 1970's.

Since the challenging and far-reaching Declaration of Venice in 1980, at a moment when the formalisation of a common foreign policy was practically non-existent, a more engaged policy was initiated. The 1989 Madrid Council and its declarations bore witness to the commitment to look for a just and lasting solution to the conflict, based on the right for self-determination of the Palestinian people, and the right of Israel to exist and live in peace, within the context of security for all. After a very long list of peace initiatives and "plans", over decades of strife, the Madrid Conference finally created and launched in 1991 what was hoped would be the decisive effort leading to the shared goal of such a peace. The framework was complex and delicate, and would later be developed by the key agreements between Israel and the Palestinians.

When the launching of the MEPP took place, Europe was not the main actor. As someone said at the time, "we provided in Madrid the concert hall and the seats, but the music had to be provided by others, the sponsors and mostly by the parties themselves". This is rather unfair. Many people failed to perceive or did not want to acknowledge the discreet and yet constant European efforts helping to catalyse the will and the decisions of the parties, as well as the extent of the economic co-operation commitments and the decisive input in the slow unfolding of the realities of the region.

During the author's years as Ambassador to Israel, he heard many times, even from some of its front line statesmen two arguments; firstly, that Europe, because of its past or of a pretended bias in favour of the Arabs, is "not reliable"; secondly, that because of its difficulties in shaping a common foreign policy, Europe "cannot deliver". These two ideas were set in comparison with the US, considered as the sole efficient and reliable "honest broker". One could recall Henry Kissinger's noted comment: "Tell me which is Europe's telephone number?". Since the times of Ben Gurion and Golda Meir this sort of reasoning was more or less present in Israeli thinking, together with the feeling that, except for the special relationship with the US,

Israel was mainly on its own, Israel being the only judge of its own security, isolated and surrounded by a continuously hostile Arab world. Camp David had reached a formal peace between Egypt and Israel, but only a "cold peace", a peace that had not developed into real co-operation, and had not reached deep into the hearts of the people. Even an exceptional man like Rabin shared some of these views, although he later changed considerably his perceptions.

On the other side the Arab perception has also frequently been that the US, though a necessary partner, sponsor and efficient broker in the MEPP because of its superpower status and its vital interests in the region, is not necessarily an "even handed broker". This is due to its traditionally special political and strategical relationship with Israel and the implications of Israeli issues and interests in internal US policy, at the level of public opinion and in the frame of the relationship between Congress and the Administration.

The perception of a US biased towards Israel in the MEPP is something that has gone through different levels and moods, depending on the evolution of the situation, i.e. the changing attitudes of the US towards the Palestine Liberation Organisation (PLO), in connection with Israel's own changing attitudes with regard to the Palestinian question. Yet at the same time, the Arabs are also well aware of the peculiarly exclusive power and capacity of the US, because of their special relationship with Israel, to influence Tel Aviv and, therefore, the MEPP. It is a question of perception to determine which of the two sides, at a given moment of political circumstances within the complexity of relations between the US and Israel, has had a greater possibility or will to exercise that power.

Since the disappearance of the effects of bipolarity in the region and the Madrid Middle East Peace Conference in 1991, the mood has certainly changed: there have been moments of increasing hope, like those of 1995, with the signing of the Interim Agreement in Washington. Yet since 1996 a climate of slow-down and crisis in the process has prevailed.

In any case, the reality, as illustrated by the breakthrough in the MEPP introduced by the Madrid Conference, after so many decades of strife and dozens of failed initiatives and peace plans over the years, (some 56 have been accounted for), is that although the core elements of peace have to be achieved by the parties within the established frame of bilateral negotiations, the role of the multilateral lanes and of the co-sponsors and other main international contributors, acting as catalysers for the appropriate climate, is crucial. In fact, it would have proved very difficult, even impossible in the very short term, for the parties alone, to engage in such a complex and delicate effort, or to maintain its momentum.

The nature of the bilateral conflict and the respective vital interests of the parties, considered in the wider regional context, with all the different factors present (security, sovereignty, territorial, economic and human aspects), create an intricate web of domestic or foreign constraints. In this context the negotiation of a just and durable peace requires a framework of equal partners and a willingness to engage in mutual concessions or transactions. Otherwise one would not be looking for a negotiated and stable peace, but for an imposed one that, by its own nature, would be a fragile one. It should not be forgotten that the signing of peace, even with all its difficulties, is a much easier task than the building of peace, which goes far beyond the former, and must involve not only the political will, codified in the agreements or treaties by the political leadership, but also the acceptance, co-existence and co-operation among the respective civil societies.

The "Oslo Agreement", signed in Washington (1993), introduced, through mutual recognition between Israel and the PLO as partners in the bilateral negotiations, a sense of at least formal equality, but this has to be nurtured by both parties and must be morally and politically bolstered externally.

Paradoxically, at the time of the East-West conflict, the impact of bipolarity on the region played a role which, although frequently obstructive to the MEPP, could also provide an element of equilibrium between parties which, because of their own condition, situation and relative potential, are essentially unequal. Nobody could, for instance, take Israelis and Palestinians under occupation as equal parties. The end of the Cold War period induced a void and a new structure of power in the region that, as in many other areas, reinforced the global role of the US (the Gulf War is an example). At the same time, the search began for what has been defined as a new international order whose conception and guiding lines, as seen and proposed by the western societies, also imply the building of a multipolar structure, anchored in common basic principles and in a real partnership. The emergent role of the EU is in this sense not only instrumental in the MEPP and in the developments in the Middle East region, but also an important and substantial element *per se* and in the frame of a positive projection of the western alliance and the transatlantic co-operation.

2. EU-US CO-OPERATION IN THE MIDDLE EAST: FROM THE "TRANSATLANTIC DECLARATION" TO THE "NEW TRANSATLANTIC AGENDA"

Over the years a wide range of consultation mechanisms have grown up to foster dialogue between the EC-EU and the US and to meet the different needs of co-operation which have been of considerable use in co-operation on the MEPP. These contacts were formalised in the 1990 "Transatlantic Declaration", which started from a number of shared objectives and provided for:

(1) bi-annual consultations between the President of the Council, the Commission and the US.
(2) bi-annual consultations between the Foreign Ministers (at that time still

in the European Political Co-operation (EPC) framework), the Commission and the US Secretary of State.

(3) ad-hoc consultations between the Foreign Minister of the Presidency, or the Troika and the US Secretary of State.

(4) bi-annual consultations between the Commission and the US government at sub-Cabinet level.

(5) briefings by the Presidency to US representatives on European political co-operation meetings at Ministerial level.

(6) in addition many Troika contacts at political director and expert level as well as contacts and briefings between the respective diplomatic Representatives in various capitals.

As a development of the "Transatlantic Declaration" of 21 November 1990, the present basis of EU-US political relations is the "New Transatlantic Agenda" and the "Joint EU-US Action Plan", adopted on 3 December 1995 by the US, the European Council and the European Commission, on the occasion of the semestral Summit that took place in Madrid under the Spanish Presidency of the EU.

As already pointed out, the Mediterranean and the Middle East have been for a long time among the important issues of the transatlantic relationship. After the crisis following the invasion of Kuwait by Iraq (2 August 1990) transatlantic co-ordination helped to set up the international coalition to face the consequences of that challenge, that led to the so called Gulf War in January-February. After its end, this co-operation was also instrumental to set into motion a revival of the MEPP that finally led to the completely new approach of the Madrid Peace Conference in 1991, based on the double frame of bilateral and multilateral venues. All this was possible by a series of key developments, among them the crucial changes in the Eastern European scenario.

The EU gave constant support during this period, and subsequently, to the initiative taken in 1991 (Madrid Conference) and developed by the US, integrating the EU economic contributions as the major donor into the priorities and orientations primarily defined by the US. The EU has also given a concrete backing, appreciated by the concerned parties, to each phase of the MEPP, working for its consolidation. It gave its support to the "Cairo Agreements" between Israel and the PLO on Palestinian Autonomy (May 1994), to the installation of the "Palestinian Authority" (July 1994): and the signature of the Peace Treaty between Israel and Jordan (October 1994). In 1994 the EU continued to be the main economic contributor to the Palestinian territories with US$ 450 million. The European Investment Bank (EIB) signed in 1995 an agreement with the Palestinian Authority granting 250 million Ecu to finance development projects in the Palestinian Territories.

The EU has also played an active role in the multilateral tracks of the MEPP, especially in the Regional Economic Development Working Group (REDWG). It has been the biggest contributor both on a collective and on a bilateral basis. There has been also a constant effort to be politically present in the region, at a moment when it had to face other challenges in its own continent. It would be possible to recall the long list of démarches made to the parties to the process, even during difficult moments, the numerous trips and contacts to smooth this or that aspect of the developments, as well as the leading role entrusted to the EU by the parties, for instance concerning the Palestinian elections.

The MEPP further developed in the Israeli-Palestinian track with the "Oslo Agreement" (1993) and the signing in Washington of the "Interim Agreement" (28 September 1995), with the EU attending and signing it as special witness. An important role was to be played by the EU in the preparation, co-ordination and observation of the elections for the Palestinian Council.

In the field of economic assistance to the Palestinians, the EU and the US co-operated in the Ad Hoc Liaison Committee and other donor gatherings needed to support the next phases of the Palestinian self-rule, and they worked together to establish a regional financing mechanism for the Middle East and North Africa.

Meanwhile, the agreement on the "Renewed Mediterranean Policy" of the EU was approved in December 1990, including a financial co-operation up to 4.405 billion Ecu for the period 1992-96, which meant an increase of 150 per cent over the previous period. More recently, the European Councils of Lisbon (June 1992), Corfu (June 1994) and Essen (December 1994) gradually defined the orientations for the Barcelona Euro-Mediterranean Conference (27-28 November 1995), held under the Spanish Presidency, and the "Barcelona Declaration" establishing a global partnership between the EU and its 12 Mediterranean associates. The Cannes European Council (June 1995) had approved an economic package of 4,685 billion Ecu in aid for development to the Mediterranean basin countries for the period 1995-99, plus the loans to be granted under special conditions by the European Investment Bank.

The "Barcelona Declaration" (28 November 1995) clearly states that "this Euro-Mediterranean initiative is not intended to replace the other activities and initiatives undertaken in the interests of peace, stability and development of the region, but that it will contribute success". It adds that the participants "support the realisation of a just, comprehensive and lasting peace settlement in the Middle East based on the relevant United Nations Security Council resolutions and principles mentioned in the letter of invitation to the Madrid Middle East Peace Conference, including the principle land for peace, with all that this implies". The relevant point is that all the relevant parties to the MEPP (Israel, Palestinians, Jordan, Syria and Lebanon) are members of the Barcelona Process.

Following shortly after the Barcelona, the "New Transatlantic Agenda" of 3 December 1995 included the following paragraph regarding the Middle East Peace Process:

We reaffirm our commitment to the achievement of a just, lasting and comprehensive peace in the Middle East. We will build on the recent successes in the Peace Process, including the bold steps taken by Jordan and Israel, through concerted efforts to support agreements already concluded and to expand the circle of peace. Noting the important milestone reached with the signing of the Israeli-Palestinian Interim Agreement, we will play an active role at the Conference for Economic Assistance to the Palestinians, will support the Palestinian elections and will work ambitiously to improve the access we both give to products from the West Bank and the Gaza Strip. We will encourage and support the regional parties in implementing the conclusions of the Amman Summit. We will also continue our efforts to promote peace between Israel, Lebanon and Syria. We will actively seek the dismantling of the Arab boycott of Israel.

Many other common engagements of the Agenda could also be applicable to the MEPP, for instance:

We will co-operate to ensure: (1) respect for human rights, for the rights of minorities and for the rights of refugees and displaced persons, in particular the right of return ....

The "Joint Action Plan" included in Part I, paragraph 2, the following:

2. Promoting the Middle East Peace Process
We will work together to make peace, stability and prosperity in the Middle East become a reality.
To this end, we will
(1) continue our support for Palestinian self-government and economic development;
(2) support the Palestinian elections which should contribute to the Palestinian democratic development;
(3) play an active role at the Conference for Economic Assistance to the Palestinians;
(4) work ambitiously to improve the access we both give to products from the West Bank and the Gaza Strip;
(5) encourage Jordanians Palestinians, Israelis and Egyptians to establish comprehensive free trade agreements among themselves;
(6) support the regional parties in their efforts to establish road links, electricity grids, gas pipelines and other joint infrastructure necessary to foster regional trade and investments;
(7) encourage and, as appropriate, support the regional parties in implementing the conclusions of the Amman Summit.
In addition, we will:
(1) continue our efforts to promote peace between Israel, Lebanon and Syria;
(2) actively seek the dismantling of the Arab boycott of Israel.

The Conclusions of the Presidency at the Madrid European Council (15-16 December 1995) took note of the importance of the signature of the New Transatlantic Agenda and Joint Action Plan, considering that the texts agreed represented a qualitative leap forward towards the strengthening of the EU-US relations, entering a new phase of consultations, concertation, and common action. At the same time the Conclusions expressed satisfaction for the signature in Washington (28 September 1995) of the Interim Agreement between Israel and the PLO, deep sorrow for the assassination of Prime Minister Rabin and backed the engagement taken by the new Prime Minister, Peres, to carry on the MEPP with the same determination. They also expressed satisfaction for the progress in the Amman Economic Summit and hoped for positive results in the forthcoming Ministerial Conference for Assistance to the Palestinian People (Paris, 9 January 1996).

3. EU-US ACTION IN THE PEACE PROCESS SINCE 1996

A clear political backing of the MEPP and of the roles played by Shimon Peres, Yasser Arafat and King Hussein was given by the EU Presidency Declaration of 10 March 1996, after the appalling bombings in Israel, and the closure of borders, with a strong appeal to all parties concerned, reaffirming its basic stance. It also announced a number of actions and diplomatic steps. Regular contacts between the EU and the US at different levels continued.[3]

The European Council of Florence (21-22 June 1996) in its Declaration on the Middle East had strongly reaffirmed:

> that peace in the Middle East region is a fundamental interest of the European Union. The Peace Process is the only path to security and peace for Israel, the Palestinians and the neighbouring states. The European Union remains dedicated to supporting it. Alongside the Co-operation Sponsors, the European Union's aim is that Israel and its neighbours may live within secure, recognised and guaranteed borders and the legitimate rights of the Palestinians shall be respected.

It encouraged all parties to:

> re-engage themselves in the Peace Process, to respect and implement fully all the agreements already reached and to resume negotiations as soon as possible on the basis of the principles already accepted by all parties under the Madrid and Oslo frameworks. These cover all the issues on which the parties have agreed to negotiate, including Jerusalem, noting its importance for the parties and the international community, not least the need to respect the established rights of religious institutions.

It also recalled the essential principles on which successful conclusion of the negotiations should be based:

> They have been enshrined in United Nations Security Council Resolutions 242, 338 and 425. The key principles, self-determination for the Palestinians, with all that it implies, and land for peace, are essential to the achievement of a just, comprehensive and durable peace.

It also reaffirmed that on this basis the EU would:

> continue to support the early resumption of the final status negotiations which opened on 5 May and the negotiations on … fully respecting the territorial integrity, independence and sovereignty of Lebanon. The European Union remains committed to supporting the cease-fire between Israel and Lebanon … appeals to all parties in the region to avoid and prevent actions which would prejudice the successful resumption of negotiations and thereby impede the course of the Peace Process … would continue to do everything possible to ensure that the work already begun is pursued and brought to its conclusion.

The general elections in Israel (29 May 1996), and the coming into power of the Coalition Government led by Prime Minister Netanyahu, with a will to square its stronger security concerns with Israel's previous commitments,

---

[3]   Secretary of State Warren Christopher met, for instance, with EU Ambassadors on 11 March 1996, and among other issues the MEPP and the Sharm el Sheick Conference on terrorism were discussed. The EU Declaration of Palermo was appreciated.

introducing in the MEPP emphasis on vague new concepts such as reciprocity, mutuality and peace without preconditions, as well as subsequent events, introduced a slow down of the MEPP. This further emphasised the need for a co-operation between the EU and the US , and other sponsors, in order to keep the MEPP alive, to renew confidence, and to put it back on track and recover its momentum.

The EU-US "open channel" of consultations was activated with a meeting in Washington (26 July 1996) between Assistant Secretary of State, Ambassador Pelletreau, and the Middle East Director of the Irish Presidency; in this meeting due attention was given to the importance of a well functioning Transatlantic relationship to the MEPP which had been the cause of some misunderstandings in the previous months and of a renewed European feeling of frustration at what frequently seemed to be a unilateral, and excluding attitude of Washington towards the EU.

The importance of the EU's role in this situation was also enhanced by the fact that for the six coming months, due to the electoral campaign, the US would have difficulties in fully playing its role in the MEPP. For this reason, it was felt, especially by the Palestinians, that the EU had a moral and political obligation to act more consistently in the MEPP.

With this in mind, on the occasion of the General Affairs Council of Luxembourg (1 October 1996) the EU "appalled by the recent violence and the resulting casualties in Jerusalem and throughout the West Bank and the Gaza Strip", issued a Declaration to the MEPP with a strong call upon both parties to abide by UN Security Council Resolution 1073 (28 September 1996), and to exercise the utmost restraint and to refrain from any actions or words which might lead to further violence.[4] The Declaration pointed out that the EU had discussed its concerns at meetings in New York with Israeli Foreign Minister Levy and in Luxembourg with President Arafat, and that the recent incidents "were precipitated by frustration and exasperation at the absence of any real progress in the Peace Process and firmly believes that the absence of such progress is the root of the unrest". It called on Israel to match its stated commitment to the Peace Process with concrete actions to fulfill its obligations, as well as to refrain from any action likely to create mistrust about its intentions, and on both parties, under the terms of the Declaration of Principles, "not to take any action which would prejudge the outcome of the Permanent Status Negotiations", affirming that it "will work to ensure that this commitment is implemented by both sides".[5] It

---

4   "It urges both sides to avoid resorting to disproportionate force, in particular the use of firearms, tanks and helicopter gunships. It calls on the Government of Israel to prevent its forces from re-entering autonomous areas in Zone A, contrary to the spirit and the letter of the interim Agreement. It further calls on the Palestinian Authority to exert full control over Palestinian forces and to maintain calm in the autonomous areas".

5   "As it declared at the Florence European Council in June 1996, peace in the Middle East is a vital interest of the European Union. Accordingly, the European Union is ready to play an active part in efforts to recommence the negotiations, commensurate with its interests in the region, and on the basis of its major contribution to the Peace Process so far".

furthermore called for "the cessation and reversal of all acts that may affect the status of the Holy Places in Jerusalem", reaffirming its policy on the status of Jerusalem.[6] It also stressed "the importance of the Euro-Mediterranean Association Agreement which is based on a common commitment to the Peace Process".

The EU expressed its belief that urgent progress in the a number of areas was crucial to the Peace Process:

(1) timely implementation of the agreements reached;
(2) positive steps to alleviate the economic problems of the Palestinians (the Council responded favourably to the request of President Arafat for an additional 20 million Ecu assistance);
(3) resumption of full co-operation in order to ensure internal security both in Israel and in the areas under Palestinian authority;
(4) refraining from measures that could prejudge the outcome of the final status negotiations, including annexation of land, demolition of houses, new settlement construction and expansion of settlements;
(5) engagement of the next stage of negotiations as set down in the Declaration of Principles.

A few days later, the Dublin European Council (5 October 1996) took particular interest in the situation of the MEPP, believing that it was time for the EU to enhance its own role with an active and concrete contribution, alongside the other partners of the region, to promote the relaunching of the Peace Process, as the regional parties had demanded, reaffirming what had been said in Florence and again in the Declaration of 1 October, that peace in the Middle East is a fundamental interest of the EU.

To this end the EU appointed Ambassador Moratinos on 21 October 1996 as the European Special Envoy (EUSE) for the MEPP. It was an important move, though this was not necessarily well perceived by all. The previous impression from the US was that they would certainly not object or oppose such a nomination, but in some American minds the idea prevailed that it could prove to be a self-defeating move for the EU. From their point of view it could demonstrate the (apparently) inadequate capabilities of the Europeans to perform a substantive political role in the short term, since the parameters of the negotiation process were already established (as in the case of Jordan), to some extent well under way (Palestinians), or conceptually framed (Syria). They thought that, on the contrary, the EU's role could be much more useful by contributing in the medium and long term to the building of the future architecture of the region. On this line, the State Department Spokesman expressed on 22 October 1996 mixed feelings: the

---

[6] "East Jerusalem is subject to the principles set out in UN Security Council Resolution 242, notably the inadmissibility of the acquisition of territory by force, and is therefore not under Israeli sovereignty. The Union asserts that the Fourth Geneva Convention is fully applicable to East Jerusalem, as it is to other territories under occupation".

collaboration of the Europeans, he said, is fundamental; the US want Europe to be engaged in the MEPP; all the recent trips of European leaders were positive; saying that "the Europeans are part of this effort since they were already present in the Madrid Conference" he nevertheless added that "with regard to the negotiations that are taking place in Taba and Eilat, Palestinians and Israelis have chosen the US, and only the US for these conversations, this is the decision of the parties and probably is the best one, in any case we have to proceed forward on this base". He said that Secretary of State Warren Christopher had sent messages to several European colleagues, inspired by this philosophy. The US obviously wanted all possible help in their efforts, and could accept any European initiative as far as it did not invade what they considered to be their own field of exclusive responsibility.

In February 1997 the EUSE visited Washington where he had extensive contacts with his US counterpart, Ambassador Dennis Ross, and other State Department high officials that would be followed by other regular consultations. The "complementarity" of the EU and the US action in the various tracks of the MEPP was considered. This was followed by the talks of the Troika of regional Directors (8 March 1997) in Washington, shortly before the meeting of the "Summit of Peace Makers" held in Cairo (13 March). As the press statement on the talks reflected, the idea of an "open channel of communication" for enhanced EU-US co-operation and co-ordination was considered.

There is evidence that, in the improved framework of consultations, the EUSE's work has been perceived as more than instrumental. Since then, for well-known reasons, a difficult period started. After the March 1997 Hebron issue and a relatively passive attitude taken by the US, their diplomatic return on the scene was started by the visits of US envoy Dennis Ross in August 1997. These trips were also meant to prepare a new attempt at a breakthrough in the MEPP that was going to be the visit of the US Secretary of State, Madeleine Albright. The fruitful and constant contacts with the parties carried out by the EUSE during this time were appreciated by all parties.

The European work in favour of the MEPP was also at the origin of the letter sent by the Minister of the Dutch Presidency, Van Mierlo, to the Secretary of State Albright, on 8 April 1997, at a time of the soaring crisis on the Har Homa issue. Once again the EU conveyed its reflections and insisted upon the need for a larger transatlantic co-operation. This was followed by the visit of Prime Minister Netanyahu to the Netherlands on 10 April 1997.

The Conclusions of the Presidency at the Amsterdam European Council (16-17 June 1997), included in Annex III a "Call of the European Union in favour of Peace in the Middle East" which reaffirmed all the basic elements of the EU's position on the MEPP. The work of the EUSE can been perceived in this European initiative.

On September 1997, acting on behalf of the EU Presidency, Luxembourg Minister Poos sent a new communication to the Secretary of State, reaffirming the will of a collaboration and complementarity, together with two concrete ideas to foster the MEPP: that of a "code of conduct" to be suggested to the parties; and the creation of a Permanent Committee on Security[7].

In 1998 the lack of progress in the Middle East Peace Process and the threat that this poses to the stability and security of the region has been a source of persistent and grave concern. The EU has continued, through the efforts of its Special Envoy for the Middle East Peace Process, through its diplomatic relations and economic involvement, and through its relations of friendship and trust with the various parties, to work with the parties concerned both in the region and outside to help rebuild trust and confidence, and to relaunch the Peace Process and help those striving to carry it forward. The contacts with the US and the backing of the American initiative have been meaningful. The EU has followed closely the developments of this initiative: meetings of the Secretary of State Madeleine Albright with Prime Minister Netanyahu and Chairman Arafat on 18 December 1997 with the proposal of the four point agenda (security, credible further redeployment, time out and accelerated permanent status talks); meetings of President Clinton on 20 February and the visit of Prime Minister Netanyahu to Washington; and London encounters of 4-5 May. Among the multiple EU actions the strong involvement of the Presidency in London talks, following the visits to the Middle East of the President of the Commission (6-13 February) and of the President of the Council (17-21 April), can be recalled.

The European Council of Luxembourg (12-13 December 1997) had established a frame of orientations for a policy of the EU directed at reestablishing confidence among the parties and facilitating the peace progress. At the Cardiff European Council on 15 and 16 June 1998, the Heads of State and Government of the European Union underlined the need for all concerned to show courage and vision in the search for peace, based on the relevant UN Security Council resolutions and the principles agreed at Madrid and Oslo, including full implementation of existing commitments under the Israeli/Palestinian Interim Agreements and the Hebron Protocol. They called on Israel to recognise the right of the Palestinians to exercise self-determination, without excluding the option of a State. At the same time, they called upon the Palestinian people to reaffirm their commitment to the legitimate right of Israel to live within safe, recognised borders. In this context the Union recalls its opposition to Israeli settlements in occupied Arab territories and to any change in the legal or demographic status of Jerusalem and its attachment to security co-operation.

---

[7] Among the possible tasks the following main ideas and aims could be considered: 1. to institutionalise Israeli/Palestinian security co-operation in a permanent and joint mechanism that could be maintained in any circumstances; 2. it would symbolise the commitment by both parties to joint crisis management under specific lines such as the EU's proposed code of conduct, allowing the parties to address together any security incidents and to prevent them from affecting the whole negotiating process.

The basic requirements for peace are well known: the right of all States and all peoples in the region to live in peace within safe, recognized borders, respect for the legitimate aspirations of the Palestinian people to decide their own future, the exchange of land for peace, the non-acceptability of the annexation of territory by force, respect for human rights, the rejection of terrorism of all kinds, good relations between neighbours, and compliance with existing agreements and the rejection of unilateral initiatives which might pre-empt negotiations on the Permanent Status.

4. FACING THE FUTURE

In conclusion, it seems that all the parties have understood the aims of the EU's policy in favour of the MEPP and want more European presence and more European commitment in that unfinished task of bringing a future of peace, economic prosperity, stability and freedom to the region.

With regard to the co-operation in the Arab world and the Mediterranean, and especially in relation to co-operation for development, it is essential that the action of the EU and the US in these areas be parallel, or complementary, but never opposed or competing. They should be guided by the criteria of concertation and co-ordination established in the Transatlantic Declaration and Joint Action Plan.

When the pending phases of the MEPP start, and it is hoped that this will soon be feasible, especially the Israeli-Palestinian negotiations on the permanent status, the core issues will have to be faced. Some are strictly bilateral (and it is up to the parties to decide upon these), but have also regional implications (such as the question of the refugees, water, or economic issues). The question of the future Jerusalem has a political, territorial and sovereignty component that is strictly bilateral: but it also has a religious-cultural side that goes beyond the parties and in which a large part of the international community, as well as the three great monotheistic religions, have important interests at stake.

In any case, in order to deal with the most crucial bilateral and regional aspects, such as security, with all its implications in the various fields, the parties will presumably need an important moral and political backing, maybe assistance in providing ideas or advice that will create and maintain the necessary favourable climate, as well as continued economic, and, in some cases, technical assistance or expertise, for the process of reaching peace as well as for the long term task of building it up. As an immediate, interested and potentially affected neighbour that is trying to create a new kind of global partnership linking both sides of the Mediterranean, embodied in the Barcelona Process, Europe has, with others, an important and concrete role to play.

Co-ordination and concertation should not remain at symbolic level, limited to a mere, if privileged, exchange of information. The importance of common Euro-American interests at stake call for substantial complementarity. Moreover, Europe cannot continue forever to finance a peace process from which it sometimes feels politically excluded and the stagnation of which is a potential threat to long range initiatives of its own, such as the Barcelona process.

The EU fully supports renewed US commitment to the peace process and it is sincerely hoped that it will fully succeed. However, given the increasing complexity of the situation both on the ground and in the American domestic arena, the Union should prepare for the possible failure of ongoing efforts.

If that were the case, there would be room for other European initiatives which, in the spirit of substantial complementarity, could help the US to relaunch the peace process.

In the past there have been some indications regarding the possibility of convening, a sort of Madrid II Conference, together with the sponsors and the relevant regional parties, under the terms of the American and the Soviet invitation letter of 18 October 1991 which did not exclude such a possibility, provided there is a consent of all the parties involved. This would be aimed at recovering and strengthening the process, on the base of the spirit and principles that inspired its launching and its development in the agreements subscribed by the parties. The Franco-Egyptian idea, joint call for peace of 18 May, of a Conference of "peace savers", with an eventual second phase with the parties, could be a step in that direction. Another possibility would be to undertake a process of "thinking-together" with a view to search for possible "synergies" between the multilateral track of the peace process and the potential of the Barcelona process. Both ideas could possibly be integrated into a single, ambitious initiative.

As experienced in the II Euro-Mediterranean Conference in Malta (15-16 April 1997), the situation created by the ailing MEPP has negatively influenced the development of Chapter I of the Barcelona partnership (Political and Security). This has been so especially with regard to the work for a future Charter on which could be based a "common area of peace and stability", and to some extent concerning the adoption of confidence and security-building measures. Barcelona was actually conceived in 1975, when the achievement of the MEPP seemed close, as a *post pacem* instrument.

Nevertheless, the *ad hoc* Euromed ministerial sessión of June 1998 in Palermo positively proved the will to preserve and develop the ongoing, gradual and long-term process within the globality of the Barcelona Declaration and its three Chapters. Not only can the Barcelona process help the MEPP, it is today the only forum where all the parties sit together, by nurturing the appropiate climate, and contributing through those "synergies". It will also play an important role, once peace is achieved bilaterally by the parties, in keeping up and building that peace. The will to create the future Euro-Mediterranean Charter exists, and, though arriving at it may be difficult, it could provide a framework of comprehensive guarantees for peace and stability.

Chapter 5

EU-US Co-operation in the Framework of the United Nations

Sir David Hannay

1. INTRODUCTION

Before one addresses the potential for and desirable objectives of European Union-United States co-operation at the UN one needs to take a wider view on the scope and nature of EU-US co-operation over foreign policy issues as a whole and also on the general methodology of EU-US foreign policy co-operation. The United Nations does not exist in a vacuum; nor, although its detractors would allege that it does, does it simply churn out wordy and worthy resolutions which disappear as quickly as they emerge, into the diplomatic waste paper basket. In recent years the UN has authorised the use of force against aggressors and those who put international peace and security at risk; it has imposed mandatory economic sanctions on several countries; it has mounted a wide range of peacekeeping operations, some more successful than others; it has attempted to mobilise a global response to some of the major challenges of the present day environmental degradation, excessive population growth, the abuse of human rights. These are all serious issues of foreign, and economic and social policy which directly engage the interests of the EU and its Member States and of the US, in some cases to the extent of using military force. It is, therefore, no good hoping that satisfactory EU-US co-operation in New York, Geneva or elsewhere on UN issues will simply emerge as if by magic from some piece of consultative machinery like weekly meetings of UN Ambassadors. Such co-operation will only occur if the ministers in capitals, who send UN Ambassadors their instructions, communicate effectively together and if their ministries are in continued contact over the handling of the questions of the day. Otherwise all the good intentions and hard work of UN Ambassadors will founder on the rocks of conflicts of interest or appreciation which inevitably occur when such major issues of foreign policy have to be decided.

2. EU-US FOREIGN POLICY CO-OPERATION AND THE CFSP

The point of departure for any wider consideration of EU-US foreign policy co-operation has surely to be that this relationship has been, is now and will continue for the foreseeable future to be the single most important external relationship in the fashioning and execution of Common Foreign and Security Policy (CFSP). There will of course be many other relationships which will need careful nurturing and development, with Russia, with Japan, with China and with the leading countries of the developing world but none of these will equal in significance or complexity the relationship with the US. From the earliest days of European political co-operation in the 1970's this relationship has shown how troublesome it can be to operate. Henry Kissinger's famous complaint about not knowing whom to contact was matched by Richard Holbrooke's jibe that Europe was sleeping when Greco-Turkish relations reached a critical point in early 1996. On the European side complaints about being taken for granted and not being properly consulted by the US are so legion that they are hardly worth enumerating. The hard facts are that both sides have a good deal of right on their side in their complaints; that no useful purpose is served by exchanging one-liner criticisms of the way the institutions of the other work, or fail to work; and that experience shows that both the EU and the US are still far from being properly organised to achieve successful co-operation in fast-moving and sensitive foreign policy crises.

The debate on the European side on how this relationship should be organised has been bedeviled from the outset by two opposed schools of thought. The first has insisted that the Europeans must begin by formulating their own policy on an issue and only then deal with the US; that such dealings must be institutionally constrained through the EU Presidency or the Troika; and that any development that seems to cut the US in on any part of CFSP as a kind of shadow member must be eschewed. The second school of thought points out that it is often necessary, as part of formulating an EU policy, to know first authoritatively what US policy on the matter in question is; that on matters which are going to involve actual co-operation between EU members and the US, perhaps even extending to military or quasi-military action, it makes sense to begin working together from the outset and that, in any case, it is an illusion to suppose that one can keep the US, with its worldwide diplomatic network, completely out of any EU discussions. It is better to organise their involvement rather than to watch it develop in the well-tried, subterranean and opaque channels which are daily used now. As so often the discussion between the two schools tends to become excessively scholastic and to bear little practical relevance to the subject matter being discussed. An acceptable method of co-operating between the EU and the US is unlikely to be found at either end of the spectrum of choice.

But the debate is also troubled by a good deal of spurious rhetoric. It is argued that Europe must learn to handle things "on its own", whatever that may mean in a complex crisis in which both the EU and the US are involved. That view was prevalent from the outset of the crisis in the former Yugoslavia. It is also argued that what Europe lacks is the "political will" to operate a foreign policy, as if some institutional change within the EU could mysteriously create a willingness to engage troops in battle or to impose economic sanctions where none previously existed. On the US side the workings of Congress are somehow required to be exempt from the discussion of co-operation within a framework of international law. But the reality of some recent developments shows how flawed most of this rhetoric is. So far as Europe doing things on its own is concerned, there are two major snags. The first relates to the resources, diplomatic, economic and military, which are available to deal with a particular crisis or situation. No-one doubts that Europe has a lot of economic clout and that a number of its Member states can make an effective military contribution. But how often are its means now and in the near future going to be sufficient on their own to handle a crisis? How often will it not make more sense to marshall all EU and US resources behind a single policy option? That brings out the second snag. If the US is not involved as a co-participant with the EU in some major international operation, then it is all too likely to be prayed in aid by one or more of the parties to the dispute to offset the pressure and actions of the EU. These were the considerations which led to the Europeans again and again, from the beginning of the Clinton Administration, to seek the full participation of the US in the efforts to resolve the crisis in Bosnia. It can be argued that it was the failure to organise such a joint effort, motivated as much as anything by US reluctance to engage its troops on the ground, which, to a greater extent than the merits or demerits of the policies espoused by the EU and the US, resulted in three years of frustration and friction for the whole international community and the not wholly justified public impression that the EU was somehow responsible for the failure to bring the war in Bosnia to an end. It is, unfortunately, only too easy to think of plenty of other potential foreign policy crises, in and around the former Soviet Union, in the Middle East, in East Asia, to give only the more obvious example, where failure by the EU and the US to work closely together could result in the frustration of the policies of both of them.

If the need to co-operate is evident, the means to achieve such co-operation is by no means straightforward. The pitfalls posed by the two extreme schools of thought referred to before will need to be avoided. There needs to be some machinery for contact both at the political and at the technical levels, with the latter providing scope for discussion on an informed basis of both military and economic aspects of a problem. There needs to be provision for a more intensive sharing of the underlying analyses of various situations, including, where possible, exchange of highly sensitive intelligence material. It is probably wiser for a non-practitioner not to venture further into attempting to prescribe how all this can best be achieved. Suffice it to say that in the absence of some standing machinery to concert EU and US policies it is highly unlikely that the degree of co-operation both sides aspire to in public statements will actually be achieved. Nor will the idea of such concertation taking place under the auspices of an existing international organisation such as NATO, crucial though the involvement of that body will be to the successful handling of some of the problems that will arise, be likely to prosper.

3. EU-US CO-OPERATION ON GENERIC ISSUES

Reverting now from the more global aspects of EU-US co-operation on foreign policy to the specifics of co-operation at the UN, one can see that many of the same problems occur in microcosm and need to be addressed. In analysing these UN problems it is probably simpler to separate them out into two main categories. The first of these relates to what could be called generic UN issues; how the organisation is financed; what it should be seeking to do both in the fields of international peace and security and of development, the two main tasks given to the UN under its Charter; what reforms are needed to the organisation and its agencies to make it more efficient and effective; whether, and if so how, the Security Council should be enlarged. The second category relates to specific issues of foreign or economic or social policy that come forward, questions of human rights, the prevention of the proliferation of weapons of mass destruction and progress towards disarmament, or environmental and population policies whose future development will crucially affect the whole international community.

So far as generic UN issues are concerned, it needs to be recognised from the outset that there are substantial differences of approach between the EU and the US and that these differences have been tending to widen in the last few years. Partly this reflects a fundamental difference of attitude which separates a super-power, and there is only one now, which finds it difficult to accept the constraints of supra-national decision-making and law, from a grouping of middle-ranking countries, each one of which has long since abandoned the illusion that it can on its own further and protect its principal national interests. Partly, also it reflects the working of the US Constitution which makes it inherently difficult for the executive to commit itself credibly on matters of supply or to accept the supremacy of international law. This difference of attitude is not going to be washed away by any amount of diplomatic sleight of hand, if only because on the US side it reflects a genuine, if regrettable, loss of public support for the UN which it will take much time and effort to remedy. The Europeans on the other hand, while also disappointed by some of the developments at the UN, and in particular the shortcomings of some of the more ambitious peacekeeping missions, are generally more inclined to give the UN the benefit of the doubt. They see the UN as an integral and significant part of their overall foreign policy approach, not as an optional extra to be turned to only if it looks likely to produce the right answer to a pressing problem. They want to remedy its defects as an instrument for peacekeeping and conflict prevention; not discard it because it has failed to achieve a 100 per cent success record. They want to strengthen the force of international law as represented by the International Court of Justice and an International Criminal Court.

It would be realistic to assume that not all EU-US differences over generic UN issues can be resolved by consultation but it would be a policy of despair and one likely to be increasingly damaging to overall EU-US foreign policy co-operation simply to take them as given and not try to do anything about them. In relation to finance the Europeans have, in fact, put on the table in New York proposals which would substantially lighten the peacekeeping burden on the US and produce a system for calculating the sharing out of peacekeeping costs in the future which would accurately and objectively calculate each country's capacity to pay, with adjustments taking place promptly and automatically to reflect changes in the prosperity of different countries. In return a commitment is sought to paying off arrears, to prompt and full payment in the future and to a series of disincentives for countries which do not fulfil commitments. There should on this issue be a basis for serious negotiation once the US presidential election has taken place. The Europeans themselves would, under their own proposal, be accepting a system which raised their contribution, so they hardly need to apologise for wanting to settle the question. On the wider reform of the UN and its agencies, the EU and its principal Member States have now established common ground with the US on the broad lines of what is needed at the 1996 G-7 Summit meeting at Lyons. It will not be easy to persuade other UN members to accept all these prescriptions but a joint effort to do so over a period of years makes far more sense than a stand-off, with the EU defending a status quo which they know contains many imperfections and the US launching sporadic unilateral sallies which do more damage than they achieve effective reforms. This sort of approach applied to other generic UN issues should produce dividends over time and there is really no satisfactory alternative to it. It is, after all, a crucial EU interest that the US should feel more comfortable with the UN and that US public support for the organisation should be restored. A UN from which the US becomes increasingly alienated will be to some extent a repetition of the mistakes of the 1920's and will not be a UN capable of undertaking the tasks which the EU wants to see it do.

4. EU-US CO-OPERATION ON POLICY ISSUES

But the headlines at the UN will always be dominated not by issues of organisation and institutional reform but by the way the policy issues of the day, whether they be threats to international peace and security or to the environment of the planet, are handled. That also will be the yardstick for its public support. It is on these specific issues that EU-US co-operation at the UN will need to focus if it is to be an effective reality and not just a series of diplomatic pirouettes. On many issues the EU and the US have a natural tendency to see eye to eye. For both the spread of democracy, the halting of human rights abuses, resistance to aggression and terrorism and the prevention of the spread of weapons of mass destruction are central to the formulation of their foreign policies. But when it comes to taking measures against actions which attack or undermine these broad objectives there are frequently differences of emphasis which can widen into policy splits. Only the very closest EU-US concertation, not just in New York and Geneva but between capitals and political leaders will prevent this occurring. It certainly can be achieved and has been frequently in recent years. The solid front against Iraq's aggression in Kuwait, the support for peacekeeping operations from Namibia and Cambodia to Haiti and El Salvador, the measures taken against Libyan terrorism, the successful campaign to prolong indefinitely the Nuclear Non-Proliferation Treaty all stand as examples of that. But there have been failures too; confusion and tension over how best to handle the problems in the former Yugoslavia; disagreement over how to treat Cuba; the differences over how far to go in introducing binding obligations to protect the world's environment. What is rather clear from the examples of both successes and failures in EU-US co-operation at the UN is how crucial such success or failure is to the success or failure of UN action in the case in point. This is not surprising. The EU and its Member States and the US are by a long way the largest players at the UN. In terms of peacekeeping and its finance, of the regular budget and of the back-up both by governmental and non-governmental agencies they bring the most to the table. But each, with its world-wide diplomatic lobbying network, can be formidably effective in stopping or diverting UN action of which it disapproves. So each, in most cases, has the capacity to cancel the other out; together they represent an extremely powerful combination. It is not, therefore, an exaggeration to say that a key factor in determining whether the UN tends in future to revert to the rhetorical jousting arena it was for so much of the time during the Cold War years or whether it continues to be the problem-solving instrument which it was intended to be by its Anglo-American founding fathers and which it has fitfully and patchily become since the end of the Cold War, will be the degree of success of EU-US co-operation.

It will be important however to avoid one trap in working for strengthened EU-US co-operation at the UN, namely an exclusive closed-shop attitude to the rest of the membership. It is all too easy to become so absorbed in the effort to work up common EU-US positions as to forget that there are some 170 other countries in the world, each with its views and its interests, of which full account has to be taken if the UN is to function effectively and equitably. If an attempt were to be made to impose a kind of EU-US duopoly on UN policy, it would soon break down and the only result would be a reversion to the North-South confrontation of the 1970's which did no good either to the North or to the South and certainly not to the UN as a whole. That means that both the EU and the US need to keep their doors and their ears open to the views of the rest of the membership and that any intensification of EU-US co-operation must be matched with a strengthening of consultative links with countries outside their magic circle.

How then is this strengthened EU-US co-operation to be achieved? Obviously a heavy burden will fall on the UN Ambassadors and their staff at the different UN headquarters; and it already does so. A balance will need to be struck here, as in the wider arena, between the demands of EU joint activity and EU-US co-operation. The US cannot simply be cut in on each and every EU meeting, even if they wanted to do so. Each side will need to grow a bit more tolerant of the fact that neither is a completely free agent. Just as the EU has to accept that US positions are often the outcome of a Byzantine process of inter-departmental negotiation and dealings with the Hill in Washington which cannot be unstitched in New York in order to suit EU preferences, so the US will need to accept that EU positions result from hard-fought compromises between Member States and equally cannot be re-fashioned just to fit US policy. This does not, it is submitted, mean that a huge amount of common ground cannot be established. But it does require a greater degree of sensitivity to the problems each other has in policy formulation and a greater willingness to take account of these than has hitherto been the case. As has been said earlier, co-operation in New York, while essential, is not sufficient to ensure success. There have to be close links at the foreign ministry and political levels too. When the EU and the US meet at political level they must be ready to grapple with and try to resolve the main issues that separate them at the UN, not just decide that the subject matter is too complex and too technical and can be left to UN Ambassadors to sort out. Clearly if some standing machinery is established to manage day-to-day EU-US foreign policy co-operation it will need to handle a number of UN issues both of a general and a specific type.

It is sometimes suggested that the Security Council is different and is quite outside the scope of EU-US foreign policy co-operation, since the EU, as such, is not, and is not likely in the near future to become, a member of the

Security Council. In reality the distinction is not so clear cut. The Maastricht Treaty provided for intensified co-operation between the EU members of the Security Council and those that are not members; and the EU frequently takes positions and even decides joint actions on matters that are under discussion within the Security Council. In these circumstances the EU members of the Security Council already work very closely together and should increasingly do so in future; and collectively they will clearly need to work more closely with the US if EU-US co-operation at the UN is to be a reality. A good deal of experience was gained of this during the handling of the Bosnia crisis and the main difference is that the EU side of the discussion is not handled by the EU Presidency but by the EU members of the Security Council, both the permanent and the non-permanent members. Even within informal meetings of the Permanent Members of the Security Council, currently five with two EU members, but at some date in the near future likely to be more numerous in both categories, it is perfectly possible to achieve both a reflection of EU policy positions and a high degree of EU-US co-operation. It is not the institutional characteristics of the Security Council which are the main limiting factor in such co-operation.

5. CONCLUSION

Enough has been said in this article to show the extent to which the UN will be a key test-bed in the years to come not only of the operation of an enduring European Common Foreign and Security Policy itself but also of the capacity to co-operate between the EU and the US. If this co-operation fails to work well at the UN, it will probably not be working terribly well elsewhere across the board. If, on the other hand, co-operation at the UN is successfully achieved in most, but certainly not all, fields then this will strengthen the overall structure of transatlantic co-operation.

PART II

THE ECONOMIC AGENDA

Chapter 6

The Transatlantic Market Place: a Challenge for the WTO?

Rolf H. Hasse

1. INTRODUCTION

Several issues are of paramount importance in ensuring the effectiveness, or indeed the future, of the transatlantic market place. These are:

(1) the importance of a liberal trade order;
(2) the necessity of positive contributions to the World Trade Organisation (WTO);
(3) the task of finishing the aims outlined in the "Marrakesh Declaration" of 14 April 1994.[1]

However, countries choose various policies and conflicting ways and means of achieving their objectives in trade affairs, particularly the countries of the so-called triad, i.e. the European Union, Japan and the United States. Two of these, the US and the EU, are the main contributors to a trade policy which is still based to a large extent on unilateralism, bilateralism and regionalisation rather than on genuine and multilateral actions and rules. Therefore the WTO, still in its infancy, is under severe pressure.

In the following, the main threats to the WTO will be pinpointed, sometimes in a provocative and contentious way, in order to alert those responsible for implementing unhelpful policies.

---

[1]　See Chapters 1-4 *ante*. See generally the Appendix *post*.

2. PROBLEMS TO BE FACED IN TRADE AFFAIRS

The WTO is designed for the 21st century as a means of revitalising a trade order based on rules and multilateralism. The Uruguay Round left huge tasks which will put enormous pressure on the WTO for the next ten years. Moreover, the WTO is challenged by the "national" trade orders which have been introduced during the last two decades. The main constructors and terminators of these nationally institutionalised trade orders are:

(1) the US;
(2) the EU; and
(3) Japan.

These countries have built up trade regimes and trade policies based on:

(1) aggressive reciprocity;
(2) unilateral action;
(3) bilateralism;
(4) regionalism;
(5) a tendency to favour quantitative restrictions; and
(6) decisions which belong to the so-called grey-zone of trade law.

Nevertheless, the future of the international trade order will depend mainly on the decisions being taken in the "Transatlantic Market Place".[2] The EU and the US represent the interest and knowledge of the virtues of multilateralism and they know best the hardships of losing the benefits of open markets and the most-favoured-nation. Japan has up to now been exploiting its opportunities as an outsider of the General Agreement on Tariffs and Trade (GATT)/WTO system. It has been taking part in GATT but its internal and external economic systems do not comply with the underlying structures and implicit assumptions of the established international economic order.[3] Therefore, the analysis and the proposals must not be concentrated wholly on the Atlantic region and their political actors. It is suggested that the "Atlantic" group of countries should be enlarged by including Japan in an initiative to be entitled TRIEMA (Trilateral Initiative for Equal Market Access). The rationale is that this core group (i.e. the EU, the US and Japan) should, together, reform the multilateral system.

---

[1]   GATT Focus, No. 107, Special Issue, May 1994.

[2]   See Wolfgang R. H. *Towards a New Transatlantic Marketplace?*, Gütersloh 1996; see also Elke T. *Die USA und die EG: Wirtschaftskooperation in einem "neuen" Atlantismus*, Ebenhausen, July 1992.

[3]   See Hasse R., Hepperle B., Wolf S. *Weiterentwicklung des handelspolitischen Instrumentariums*, Hamburg, 1994, pp. 1–208; see also Van Marion M. F. *Liberal Trade and Japan. The Incompatibility* and Krugman P. *Trade with Japan. Has the Door Opened Wider?*, Chicago and London, 1991.

3. THE "NATIONAL" CHALLENGES FOR WTO

The challenges for the WTO emerge from "national" trade orders, being created and implemented:

(1) before the Uruguay Round;
(2) during the Uruguay Round; and even
(3) after the Uruguay Round and just before the launching of WTO.

3.1 US Trade Policy

The main characteristics of the US trade policies against the spirit of multilateralism and GATT were:

(1) the unilateral actions based on the family of Section 301 laws since 1974;
(2) the bilateral negotiations and decisions of the US and Japan since the middle of the 1980's (MOSS, SII et al), especially the preference for the results-approach[4] instead of the rules-approach of GATT;
(3) the newly increased unilateral attitude to introduce and enforce economic sanctions (Helms-Burton Act or Cuban Liberty and Democratic Solidarity Act of March 1996) by systems of black-listing and extraterritorial enforcement of national regulations;
(4) a tendency towards regionalism[5] (North American Free Trade Area (NAFTA), 1 January 1994; the vision for a Pan-American Free Trade Zone from Alaska to Argentina until 2005: Free Trade Agreement of Americas (FTAA); the target for a Asia-Pacific Free Trade Area until 2010, Asia-Pacific Economic Co-operation (APEC));
(5) the policy of increasing protectionism or implementing protectionist laws (such as the Omnibus Trade and Competitiveness Act (Trade Act) 1988; the Food, Agriculture, Conservation and Trade Act (Farm Act) 1990; and the Omnibus Budget Reconciliation Act and Export Enhancement Act 1992) despite the agreement of Punta del Este (1986)[6] which aimed at a "roll back"[7];
(6) the failure to fulfill the obligations of the Uruguay Round in the areas of textile and clothing, services etc.;
(7) the failure to adjust national procedures and trade laws to the rules of the WTO, i.e. to the Dispute Settlement Systems, and the threat of an

---

[4] See Tyson L. A. *Who's Bashing Whom? Trade Conflict in High-Technology Industries*, Washington DC, 1992. Moss: Market Oriented Sector Selective (1985/86); SII: Structural Impediment Initiative (since 1989).

[5] WTO, *Regionalism and the World Trading System*, Geneva, April 1995, p. 33.

[6] For the text of this agreement see Jackson J. H. *The World Trade Organization, Constitution and Jurisprudence*, London 1998, (Pinter), pp. 180–189.

[7] See Tables 1 and 2 *post.*

American rejection in case of judgments against the US (a "three-strikes out" attitude) which is jeopardising the WTO;

(8) the initiative for a Transatlantic Free Trade Area (TAFTA) which is presented as a means for global liberalisation but may well fuel discrimination; and

(9) the most recent example of a bilateral and results-approach agreement: the US-Japan Agreement on Automobile and Automobile Parts of 21 October 1996.

3.2 EC Trade Policy

The EC trade policy was very similar to US trade policy until 1994: aggressive reciprocity, regionalism, a policy of increasing protectionism and reluctance to dismantle trade barriers. The more recent trends are focused upon below.

(1) During the 1980's the EC increased the level of protectionism before Punta del Este 1986 which it had been keeping for many years: there was no "roll back"[8].

(2) The EC has been continuing its policy of regionalisation by a series of new bilateral (such as the Europe Agreements with the Central and Eastern European Countries (CEEC)) or multilateral treaties with European Free Trade Association (EFTA) countries (such as the European Economic Area (EEA) with the EFTA countries).

(3) It is of great concern that, as part of the political compromise to finish the Uruguay Round, the EC altered the rule to introduce anti-dumping actions from a qualified to a simple majority in the Council. As a result the number of cases and the volume of trade under anti-dumping suspicion and action increased considerably[9].

(4) Just as the WTO came into being, the EC introduced its "Trade Barriers Regulations" (22 December 1994) which are only partly compatible with the rationale of the WTO and its rules.

(5) Last but not least, the troublesome Banana Case[10] is an indicator of the special kind of deliberate discrimination by trade preferences.

3.3 Japanese Trade Policy

Japan is still a country whose trade order and economic structure do not fit the rationale of GATT 47 or GATT 94 despite the formal compliance of that country to these agreements.

---

[8] See Table 1 *post*.
[9] See Tables 3 and 4 *post*.
[10] The Banana Case is a major trade dispute over the EU's import régime for bananas, which has involved the EU and US for several years and has led to several GATT/WTO panels.

3.4 Conclusion

To sum up one can therefore say that the WTO came into being on 1 January 1995, but its most important members have been weakening its frame and contents.

4. OPTIONS FOR GREATER COMPATIBILITY

4.1 TAFTA, Vehicle or Obstacle?[11]

The idea of the Transatlantic Free Trade Area (TAFTA) was launched at the time of ratification of the WTO. This was a peculiar coincidence, because any free trade association includes preferential treatment and discrimination, whereas the WTO aims at revitalising multilateral trade liberalisation. That is why doubts arose about the targets of this initiative. If the supporters of TAFTA predominantly favour the aspect of a free trade zone, this will be a negative challenge to the WTO. What makes this possibility even worse is that it would be launched by the WTO's two most important members, the US and the EU. If TAFTA becomes mainly an institutional framework or a mechanism for analysing and solving conflicts, in advance or subsequently, then TAFTA is the wrong label for a promising institution. Trade relations between the US and the EC are prone to conflict, and this potential will increase when:

(1) agriculture;
(2) services;
(3) telecommunications;
(4) intellectual properties; and
(5) technical standards

are discussed to establish open markets and competition. The Transatlantic Action Plan and the Transatlantic Business Dialogue (TABD) of November 1995[12] must be seen in this context.

However, TAFTA may serve as a body to handle and remove important obstacles for any international rule. Both parties may act as a group of interested and involved countries, and their proposals may ease the negotiations in the WTO according to the Marrakesh Declaration.

However, even with these positive aims, TAFTA will continue to

[11] See Horst S., Langhammer J. R., Piazolo D. *The Transatlantic Free Trade Area, Fuelling trade discrimination or global liberalisation?*, in Journal of World Trade, Vol. 30, 1996, pp. 45-61; see also Freytag A., Zimmermann R. *Die Auswirkungen eines transatlantischen Freihandelsabkommens auf die deutsche Industrie*, Institut für Wirtschaftspolitik der Universität zu Köln, Köln, July 1996.
[12] See Gardner A. L. *A New Era in US-EU Relations? The Clinton Administration and the New Transatlantic Agenda*, Brookfield 1993.

incorporate an important disadvantage: it will be a bilateral initiative and an independent and institutional challenge to the WTO. A more multilateral framework and multilateral scope is necessary.

4.2 TRIEMA as a More Appropriate Option

The Trilateral Initiative for Equal Market Access (TRIEMA) is in some sense a proposal to enlarge the idea of TAFTA and the Transatlantic Agenda and Action Plan as a framework of conference building.[13]

If TAFTA is designed as support for the WTO then the size of the group and its fundamental basis will have to be considered. A bilateral TAFTA may be helpful but it will not be an optimal solution. A better alternative may be to include Japan, and to include all three under the roof of the Organisation for Economic Co-operation and Development (OECD). This is the central idea behind TRIEMA.

Why should such an initiative not be accused of being a dangerous alternative of negotiating trade affairs outside the WTO? This proposal is based on an analysis of the main reasons and the main solutions of trade conflicts as listed below.

(1) The trade volume between the triad is high and the main trade conflicts have been occurring between these countries during the 1980's.
(2) The trade relations inside the triad have been conflict-prone.
(3) Nearly all negotiations were carried out on a bilateral basis and in a non-co-operative manner.
(4) The results were mostly insufficient.
(5) The positions and procedures were based on strategies of aggressive reciprocity, favouring the results-approach and discarding the rules-approach.
(6) The solutions often caused troubles and suspicion on the part of third countries.
(7) Finally, the outcome and attitudes have been jeopardising the rationale of GATT.

These drawbacks may be overcome for the benefit of all triad countries and of the WTO by TRIEMA because firstly, the trilateral approach avoids the shortcomings and risks of bilateralism of any kind. Secondly, putting these negotiations under the roof, guidance and surveillance of the OECD avoids the suspicion of dominance and the overruling of the WTO. The Organisation for European Economic Co-operation (OEEC), and the subsequent OECD, have been institutions which never fostered a purely regional approach. In trade and monetary affairs they have supported

---

[13]   For more details see Hasse R., Hepperle B., Wolf S. *Weiterentwicklung des handelspolitischen Instrumentariums*, Hamburg, 1993, p. 195 ff.

international co-operation, multilateralism and convertibility. During the times of transition in the 1950's, 1970's and 1990's, they have been concentrating their policies on efforts to improve or to maintain the international framework as it is designed in the charter of the International Monetary Fund (IMF) and in GATT. Moreover, the OECD is an acknowledged institution with an efficient staff for internationally-oriented consultations and surveillance. Thirdly, the WTO is not the appropriate institution to deal with the matter outlined here. Despite the progress concerning its institutionalisation, the process to enforce WTO rules is based on the assumption that every country adopts its trade policies and its trade order to the rules of the WTO autonomously. This assumption may be too optimistic. TRIEMA is an approach to accelerate this political process. If it is left to the US, Japan and the EU, one might end up with a prisoners' dilemma due to the missing reciprocity. The national change of the trade order is an implicit renunciation of reciprocity and this will increase resistance against the change. Negotiations among the triad would avoid this trap because every party is able to balance its benefits and costs due to the fact that the main trade barriers impede, in particular, the trade between the triad countries. Fourthly, the TABD of November 1995 is an insufficient substitute for TRIEMA. But it is able to support TRIEMA. It may even be better if this business dialogue were to include Japan, so as to exert pressure on TRIEMA and to have a parallel process of reciprocity, on the macroeconomic, political level and on the microeconomic, business level.

5. CONCLUSION

The WTO is a means to overcome bilateralism, regionalism and aggressive reciprocity. Moreover, it is a serious attempt to abandon a trade policy based on the results-approach and to reestablish the rules-approach. Furthermore, it is seriously challenged by the national "counter-trade rules" the triad countries established (EU, USA) or maintained (Japan) in the late 1970's and in the 1980's. The WTO relies upon a process of self-commitment, that all member countries adapt their trade rules to comply with WTO. This seems to be over-optimistic, especially if one takes into consideration the huge tasks ahead in the next ten years (agriculture, textiles, telecommunication, services, ecological and social standards). Also it does not offer efficient political procedures to close the gap between the GATT 94 and the "counter-trade rules". An institutionalised process of political negotiations is necessary to improve the international trade order and to enforce the WTO. The national-oriented approach of transformation of the WTO is impeded by the lack of reciprocity.

To overcome these obstacles a Trilateral Initiative for Equal Market Access (TRIEMA) is suggested among the countries of the triad (EU, Japan,

USA). Under the roof, guidance and surveillance of the OECD the triad countries may negotiate the strategy to transform their trade orders and to put them into compliance with GATT 94. The role of the OECD is to avoid suspicions of dominance, to guarantee results which comply with multilateralism, non-discrimination, the most-favoured-nation clause and reciprocity and to procure a highly skilled staff and protected environment.

The approach of TAFTA is too narrow, and too bilateral. This verdict is correct even if TAFTA does not aim at regional trade preferences but instead concentrates its tasks on negotiating potential or actual trade conflicts on this bilateral basis. The TABD may be of great importance and support. It may help to enforce the process of adjustment of the national trade orders. An even better choice may be to extend this dialogue to the triad. In this case the improvement of the international trade order and the enforcement of WTO may occur on two interrelated levels: on the macroeconomic, political level within TRIEMA; and on the microeconomic, business level within the Business Dialogue.

From this parallelism, a positive impact and a change of trade policies and attitudes may be expected. The globalisation of trade flows, and especially the globalisation of production with its increasing flows of intra-firm trade, will destroy the traditional patterns of protectionism. Whereas the governments are still thinking in more traditional patterns, already businesses are pursuing different patterns of international trade.[14] This change of trade policies must be demanded from the business level and the core group of the world economy, the triad countries. They may introduce this shift which is in full compliance with the WTO and will help to enforce its rule.

TABLE 1

Trade Coverage Rates of Selected NTMs[15] Applied by Developed Countries[16],
1981–1990 (1981 = 100)

Country	1981	1984	1986	1988	1989	1990
Total	100,0	104,1	103,3	105,3	104,6	103,1
EC-12	100,0	111,7	108,9	108,6	108,5	109,0
Japan	100,0	100,1	97,2	96,8	96,7	96,7
USA	100,0	97,7	101,1	100,7	110,4	106,0

Source: IMF, Issues and Developments in International Trade Policy, Prepared by a Staff Team led by Margaret Kelly and Anne Kenny McGuick, Washington, D.C. 1992, S. 116.

---

[14]   See Hasse R. *Globalisierung versus Protektionismus*, in Biskup, Reinhold, ed., Globalisierung und Wettbewerb, 2. ed., Bern-Stuttgart 1996, pp. 316; Times of July 1995; San Francisco Chronicle of July 10, 1995 ("Underwear Makers say Import Quotas Are Pain in Butt").

[15]   Only "core-NTMs".

[16]   EC-12, Austria, Canada, Finland, Japan, New Zealand, Norway, Switzerland, USA.

TABLE 2
Initiations of Section 301 by Year, 1984–1993

	Sec 301	Super 301	Special 301	Total
1984	3	-	-	3
1985	5	-	-	5
1986	6	-	-	6
1987	4	-	-	4
1988	8	-	-	8
1989	3	6	-	9
1990	3	-	-	3
1991	4	-	2	6
1992	2	-	1	3
1993	1	-	1	2

Source: GATT, Trade Policy Review Mechanism, USA, Geneva 1994, p. 104.

TABLE 3
EC: The Number of Anti-dumping Actions, 1991–1994

	7 February 1994	23 April 1992	1 January 1994	12 December 1994
Definite duties	289	373	542	450
Provisional measures	22	10	25	34
Other duties	28	51	55	53
Initiation	71	83	69	871
Total measures	410	517	691	1.408

TABLE 4
EC: Anti-dumping Measures Against Consumer Products, 1991–1994

	Number of Initiation	Export-countries	Good/country-combination	Import-volume (1000 Ecus)
1991	4	3	7	451.994
1992	5	7	13	482.398
1993	4	6	8	906.164
1994	9	11	25	1.294.264
Total	22	27	53	3.134.820

1994: Measures in force initiated in the period 1991–1994

	19	14	56	2.450.881

Source: Caspari, Stefan, Willkommener Schutz der europäischen Industrie, in: Handelsblatt of 14 March, 1995.

Chapter 7

EU and US Agricultural Policies and Their Impact on Bilateral Relations in the Framework of the WTO

Wayne Moyer

1. INTRODUCTION

Both the European Union and the United States have significantly reformed their agricultural policies during the 1990's, catalysed by the enormous and growing costs of farm support and by the perceived need to liberalise international agricultural trade in the context of the Uruguay Round of the General Agreement on Tariffs and Trade (GATT) and the creation of the World Trade Organisation (WTO). The MacSharry reforms of the EC's Common Agricultural Policy (CAP) were approved by the Council of Ministers in 1992, changing the CAP in such a way that the EC could accept the final Uruguay Round Agreement for agriculture. The US reform came during the spring of 1996, with President Clinton's signature in early April of the US Federal Agricultural Improvement and Reform Act (FAIR). This legislation brings domestic farm policy more into conformity with the obligations of the Uruguay Round Agreement.

The MacSharry reforms and FAIR both move substantially in the direction of decoupling farm support from how much farmers produce and both create more market-oriented agricultural policies. There are other similarities as well. However, there are significant differences which will probably have opposite effects on bilateral relations in the context of the WTO. It will be argued that while MacSharry has worked to moderate US-EU disputes, FAIR will probably work to aggravate them, though this will depend on world market conditions. With the Uruguay Round agreement in place, it will be further contended that FAIR will put strong pressure on the EU to emulate the US, pressure which could have been more easily resisted prior to the Uruguay Round.

2. THE MACSHARRY AND FAIR REFORMS

The discussion begins by detailing how the MacSharry reforms and FAIR changed the traditional US and EU farm support mechanisms. The traditional CAP mechanism for the support of cereals was to set an intervention price at a level deemed by the Council of Agricultural ministers sufficient to provide adequate income support for farmers.[1] This became a floor price, which farmers were guaranteed, in that the EC would buy up whatever quantity was necessary to keep the market price in Europe from falling below the intervention price. The intervention price was generally much higher than the world price, creating strong incentives for over-production, since farmers would be guaranteed the intervention price for whatever quantity they produced. This price was protected by a variable import levy, which essentially kept cereal imports out of the EC (except in the rare instance that the domestic EC price rose above an import threshold price set significantly above the intervention price). As a result of high intervention prices, the EC accumulated an increasing grain surplus that it had to dump on the international market using export subsidies. This created conflict with the US, which coveted the same markets and began an export subsidy war. The costs of intervention, storage and export subsidies placed a significant burden on the costs of the CAP, which could not be sustained. An effort was made to control the cost escalation with the 1988 Brussels Stabilizers Agreement, which set maximum guaranteed quantities for compensation and introduced voluntary set-asides, but these measures did not stop the growth of the surplus or the escalation of the EU budget costs.[2]

The pre-MacSharry CAP was thus untenable in that its high costs were totally inconsistent with EC enlargement and with deepening European integration. The CAP also blocked completion of the Uruguay Round, in that the US and a group of grain exporting nations known as the Cairns group were unwilling to sign a trade liberalisation agreement which did not

---

[1]   This support mechanism was applied primarily to cereals. Other mechanisms were applied to other products. This mechanism will be focused on because of the importance of cereals to both the MacSharry and FAIR reforms. For discussion of the traditional CAP price support mechanisms, see Harris S., Swinbank A. and Wilkinson G. *The Food and Farm Policies of the European Community*, Chichester and New York, John Wiley and Sons, 1983, especially Chapter 3.

[2]   For discussion of the 1988 Brussels Stabilizers Agreement, see Moyer, W. H. and Josling T.E. *Agricultural Policy Reform: Politics and Process in the EC and the USA*, New York and London: Harvester Wheatsheaf, 1990, pp. 78–98.

include agriculture. The MacSharry reforms, proposed by EC Agriculture Commissioner Ray MacSharry, attempted to deal with both the domestic cost and Uruguay Round problems.[3] They lowered intervention prices much closer to world price levels, providing farmers with compensatory payments based on the average acreage they had farmed in the immediately preceding years. In return for support, a programme of mandatory set-asides was created, whereby farmers were obligated to remove a percentage of their land from production to reduce the surplus.

The context of FAIR in the US appeared quite different. US government support for farmers in the 1970's and 1980's relied much less heavily than the EC on fixing commodity prices. Price support comparable to the EC intervention price existed in the loan rate which was the price farmers could be assured if they placed their crops in storage.[4] It functioned as a floor price, since farmers could forfeit their crops to the government if market prices fell below the loan rate. US loan rates differed from EC intervention prices in that they generally were set close to world market levels, so did not have the same kind of market distorting effects. The principal subsidy to farmers came from deficiency payments (cheques from the government), which represented the difference between the loan rate price and a much higher target price, which was set at a level deemed sufficiently high to ensure adequate farm income. Farmers had only limited flexibility in what they could plant to receive deficiency payments and they had to set aside a percentage of their land determined by the Secretary of Agriculture. Deficiency payments created incentives for overproduction, requiring export subsidies. They placed a heavy burden on the US treasury, even though this burden was somewhat limited by the 1985 and 1990 farm bills, which restricted the acreage qualifying for deficiency payments.[5]

The costs of farm support became an increasingly sensitive issue in the late 1980's and early 1990's as the US government attempted to come to grips with its enormous budget deficit. The incentives for action increased with the 1994 election of a Republican congress ideologically committed to cutting the deficit through reduced government spending. Shortly after the election, Congressman Pat Roberts (R-Kansas), the new Chairman of the House Agriculture Committee proposed what he called "Freedom to Farm" legislation, which became the basis for the US Federal Agricultural |

---

[3] For discussion of the details of the MacSharry reforms, see De Benedictis M., De Filippis F. and Salvatici L. *Nature and Causes of CAP: Changes in the 1980's and a Tentative Exploration of Potential Scenarios*, in Anania G., Carter C. A. and McCalla A. F. *Agricultural Trade Conflicts and the GATT: New Dimensions in US-European Agricultural Trade Relations*, Boulder, Colorado, Westview, 1994, pp. 125–159. For a recent report on progress in their implementation, see Madill M. L. *EU Enters Final Stage of Agricultural Reform Program*, US Department of Agricultural Outlook, August 1995, pp. 15–18.

[4] For discussion of US agricultural price support mechanisms, see Moyer, W. H. and Josling T. E. *Agricultural Policy Reform: Politics and Process in the EC and the USA*, New York and London: Harvester Wheatsheaf, 1990, Chapter 5.

[5] For discussion of 1985 and 1990 US farm bills, see *ibid* Chapter 7.

Improvement and Reform Act. FAIR does away with deficiency payments and with land set-asides, allowing farmers to plant whatever they want (except for fruits and vegetables) on as much of their acreage as they want, then sell what they produce for the best price they can get. In return for weaning them from the benefits of farm programs, farmers will receive compensatory payments which will gradually decline over the seven years of the farm bill.[6]

Interestingly, the most fervent advocates of FAIR were not legislators who in the past had been most critical of farm subsidies, but rather those who had been most supportive. This stemmed from a very significant change in the economic environment which occurred just as Congress was considering its 1996 farm legislation. Agricultural commodity prices rose steadily, caused both by poor harvests and by increased demands for grain and oilseeds coming mostly from the rapidly developing nations of Asia. Rising farm prices created an unlikely alliance between the farm lobby and agricultural reformers. FAIR was acceptable to the reformers, because it held out the possibility of the elimination of traditional farm programs, albeit after a period of transition. It was acceptable to the farm lobby in that it would actually provide more benefits to farmers in the short run than traditional legislation, in a high farm price environment, where deficiency payments would decrease or be non-existent.

pre-Asian crisis

3. MACSHARRY AND FAIR COMPARED

The effects of the MacSharry reforms and FAIR are compared in Figure 1. MacSharry and FAIR are similar in that both pieces of legislation pay farmers compensatory payments, which are not linked to how much the farmers produce. They are also similar in that EU and US compensatory payments actually increase farm policy expenditures in the short run in the expectation of cost savings in the long run, when compensatory payments are phased out and agriculture becomes fully market orientated. For the EU there is an expectation that compensatory payments will eventually be stopped, but no deadline has been set. For the US, compensatory payments will expire after seven years.

---

[6]   For details of FAIR, see Hosansky, D. *Farm Policy on the Brink of a New Direction*, Congressional Quarterly, March 23, 1996, pp. 786–788, Hosansky D. *House Easily Clears Rewrite of Decades-Old Farm Laws*, Congressional Quarterly, March 30 1996, pp. 874, 875, and AgraEurope, May 3 1996, P/1-P/3. For discussion of the development and politics of FAIR see Orden D., Paarlberg R. and Roe T. *Can Farm Policy Be Reformed*, Choices, First Quarter, 1996, and Orden D., Paarlberg R. and Roe T. *A Farm Bill for Booming Commodity Markets*, Choices, Second Quarter, 1996.

Figure 1 – MacSharry and FAIR Agricultural Policy Reforms Compared

	MacSharry	**FAIR**
1. Market orientation	Reduces market price and pays hectarage compensatory payments. Set-aside compulsory	Removes acreage restrictions and provides declining acreage payments
2. Short and long term costs	Short term budget costs incurred to achieve policy reforms which should reduce long term consideration	Short term budget costs incurred to achieve policy reforms which should reduce long term costs
3. Effect on production	Lowers production by reducing price incentives and by creating mandatory set-asides	Increases production by increasing planting flexibility and allowing Conservation Reserves Programme (CRP) land to be brought into production
4. Effect on world market prices	Raises world commodity prices	Lowers world commodity prices
5. Effect on farming regulation	Increases farming regulation. Mandatory set-asides	Decreases farming regulation. Farmers given flexibility to plant what they want on as many acres as they want
6. Effect on bilateral relations	"Accommodates" US by restricting output and allowing Uruguay Round Agreement	"Challenges" EU by moving to greater market orientation, creates possibility of increasing US world market share at the expense of EU

The US and EU reforms have different effects on production. MacSharry, by mandating set-asides and lowering intervention prices, works to limit production. FAIR works to increase production in that it eliminates land set-asides and even allows farmers to remove land from the conservation reserve programme and return it to production. The increased flexibility which US farmers have in deciding what to plant will also increase production in crops for which prices are high, though it will tend to reduce it in other crops where prices are low.

The effect on world prices is also different. MacSharry, by restricting production, has tended to raise world prices for agricultural commodities in that less surplus is produced to dump on the international market. Decreased EU intervention prices, along with increased world prices and a decreased surplus to export have reduced the need for the EU to pay export subsidies. FAIR has an opposite impact. By stimulating agricultural production, this farm legislation will tend to lower world prices. The export subsidy burden created by increased production remains manageable in that US domestic prices will be close to world market prices. To ensure that the US can export any surplus and remain competitive in international markets, FAIR preserves export subsidies in the form of the Export Enhancement Programme. Though the funds authorised for this programme are considerably reduced in 1996 and 1997 from the levels generally employed in the last ten years, in the expectation that tight world grain supplies will keep world prices high, they increase rapidly in the period from 1998 to 2002, reaching the limit allowed under the Uruguay Round Agreement. Further insurance is provided by provision for marketing loans for maize, wheat, soyabeans, cotton and rice, which are also export subsidies in that the US government makes up the difference between what farmers get for their product on the international market and the loan rate that the government guarantees.

Finally, the MacSharry reforms increase the regulations under which EU farmers labour in that they require land set-asides, thus increasing the administrative burden for the CAP. FAIR decreases farm regulations and the administrative burden in that farmers no longer have to set aside land and can grow pretty much what they want.

4. IMPACT OF MACSHARRY AND FAIR ON BILATERAL RELATIONS

The MacSharry reforms worked to improve bi-lateral relations between the EU and the US in that they went a long way toward removing the thorniest issue between the two entities, the dumping of EC surpluses on international markets using export subsidies. Lowered intervention prices and mandated set asides have reduced the surplus and hence the need for export subsidies. They also have allowed the EU to meet the terms of the Uruguay Round Agreement to lower domestic supports by 20 per cent, to reduce import restrictions by 36 per cent overall, and a minimum of 15 per cent, and to reduce export subsidies by 36 per cent in terms of cost and by 21 per cent in terms of quantity exported with subsidies.

FAIR's impact on US-EC relations is less easy to predict. One must consider the effects of the 1996 US farm legislation on the budget cost of the CAP and the effects on world market share in the context of both high and low world prices. As long as world agriculture commodity prices stay high, the EU budget cost effect will be minimal. High prices are indicative of high demand in the outside world for agricultural products. Hence, as long as they last, adequate international demand will exist to absorb whatever surplus is produced in the US and the EU. Farm incomes in Europe and the US will remain at acceptably high levels, at acceptable cost to the US and EU budgets.

However, the market share effect is not insignificant. In a high commodity price situation, the EU will reduce set-asides to near zero levels, but US production is likely to increase more significantly because of the flexibility which US farmers have in choosing which crops to plant. Also the total planted acreage will probably increase more significantly in the US than in the EU because of the enormous productive acreage in the conservation reserve which could be brought back into production in addition to the land placed in production by the elimination of required set-asides. Thus the US is likely to garner a larger share of growing international markets than the EU, which will probably be unacceptable to the EU, particularly to France.

The impact on bilateral relations will be even worse if world agricultural commodity prices decline in a significant way prior to the expiration of FAIR in 2002. In a declining commodity price situation, FAIR represents a direct challenge to the EU. There will be some tendency to reduce US farm production induced by lower world prices, but this effect will probably be more than counterbalanced by the production increasing effects generated by the elimination of acreage reduction programs and of continuing to farm conservation reserve land brought back into production by recent high prices. Thus, the US, with overall increased production, will directly contest the EU for declining world markets. Traditionally, the EU would respond to the challenge by increasing its export subsidies, but this option is no longer as available as it once was because of the commitments made under the Uruguay Round.

5. OPTIONS FOR THE EU IN RESPONSE TO FAIR

To be sure, the EU will be under pressure to protect its market share of world agricultural trade by subsidising exports to the maximum extent permissible under the Uruguay Round Agreement, but this will raise the budget costs of the CAP, already bloated by compensatory payments. If world prices are low, the EU may not be able to market the surplus generated by current price supports. If the EU cannot market its surplus, it could store the surplus and build up stocks, or, it could increase mandatory set-asides and compensatory payments. Both of these options appear problematic in that they add significant costs to the EU budget.

The undesirability of these options leaves only a fourth option, EU emulation of US policy in eliminating price supports and set-asides, giving

European farmers the freedom to plant what they want, on whatever acreage they want, yet giving them compensatory payments to ease the transition. The net effect will be to facilitate the restructuring of EU agriculture and to create more efficient production which can compete effectively on world markets. This option helps the EU in its competition with the US for world market share even in the situation of high world commodity prices. Though this option would doubtless generate serious opposition from the EU farm lobby and might increase tensions between EC members who would gain and those who would lose from agricultural restructuring, it would still be attractive as a means to better control government spending for agriculture and would facilitate the entry of the countries of Central and Eastern Europe into the EU. Interestingly, the acceptance of option four is more likely in the context of the Uruguay Round agreement and the WTO than it was before, in that option one, unlimited export subsidies, is no longer available.

The July 1997 Agenda 2000 proposals provide evidence that the European Commission understands the problem and wishes to move EU policy in the direction of option four. Agenda 2000 provides a major package of agricultural policy reforms comparable to the MacSharry reforms of 1992. The centrepiece of these proposals is an initiative to bring the EU market price for cereals down close to world market levels, thus making export subsidies largely superfluous and avoiding the limitations on subsidized exports imposed by the Uruguay Round and by the next Round of WTO trade talks which begins at the end of 1999. Significant new changes in the CAP are inevitable in light of the impending eastward enlargement of the EU, the next round of WTO talks and the US's switch to a more market-oriented agricultural system in the framework of the 1996 Federal Agricultural Improvement and Reform Act.

PART III

THE JUSTICE AND HOME AFFAIRS AGENDA

Chapter 8

Transatlantic Relations in the Fields of Justice and Home Affairs–can the EU Really Deliver?

David Cullen

1. INTRODUCTION

The adoption of the New Transatlantic Agenda (NTA) in December 1995 has, among other things, provided the United States and the European Union with a comprehensive framework for co-operation in the fight against international organised crime, terrorism, drug trafficking and on illegal immigration and asylum matters. In the context of the EU these subjects fall under the umbrella heading of Justice and Home Affairs (JHA).[1] Co-operation in the fields of JHA at the EU level is governed by provisions of the Treaty on European Union (TEU), in particular, Title VI TEU (more commonly known as the Third Pillar). The inclusion of these matters in the NTA, as priority areas for EU-US co-operation, is of great significance. However, progress towards joint action, it has to be said, will constitute one of the biggest challenges for the EU in the near future.

Co-operation in JHA issues has existed for some time now between the US and individual EU Member States but not with the EU itself. The NTA highlights for the first time US recognition of the need to deal with the EU as a separate entity and not solely (as has been the case in the past) with its

---

[1] Justice and Home Affairs within the EU generally refers to: asylum policy; rules governing the crossing of external borders; immigration policy; combating drugs policy; combating fraud on an international scale; judicial co-operation in civil and criminal matters; customs and police co-operation. See the Appendix *post* where the NTA is set out in full.

individual constituent Member States. From the EU perspective, implementation of the areas of the NTA dealing with JHA will not be as
straightforward as it may seem. The Third Pillar on JHA co-operation, it
should be recalled, is a recent addition to the European integration process
and, moreover, is still subject to considerable debate (among Member States)
as to its role and long term standing in the EU. Since the entry into force of
the TEU, the ability of the EU to take concrete action in the fields of JHA
has been called into question. This lack of progress within the EU is primarily
a result of institutional and legal shortcomings of TEU but is also due to
divergences among Member States, some of whom would argue that these
areas fall within the realm of national sovereignty and that consequently
competence to act should remain with the Member States and not be
transferred to the level of the EU. Such internal complexities are bound to
affect, in some way or another, the EU's ability to implement the JHA
provisions of the NTA: the question is how and to what extent.

This chapter thus aims at assessing the ability of the EU to implement the
JHA provisions of the NTA in co-operation with the US. To do so one needs to
have a clear understanding of the background to JHA co-operation in the EU.
This will be followed by a closer examination of the JHA provisions in NTA
and progress in their implementation. In addition to an overview of JHA
co-operation in general the example of drugs control co-operation will be
explored in greater detail. The choice of drugs control as a case study into
EU-US co-operation in the fields of JHA stems primarily from the fact that it
is one of the few areas where at least some visible progress has been achieved
since the announcement of the NTA, reflecting a strong commitment on both
sides to see progress in this area. The dispersal of drugs-related provisions
throughout the Treaty will also highlight the limits of external EU action in the
quasi-intergovernmental Second and Third Pillars as opposed to the more
supranational First Pillar. The concluding part of this chapter shall look at the
weakness of the Third Pillar structure, the possible modifications resulting
from the 1996/97 Intergovernmental Conference (IGC) and how this may
affect EU relations with the US in particular and third countries in general.

2. EUROPEANISATION OF CO-OPERATION IN JHA

For a long time areas of JHA remained outside the formal domain of
European integration. Justice and Home Affairs was (and still is) seen as
touching the sensitive but nonetheless abstract concept of national
sovereignty. As in the case of defence, for instance, much fuss was made
about the need to ensure that the nation states would remain the ultimate
decision makers in areas of so-called "high politics" such as internal security,
terrorism, drug trafficking and other forms of international crime. This belief
in the need to by all means ensure that such areas did not become subject to

the rigid supranational-like legal regime of the European Community persisted for some time.

This belief did not however impede co-operation among Member States on a purely intergovernmental level, a co-operation which became more urgent in the 1970's and 1980's due in large part to increased "Euro-terrorism" and terrorism from the Middle East.[2] This intergovernmental co-operation extended to third countries as well such as the US.

With the reaffirmation at the EC level of the need to ensure free movement of persons (one of the four fundamental freedoms), the abolition of internal national borders and their replacement with adequate compensatory measures, came the increased urgency to establish a more global and coherent form of co-operation. This need was exacerbated by the end of the Cold War and the ensuing problems (influx of migrants, refugees, traffic in illegal substances etc.) and the rapid growth in international organised crime. In short, the need to co-operate more closely at the European level was finally acknowledged (in varying degrees by different Member States), and, following Maastricht, was formally incorporated into the TEU. The plethora of intergovernmental and semi-communautaire working groups dealing with JHA issues were grouped together under a hybrid Third Pillar. The Third Pillar (Title VI TEU), owing to the particularly sensitive nature of JHA, did not fall under the legal framework of the EC Treaty or the First Pillar[3], rather it reflected some form of compromise "institutionalised intergovernmentalism". The main characteristics of this hybrid Title VI or Third Pillar comprised: the creation of new legal instruments (joint actions, joint positions) alongside more traditional intergovernmental ones (conventions, resolutions, conclusions, declarations, etc.), the predominance of the unanimity rule and other intergovernmental characteristics, but also more relevantly, the incorporation of these areas of JHA into the single institutional framework of the EU (Article C TEU), a formalised but restricted role for Community bodies such as the Commission and Parliament, and Court of Justice, a strengthened role of the Council, and the inclusion of provisions linking some areas in the Third Pillar to the First Pillar, to name but a few.

Even though the Third Pillar was quite clearly a compromise package deal between those countries (Germany, Belgium, the Netherlands) who wanted to see provisions on this area wholly included in the EC Treaty, and others (e.g. the United Kingdom and Denmark) who sought its inclusion exclusively in a separate pillar and thus allowing for purely intergovernmental

---

[2]   Resulting for instance in the creation, among Member States, of informal, intergovernmental (and often non-transparent) fora of co-operation such as Trevi, GAM, Judicial Co-operation in EPC, and later CELAD.

[3]   This meant that the traditional Community legal instruments (regulations, directives and decisions) as provided for in Article 189 EC would not apply to any of the areas referred to in the Third Pillar or Title VI TEU.

co-operation, it was nonetheless hailed as a great success. However, in the first few years, the Third Pillar did not live up to its expectations. The lack of progress, and the lack of ability to ensure that acts get through their draft stage and are ultimately ratified, may simply be put down to teething problems and institutional shortcomings in the Third Pillar, or may be the result of more deep-rooted problems. The first reactions by practitioners and academics alike have been for the most part negative. Frustration over the lack of any significant progress during the first two years was illustrated in the Reports of the Institutions in view of the 1996 IGC. The entry into force of the Schengen Implementing Convention[4] (26 March 1995) simply reinforced the belief among many that the provisions of Title VI TEU were simply ineffective and no longer appropriate in terms of ensuring a greater and more coherent form of co-operation in the fields of justice and home affairs. It is evidently clear to all that the Third Pillar is the result of a compromise between those parties that wanted to see some if not all JHA areas incorporated within the legally binding supranational framework of the EC and those who considered areas of JHA to be central to a nation state's sovereignty and thus argued that these areas should remain wholly within a loosely-formed intergovernmental co-operation structure. The functioning of this inherently flawed model has thus been affected by the divergent conceptions of its role and long term standing in the EU (i.e. whether the Third Pillar should be seen as a permanent structure alongside, but ultimately apart from the EC Treaty or whether it is a temporary measure until such a time as it is politically acceptable to disband the structure and incorporate all areas of JHA into one, overarching legal framework).

It was hoped, nonetheless, that the creation of the Third Pillar of the EU would provide greater coherence, efficiency and effectiveness in the treatment of JHA at the European level and that this would facilitate co-operation in those "internal security issues with a potentially international dimension"[5] between the EU as a whole and third countries. Subsequent to the entry into force of the TEU the Council of Justice and Home Affairs Ministers has met quite regularly. The need to co-operate more closely with third countries, including the US, has come up on various occasions in discussions. A meeting between the Troïka[6] and the relevant ministers from several third countries would often be held straight after a Council meeting of the Justice and Home Affairs Ministers in order to "inform them of the Council's discussions and to exchange views on subjects of common interest"[7].

---

[4]   The Schengen Implementing Convention is an intergovernmental agreement among some but not all EU Member States which abolishes internal border controls and at the same time puts into place various compensatory measures such as a common external border, and increased police, judicial and customs co-operation among the contracting parties.

[5]   Anderson M. *Policing the European Union*, Clarendon Press, Oxford, 1995, p. 175.

[6]   The Troïka consists of representatives of the current, preceding and succeeding presidencies of the EU.

[7]   1710th Council Meeting–Justice and Home Affairs, Brussels, 29, 30 November 1993, 10550/93 (Presse 209), p. 6.

At the JHA Council meeting of 9, 10 March 1995, the Council agreed on the need to establish set procedures for "organising contacts with third countries in the context of the Third Pillar". This entailed contacts:

(1) by the Presidency, acting in principle through the General Secretariat;
(2) by the Presidency or the Troïka; and
(3) by the ministers.[8]

Although there have been some minor successes[9], co-operation with third countries has not advanced too far. The EU can to a certain extent be accused of overly concentrating on the internal dimension of JHA (e.g. legislative harmonisation and the creation of common standards within the EU) at the high cost of failing to properly address the external dimension.[10] However this is only partly true. It is hardly surprising that the EU has had difficulties in comprehensively addressing the issue of third country co-operation in JHA considering the structural, institutional, instrumental and (not to be forgotten) ideological difficulties in doing so. One cannot yet talk about a common security judicial space at the European level.[11] The EU has not yet established common policies in areas such as asylum, immigration, policing etc. The judicial systems differ enormously which render effective and coherent action at the level of the EU highly difficult. Such differences should not be underestimated.

---

[8]   1831st Council Meeting, Justice and Home Affairs, Brussels, 9, 10 March 1995, 5423/95 (Presse 69).
[9]   E.g. The Berlin Declaration on Increased Co-operation in Combatting Drug Crime and Organised Crime in Europe, Berlin, 8 September 1994, Council Press Release 9345/94 (Presse 182), Brussels, 14 September 1994; the EU-ANDEAN Group Joint Communication on combatting drug trafficking, Council Press Release 9977/95 (Presse 262), Brussels, 25 September 1995.
[10]   The EU has, furthermore, been accused, by third parties, of increasingly trying to create a "Fortress Europe". The main objective of this fortress approach in the area of internal security would be to neutralise any external threat, be that from clandestine immigration, organised crime, drug trafficking etc. To bring this about requires the creation of a strong external border, and the development of common policies in areas such as immigration and asylum which invariably end up being rather restrictive in nature. Agreement is often on the basis of "lowest common denominator" as was the case in the adoption of the first Third Pillar joint position (Joint Position on the harmonised application of the definition of the term "refugee" in Article 1A of the Geneva Convention of 28 July 1951 relating to the status of refugees, OJ No L63/2, 13 March 1996).
[11]   The goal of an "Area of Freedom, Security and Justice" is referred to in the draft text on the revision of the Treaties which was prepared during the Irish Presidency. See Conference of the Representatives of the Governments of the Member States, "The European Union Today and Tomorrow. Adapting the European Union for the benefit of its peoples and preparing it for the future, a general outline for a draft revision of the Treaties", "Dublin II", Brussels, 5 December 1996.

3. NEW FRAMEWORKS FOR TRANSATLANTIC RELATIONS IN THE FIELDS OF JHA

3.1 The Joint Declaration of 1990

It is important to recall that a formal framework for co-operation in JHA issues between the Member States of the EC and the US has existed for some time in the form of a Joint Declaration by the EC, the US and the Member States, adopted on 22 November 1990. This Joint Declaration[12] was not confined purely to trade aspects but also included issues of foreign policy and JHA[13]. This is quite significant as one should recall that the EU and hence the Third Pillar did not exist at that time. Since then the EC has enlarged its competences and the EU has been established with a far wider scope. So whereas a Joint Declaration was adopted by the US, the EC and also the Member States in 1990, in the NTA of December 1995 the EU and the US are the only two parties. It is true that the latter is a political and not a legal instrument. It does cover many issues which are within the competence of the Member States and as such in these areas the Member States will act. If a legal instrument as in 1990 was to be used, the Member States would have been formal parties along with the EC. It was nonetheless symbolic that the EU was accorded such a high profile role both by the Member States and the US itself.

3.2 The New Transatlantic Agenda and Joint Action Plan of 1995

Announced on 3 December 1995 by President Clinton, President Santer of the European Commission and the then Spanish Prime Minister, Felipe Gonzlez, the NTA marks the beginning of a new era in EU-US relations and is even viewed by some as a precursor to a veritable Transatlantic Treaty.

Both documents adopted in Madrid in December 1995, namely the NTA and the Joint Action, according to Horst G. Krenzler, "focus on the substance of the relationship regardless of legal constraints, leaving it to either the Community or its Member States to act on specific matters as required".[14] It is true to say that these are living documents[15] which can be "chopped and

---

12   Published in Bull. EC 11, 1990, pp. 90–91.
13   Under the title "Transatlantic challenges", sensitive issues such as "combatting and preventing terrorism", "putting an end to the illegal production, trafficking and consumption of narcotics and related criminal activities, such as the laundering of money; co-operating in the fight against international crime" among others had been addressed.
14   Krenzler H. G. remarks made at the Conference "*The New Framework for EU-US Relations*", Brussels, 4–5 July 1996.
15   According to Krenzler and Schomaker, when the moment came to negotiate both the NTA and the Action Plan, flexibility seemed to be the order of the day. They further remark that "In a situation where leaders on both sides of the Atlantic intended to send a political signal rapidly, an instrument which did not have to be submitted to the long and sometimes ... approval procedures of the US Congress, the European Parliament and all the Parliaments of the Member States of the European

changed" in accordance with new political developments. The NTA and the Joint Action Plan are however very open-ended and whereas they outline areas for action, they do not specify how and when to proceed to concerted action. There is no timetable for action and in those areas where there may be a question of joint competence between the EC[16] and the Member States, it does not specify how the EU should proceed. This latter point will have to be decided within the EU itself when the situation arises.

The NTA is nonetheless of great symbolic importance in that it marks an important development in the US' perception of the EU not merely as an intergovernmental forum for co-operation among nation states or as a purely trade and economic organisation, but as an accepted and powerful political entity in itself. This recognition by the US of the EU as one whole, as an important player in the world scene in areas that go far beyond the economic sphere is highly significant. Implicitly it can be seen as a vote in favour of the establishment and development of a EU (as opposed to a EC) and its expanding remit which now touches on sensitive areas of internal affairs and foreign policy. This is not to suggest that the US is overlooking the role of the Member States (much of the Action Plan cannot be implemented without the active and formal participation of the Member States) but is simply recognising the existence of another somewhat overarching actor which has the potential of playing a meaningful co-ordinating role.

3.3 JHA Elements of the NTA and Joint Action Plan

JHA issues feature prominently in both texts (the NTA and the Joint Action Plan) under the goal of "responding to global challenges" one of the four major goals (the other three being promoting peace, development and democracy in the world, contributing to the expansion of world trade and closer economic ties and, finally, building bridges across the Atlantic by encouraging closer communication between the people) which together constitute the framework for joint EU-US action. According to the Statement of Purpose of the NTA, the US and the EU together "will fight international crime, drug trafficking and terrorism; address the needs of refugees and displaced persons".[17] The mood is ambitious and upbeat. The

---

(*Cont.*)
  Union was very attractive", Krenzler H. G. and Schomaker A. *A New Transatlantic Agenda*, European Foreign Affairs Review, Vol. 1, 1996, p. 18. See the Appendix *post* where the NTA and the Joint Action Plan are set out in full.

[16] The EC and not the EU. The EU cannot sign a contractual agreement or international agreement as it does not in terms of international law have legal personality. The EC on the other hand does have legal personality. So for instance, if an international agreement is to be signed which covers areas dealt with in the Community but also in the EU (for instance aspects of JHA or CFSP), the contracting party of the agreement on the European side will not be the EU but rather the EC and all 15 Member States.

[17] The section on "Responding to Global Challenges" also includes priorities which are not JHA-related such as the protection of the global environment and the combatting of diseases.

means by which and time frame within which both parties will "move to common action" are left quite open. Thus one avoids the thorny question of how this will be practically possible, particularly on the EU side. The rhetoric is even stronger in the Joint Action Plan in which the following remarks are made:

> We share a common concern to address in an effective manner new global challenges which, without respect for national boundaries, present a serious threat to the quality of life and which neither of us can overcome alone. We pledge our actions and resources to meet together the challenges of international crime, terrorism and drug trafficking, mass migration, degradation of the environment, nuclear safety, and disease. Together we can make a difference.

Ultimately the question that must be asked is to what extent can the divergent interests in the EU find some way in which to work together and provide a coherent front *vis-à-vis* the US.

In the Joint Action Plan, JHA issues are subdivided under three broad headings:

(1) Fight against organised crime, terrorism and drug trafficking;
(2) Immigration and asylum; and
(3) Legal and judicial co-operation.

A brief description of the priorities under each of these headings seems be useful.

(1) *Fight against organised crime, terrorism and drug trafficking.* The emphasis here is on information exchange, and improving bilateral co-operation and institutional contacts. Exchange of law enforcement and criminal justice should be fostered, particularly in the areas of scientific and technological developments, exchanges of experts and observers between institutes and agencies, and the sharing of information on, for instance, studies and analyses of emerging trends in international activity. The possibility of EU participation in the International Law Enforcement Academy is mentioned along with increased co-operation with other regional institutions such as the Italian Judicial Training Centre and the Middle and East European Police Academy. There should be increased co-operation between both parties on the provision of training, technical assistance and other equipment to third countries. Not surprisingly a great deal of emphasis is placed on the question of combatting drug production and trafficking, an area in which the need for immediate and concrete action has been recognised by both the EU and the US for some time now (drugs co-operation between the US and the EU will be assessed in greater detail elsewhere in this chapter). The multifaceted approach covers greater co-operation with international multilateral fora such as the United Nations Drug Control Programme (UNDCP), the promotion of alternative development programmes in order to counter drug production, a strengthening of the Dublin Group and the counter-narcotic measures carried out by its members, and better

co-ordination of programmes in regions such as the Caribbean and (although to a lesser extent) Latin America. Greater use should be made of EU institutions such as the European Monitoring Centre for Drugs and Drug Addiction (EMCDDA) and co-operative links with similar institutions in other regions of the world (specific reference to the Commission Interamericana para el Control del Abuso de Drogas) should be fostered. Priority is also given to concluding an agreement between the EU (more correctly the EC) and the US on chemical precursors for drug production

Both the US and the EU will discuss the possibility of facilitating further relations and co-operative measures between US law enforcement agencies and the European Police Office (EUROPOL) and once the EUROPOL eventually enters into force, consider some formal agreement allowing US access to its data.

(2) *Immigration and asylum.* Once again, the commitment to enhance exchange of information on various aspects of asylum and illegal immigration (including therein the organisation of joint conferences and seminars) is reaffirmed, as well as the need for greater co-ordination in international instances (e.g. United Nations High Commissioner for Refugees (UNHCR)) and conferences. Priority is placed, in particular, on co-operation in combatting the traffic of women, illegal immigrants etc., the establishment of common responses to refugee crisis situations, improvement of co-operation on issues such as forged identity documents and transport carrier's liability.

(3) *Legal and judicial co-operation.* Initiatives are to be taken in the area of apprehension and extradition, deportation, and mutual legal assistance so as to "ensure that international fugitives have nowhere to hide". Every effort possible will be made to strengthen international judicial assistance in the obtaining of evidence or other relevant information and in the judicial seizure and forfeiture of assets. The work of the Hague Conference on Private International Law and the International Institute for Unification of Private Law (UNIDROIT) should be fully supported and promoted.[18]

In all, approximately 28 Third Pillar issues are earmarked as items for co-operation and ultimately joint action. In many areas the EU-US have at this stage only modest expectations such as, for instance, increased exchange of information, the hosting of joint seminars commitment to greater co-ordination of policies. To a certain extent there was an awareness on the part of the US negotiators that this is an area in which one cannot expect any great progress until such time as the EU "gets its

---

[18]   The EU for its part should endeavour to present and defend, at all times possible, common positions in international fora (organisations, conferences etc.). This can be done on the basis of Article K.5 TEU.

own house in order". A few weeks prior to the announcement of the NTA in Madrid, the Deputy Assistant Secretary of State for international narcotics and law enforcement, Jonathan Winer, accepted the fact that progress may be slow until such a time as the structural problems of the Third Pillar are rooted out. Winer remarked:

> Third Pillar issues will be addressed ... But it is difficult to say exactly how far we will be able to go, other than continuing dialogue, because the EU is still trying to digest how it is going to approach Third Pillar issues and co-operate with the United States. It is clear we will continue working bilaterally with a number of EU members but it is not clear how we will integrate this with the EU ... Essentially, what the EU has said to us is, let's work on an issue by issue basis; it's premature for us to develop structural mechanisms ... What we have to do is come up with ideas and solutions that will work".[19]

The US, for its part, has also had to come to terms with the idea of dealing with only one party, the EU, in areas where previously it always co-operated bilaterally. The US made it very clear that they did not want to forego what they saw as a well-established and effective range of bilateral relations with Member States, although they did at the same time recognise the urgency of actively promoting co-operation at a regional level. However, clearly this co-operation at the regional level should not undermine the existing bilateral co-operation with individual Member States.

The NTA purports to project an image of coherence, consistency and consensus on the part of the EU. This is somewhat artificial and the ability, in practice, of the EU to proceed to common action and eventually to engage in "ambitious projects" must be called into question. It is of no secret to anyone that the Third Pillar has encountered severe difficulties in functioning efficiently and effectively. The reasons for this, as already mentioned, include the slow decision-making process (predominance of unanimity as voting requirement in the Second and Third Pillars), a cumbersome multi-level structure and the divergent positions of Member States on what they actually want out of JHA co-operation at the EU level.

As such, expectations should be modest and the best approach seems to be that of proceeding, as Winer advised, on a case by case basis. This should be borne in mind when evaluating the JHA aspects of EU-US co-operation in the framework of the NTA.

---

[19]   See Embassy of the United States of America, Belgium, press release on International Crime, *US, EU move forward in fight against transnational crime*, 14 November 1995, excerpts from an interview with Jonathan Winer, Deputy Assistant Secretary of State for International Narcotics and Law Enforcement.

4. DRUGS CO-OPERATION–A CASE STUDY INTO THE POTENTIAL AND LIMITS OF EU-US CO-OPERATION IN JHA

From the EU side co-operation on drugs was always going to be high up on its list of priorities. It is an area where the political will to tackle the problem was strong, from the outset, on both sides of the Atlantic (although the methodology and approach may differ). Transatlantic co-operation in this area did however present quite a challenge for the EU. The EU, since the entry into force of the TEU, has had to overcome an internal challenge of providing some coherence to the myriad of provisions on drugs within the Treaty.

4.1 Background to Drugs Co-operation at the European Level

Prior to the TEU, neither the Treaty of Rome nor the Single European Act 1986 contained any specific provisions on drugs. This is not to say that no action was taken at the European level. From the mid 1980's onwards there has been a flurry of activities at the intergovernmental level and also (a point which is often overlooked) at the level of the EC.

Much work had been done on an intergovernmental level among Member States under such fora as Trevi network and the GAM group. The European Parliament for its part had been particularly active in producing some seminal reports on the drugs situation in Europe (largely focusing on the public health question) and the need for a co-ordinated response to the problem. The political momentum received a jump start on 3 October 1989 through President Mitterand's initiative which called for a more co-ordinated effort at the European level in the fight against drug addiction, production and trafficking. Mitterand's plea led to the decision by the European Council in December 1989 to establish an intergovernmental forum called the Comité Européen de Lutte Anti-Drogue (CELAD). The aim of CELAD was to examine ways in which to further co-operation with drug producing and transit countries, to combat the associated money exchanges and to take action in the health sector. In 1990 it drew up the first European plan to combat drugs which was adopted by the Rome European Council of December 1990. This plan marked the first coherent and comprehensive approach to drugs control co-operation at the European level but was never going to make a huge impact as long as the Community itself did not have the competence to act on many of the recommendations. This was a co-ordinated approach lacking in powers of enforcement and depended very much on the will of the Member States to proceed. It did at least reaffirm the need and urgency to act at all levels, local, national, European and global to combat the scourge of drugs.

CELAD was also instrumental in preparing the ground for the creation of a

European Monitoring Centre for Drugs and Drug Addiction (EMCDDA). The regulation establishing EMCDDA was to be based on Article 235 EEC Treaty and thus fell within Community competence. The regulation entered into force on 30 October 1993. The main aims of the EMCDDA include: the collection and analysis of existing data; improvement of data-comparison methods; dissemination of data; and co-operation with non-Community countries.

Within the Community, there was no specific mention of drugs, yet action was taken on the basis of other provisions. For instance, control of international trade in chemical precursors[20] falls under trade policy (Article 113 EC), otherwise known as the common commercial policy, an area in which the Community has competence to act.[21] This competence allowed the Community to act at an international level (following a mandate given by the Council), most significantly in the 1988 United Nations Convention against Illicit Traffic in Narcotic Drugs and Psychotropic Substances which includes provisions on precursor control (Article 12). The Community became a party to this Convention thereby confirming its role as an actor in the international fight against drugs. Subsequently the Community adopted a Regulation on the basis of Article 113 introducing a Community system of exports of these products to third countries.[22] The EC thus is fully responsible for controlling trade in precursors to non-EU countries on the basis of this Regulation (which was amended in March 1992[23]). The importance of this legislation, at the time, should not be underestimated as it marked a new departure in which "the EC's traditional abstention from legislation in drugs matters"[24] was coming to an end. In view of the Single European Act and the emphasis on the completion of the internal market, a Directive (on the basis of Article 100A EC Treaty) was adopted in December 1992[25] on the manufacture and the placing on the market of precursors within the Community itself. This Directive complements the above-mentioned Regulation.

Money laundering, which has become so vital to sustaining the growth of the drugs trade, also falls under the competence of the Community. Following the recommendations of the G7 Financial Action Task Force,

---

[20] Precursors are legal chemicals for use in industrial production, which can also be used for the purpose of direct processing into psychotropic substances such as ecstasy or LSD or for the processing of coca paste into cocaine and morphine into heroin.

[21] According to MacLeod, Hendry and Hyett, "The case law of the Court of Justice has established that the Community has exclusive competence in the field of common commercial policy. In consequence, the Member States are no longer competent to act on their own as far as commercial policy measures are concerned", MacLeod I., Hendry I. D. and Hyett S. *The External Relations of the European Communities: a manual of law and practice*, Clarendon Press, Oxford, 1996, p. 273.

[22] Council Regulation (EEC) 3677/90 of 13 December 1990, OJ No. L 357 of 20 December 1990 (as amended).

[23] Council Regulation (EEC) 900/92 of 31 March 1992, OJ No. L 96 of 10 April 1992 (as amended).

[24] Hobbing P. *Export Restrictions on the Chemical Industry: New European Union Policy on Drugs*, 7 February 1995. Text originally published in German in Europäisches Wirtschafts - und Steuerrecht", Heidelberg, October 1994.

[25] Council Directive (EEC) 92/109 of 14 December 1992, OJ No. L 370 of 19 December 1992 (as amended).

the Council adopted a Directive on prevention of the use of the financial system for the purpose of money laundering.[26]

The Community from 1987 onwards has also become actively involved in North-South, East-West co-operation. The EC had become an active international player following the Council Decision of 26 January 1987. This Decision also "paved the way for the Community to acquire specific instruments to provide active assistance in producer and/or transit countries".[27] This has allowed the EC, through its development policy, to co-operate with developing countries in providing financial assistance for alternative development. In line with the Community's trade through development approach, the EC has signed preferential trade agreements with several Latin American countries in the framework of the General System of Preferences (GSP). One of the aims of such preferences has in part been to support alternative development in an attempt to reduce the cultivation of coca plants. In the African, Caribbean and Pacific regions where ties with the Community are stronger, the IV Lomé Convention, which regulates co-operation between the Community and these countries, "provides institutional and financial resources to further the fight against drug abuse and drug trafficking".[28] Similar assistance has been provided more recently to the countries of Central and Eastern Europe, for instance within the PHARE programme.

The EC has built up a wide range of trade agreements with countries and regions all over the world, most of which now incorporate some provisions on drugs. The external drugs policies that have been built up between the EU-EC and third countries/regions can vary quite considerably as they are often influenced by the particular sectoral policy (security, development, trade) interest in the region. According to Dorn:

> Enlargement, security and development concerns apply to many of the countries of Eastern Europe, and hence frame EU drug policies there. Security concerns of the EU, but not enlargement prospects apply to Russia ... and to the countries to the south of the Mediterranean, so security concerns frame EU drug policies in those contexts. Development and trade policies (but not security concerns) underpin the political rationale and practical application of the EU's drug policies *vis-à-vis* the Latin American countries".[29]

4.2 EU Policy on Drugs Following the Treaty on European Union

The TEU marked a fundamental step forward in a sense that it is the first time that explicit provisions on drugs are included in the formal Treaty

---

[26] Council Directive (EEC) 91/308 of 10 June 1991, OJ No. L 166 of 28 June 1991.
[27] Commission Communication to the Council and the European Parliament on a European Union Action Plan to combat drugs (1995-1999), COM (94) 234 final, Brussels, 23 June 1994, p. 42.
[28] *Ibid* p. 43.
[29] Dorn N. *Borderline Criminology: External Drug Policies of the EU* in Dorn N., Jepsen J. and Savona E. *European Drug Policies and Enforcement*, Macmillan Press, Britain, 1996, p. 243.

context. The TEU, at first sight, would seem to go some way towards facilitating a definition of coherent approach to EU drugs policies. The inclusion of a plethora of drugs-related provisions with formal Treaty bases raised hopes among many that concrete measures would be taken. However on closer examination, rather than being neatly placed in one chapter, provisions on drugs seem to be scattered in a clumsy way throughout the Treaty. All three pillars are involved in some way or another. The Third Pillar is probably the most significant innovation. No less than four out of the nine matters of common interest listed in Article K.1 have a direct bearing on the EU's drugs policy, these being K.1(4) combatting drug addiction in so far as this is not covered by (7) to (9); K.1(7) judicial co-operation in criminal matters; K.1(8) customs co-operation; K.1(9) police co-operation for the purposes of preventing and combatting terrorism, unlawful drug trafficking and other serious forms of international crime, including if necessary certain aspects of customs co-operation, in connection with the organisation of a EU-wide system for exchanging information within a European Police Office (EUROPOL).

It is not surprising that the lion's share of measures relating to drugs have been placed in a legal framework distinct to that of the European Communities (First Pillar) as these are sensitive areas in which Member States are reluctant to cede full control. It does mean however that co-ordination within the EU becomes a necessary, albeit complex requirement.

Whilst there may not be an explicit mention of drugs, the Second Pillar on common foreign and security policy will logically be involved in much of the EU's external activities regarding drug trafficking and production, as these activities will invariably overlap with external security issues. This security dimension was recognised at the Lisbon European Council of 26–27 June 1992 which identified the fight against traffic in illicit drugs as an area of possible joint action concerning third countries or regions.[30]

With regard to the First Pillar, in addition to the existing possibilities covered by the trade and development policies and Internal Market measures, a new Title (Title X, Article 129 EC) is devoted to Public Health in general. Article 129 EC makes specific reference to drug dependence. The Article further mentions the importance of fostering co-operation with third countries and international organisations. Article 129 EC (in accordance with the principle of subsidiarity) is restricted to incentive measures and recommendations.

The situation as it is now requires a great deal of co-ordination, and much of the activities at the external level will depend on the will of all Member States (as actions in the Second and the Third Pillars require unanimity).

---

[30]   At that time the Maghreb countries and the Middle East were mentioned as potential areas for future Second Pillar action against the traffic in illicit drugs.

[31]   Fortescue A. *The Legal Framework for Action in the European Union* in Estievenart G. *Policies and Strategies to Combat Drugs in Europe, The Treaty on European Union: Framework for a New European Strategy to Combat Drugs*, European University Institute, Florence, Martinus Nijhoff Publishers, Netherlands, 1995, p. 329.

Co-ordination is necessary to ensure that confusion, as Fortescue remarks, does not "flow from the fact that different aspects are to be treated under different rules of three different 'pillars'".[31] In general the Committee of Permanent Representatives (COREPER) is charged with ensuring consistency, not only in drugs co-operation but in all JHA aspects throughout the Treaty. Within the Institutions, specific horizontal groups exist to ensure co-ordination of drugs or drugs-related measures.[32]

In the Commission Communication of 1994 on a European Action Plan to Combat Drugs (1995-1999), the Commission suggests that a global EU drugs policy should entail essentially a three-pronged approach involving the reduction of the supply of drugs, the suppression of trafficking and the intensification of international co-operation. Such a three-pronged strategy, whilst all well and fine on paper, may prove to be somewhat more difficult to implement in practice.

Taking into consideration the aforementioned comments concerning the internal management of the EU drugs policy, the balance sheet of co-operation and concrete action in the framework of the NTA is not all that bad. It has correctly been identified, on both sides, as an area where substantial progress can be achieved. The two areas that were pinpointed for speedy progress (partly because some of the groundwork had already been made prior to the signature of the NTA) were the conclusion of an agreement between the US and the EU on chemical precursors and joint EU-US counter narcotics co-operation in the Caribbean Region.

4.3 EU-US Co-operation on Chemical Precursors

One should recall that this is an area in which the EC has competence to act (within the context of the EC trade policy) and, as such, a speedy agreement had been envisaged. Furthermore there has been quite a high level of co-operation and co-ordination between the EC and the US prior to the NTA. From around 1993 onwards a more concerted effort was made on the part of both sides to regularise meetings, to put more emphasis on information sharing and exchange of expertise, and to pool financial and staff resources. However, the Council was still rather reluctant to adopt a formal agreement with the US or any other third country for that matter. For some years now, there have nonetheless been regular encounters between officials from the US Drug Enforcement Agency (DEA) and from Commission DG XXI (Directorate General for Customs and Indirect Taxation). The EC and US have, for the past few years, also been organising a jointly sponsored conference yearly to which representatives from third countries and international organisations are invited. On 24-28 January 1996 the annual

---

[32]   In the Council there is a horizontal working group on drugs and in the Commission there is an Interservice Group on Drugs which play a general co-ordinating role.

conference was held in Rio de Janeiro in Brazil, and focused on "River and Cross Border Smuggling". The conference was co-sponsored by the DEA and the European Commission in co-operation with the Government of Brazil.

Pressure to act on precursors came originally from the drug-producing developing countries who wanted to see the industrialised countries or regions such as the EC and the US "do their bit to combat drug trafficking by introducing export controls on chemicals".[33] The EC countries had been particularly singled out by the US and Latin America for failure to control the export of chemicals to "high risk countries". The Regulation[34] controlling the export of precursors to third countries already mentioned above helped rectify the situation somewhat. A list of 24 so-called sensitive countries was also adopted. These countries have accepted that exports destined to them go through a selective requirement to obtain authorisation.[35]

To control even further the movement of precursors, the Community has embarked on a co-ordinated approach at the regional level with the Association of South-East Asian Nations (ASEAN) and Latin American countries, the aim being to sign a formal agreement which would cover trade control, administrative assistance and technical co-operation. Following a Joint Communication between the EU and the Andean Pact (Colombia, Bolivia, Equador, Peru and Venezuela) on 26 September 1995, the Community went on to sign, on 18 December 1995 (shortly after the announcement of the NTA), an agreement[36] on the control of drugs precursors and chemical substances with each of these countries. The agreements are the "first operational international agreements concluded by the Community on drug abuse control"[37] and contain provisions on monitoring of the trade of controlled chemical substances to prevent their diversion for illicit purposes, technical and scientific co-operation, a legal framework for the exchange of information and the establishment of a joint follow-up group to oversee implementation of the agreement. More recently on 13 December 1996 the Community signed a similar agreement with Mexico.

The agreement with the US, once it is signed, will be the seventh international precursor agreement concluded by the EC[38]. The EC-US

---

[33]   Hobbing P. *Export Restrictions on the Chemical Industry: New European Union Policy on Drugs*, 7 February 1995, p. 3.

[34]   Council Regulation (EEC) 3677/90 as amended by Council Regulation (EEC) 900/92.

[35]   See Council Regulation (EEC) 2959/93 of 27 October 1993, OJ No. L 267 of 28 October 1993.

[36]   For instance, see the agreement between the European Community and the Republic of Bolivia on precursors and chemical substances frequently used in the illicit manufacture of narcotic drugs or psychotropic substances, OJ No. L 324/3, of 30 December 1995.

[37]   Agence Europe, No 6617, Friday, 1 December 1995.

[38]   It should be noted that, since the text of this article was written, the draft EU-US Precursors Agreement referred to above has been signed. See Council Decision (EC) 97/389, OJ L164 21.6.97 p. 22, concerning the conclusion of an Agreement between the EC and the US on precursors and chemical substances frequently used in the illicit manufacture of narcotic drugs or psychotropic substances.

agreement will be different in the sense that it is seen as more of a framework agreement between two developed regions, the aim of which will be to control the export of licit chemicals produced on their territory to sensitive third countries which may eventually be used in the illicit production of drugs. It shall more than likely contain provisions which will allow for co-operation between the EC and the US concerning third countries such as the sharing of intelligence and the exchange of information on the purchase and sale of certain chemicals to "sensitive" third countries. Such a provision does not, understandably, exist in the other precursor agreements concluded by the EC. Other than the scope of the agreement, which as mentioned will more than likely include some provision on "means of mutual consultation on the legitimacy of proposed transactions in scheduled substances destined for third countries", the format and content of the EC-US agreement should not be too dissimilar to that of the previous EC precursor agreements. It should thus include provisions on trade monitoring, mutual administrative assistance, information exchange and confidentiality, technical and scientific co-operation and the establishment of a Joint Follow-up Group to oversee implementation of the agreement.

Conclusion of the agreement has dragged on a bit. From around February 1996 onwards, negotiations started with the US on the agreement. Up until May 1996, negotiations between EU experts (Commission representatives, mainly from DG XXI) and US experts (mainly from the DEA) went relatively smoothly. From May onwards divergences started to emerge, not so much on the substance (on which there is a consensus), but rather in terms of different theoretical approaches within the US Justice Department on the value of signing an agreement with the EC as a whole. Concern was voiced that by entering into formal legal arrangements with the EC, the US risked undermining the level of bilateral co-operation that already may exist between the US and Member States. Or, to put it another way, formal co-operation at the EC level may not be as efficient nor as effective as existing co-operative arrangements between the US and individual Member States.

The question must be asked here as to what extent there may have been a misunderstanding on the part of some negotiators as to the legal nature of the EC/EU set-up. If precursors fell under the Third Pillar as is the case with many of the external aspects of the EU drugs control policy, the Community would not have such an exclusive role and perhaps more relevantly, in legal terms, the Member States and not the EU would be the contracting parties of the agreement with the US.

The concern on the US side is in many ways academic as there is no evidence of any kind of precursor agreement existing between an individual

[39]   It is of course difficult to see how individual Member States of the EU could have entered into agreements with third countries in view of the fact that control in the trade of precursors falls under the trade policy of the EC, an area where (according to EC jurisprudence) the Community alone can act.

EU Member State and the US.[39] However, on the other hand, this case may reflect a more general concern in the US Administration and the Justice Department in particular, that further progress at the EU level in all fields of JHA co-operation may have adverse effects on the well-established bilateral co-operation networks that have been built up over the years with individual Member States.

Furthermore, and obviously this is harder to quantify, the US seems quite concerned to avoid a situation where formal EU-US co-operation may undermine informal co-operation networks that already exist between the US and Member States. It is hard to say whether the US favours a more informal approach to co-operation in JHA areas than the EU. It may simply depend on the particular issue that is being discussed. It is true nonetheless that it will prove far more difficult for a young political entity such as the EU (already struggling with questions of identity and legitimacy) to support the widespread use of informal co-operation with third countries in JHA issues as such informal co-operation would be void of any democratic and judicial control. The EC/EU justifiably has to be careful not to find itself in a situation where it may be accused of not being fully transparent or accountable.[40]

International chemical precursor control policies are entering into a third phase of development in which the objective will be multilateral initiatives, something which has been requested and supported by the UN. The first stage comprised of organising awareness conferences, joint seminars etc. on the need for international drug precursor control. The second stage began with the conclusion of formal bilateral agreements. The EC-US precursor agreement will provide the impulse for the development of multilateral initiatives, with the EC becoming the hub for such activities.

4.4 EU-US Caribbean Counternarcotics Co-operation

The joint EU-US Caribbean counternarcotics co-operation is cited as the first major success story in EU-US JHA co-operation since the announcement of the NTA. Once again, the seeds of co-operation were sown prior to the NTA. Nonetheless, it would be fair to say that, as in the case of the tentative precursors agreement, the December 1995 Madrid Summit and the ensuing NTA did inject the political impetus necessary to progress swiftly to concerted action. Both sides have already been active in this region. This new initiative arose out of the need to co-ordinate the various assistance programs

---

[40] This obviously is less of an issue for the US. The EU is at an embryonic stage of development wherein which it needs to nurture the trust and confidence of its citizens. Without this social legitimacy gained through popular support for the EU process, the EU has to be very careful not to be perceived as favouring an informal form of co-operation with third parties which is highly difficult to account for. This will only confirm fears both of the European Parliament and national parliaments that there is a problem of democratic deficit and accountability at the EU level.

and projects in the area. Recently, the US has been cutting back on many drug control activities in the Caribbean whilst at the same time urging the EU to take a greater lead role in the region so as to fill a vacuum that may result from the US toning down of activities. This arrangement boils down in many respects to the simple question of financial "burden-sharing".

4.5 Background to the EU-US Caribbean Drugs Initiative

The Caribbean is not a major drug producing region; the only known illicit drug to be grown in the region is cannabis. It has however become a main transshipment area for illicit drug trafficking from South America to North America and Europe[41] and also an area for drug-related money laundering. The effects on the region have been devastating in terms of socio-economic development.

DG VIII, the Commission Directorate General responsible for Development Policy, had already earmarked drugs control as a priority area for co-operation with the ACP countries. Its interest lay more on the development side of drug control and less on the law enforcement side which was considered a Third Pillar issue. In brief one could say that the Commission, and more particularly DG VIII, was already quite active in defining a coherent policy for drugs in this area before the NTA. It was not however, as of yet, a political priority on the part of the EC-EU on the whole. The joint letter by Chirac and Major along with the specific reference in the NTA certainly bolstered support for more co-ordinated drugs control initiatives and provided the necessary political weight to convince doubters within the Commission that drugs control in the Caribbean deserved to be accorded such priority status.

4.6 Letter by John Major and Jacques Chirac to Jacques Santer, December 1995

Prior to the Madrid European Council, Major and Chirac wrote a joint letter to the President of the Commission, Jacques Santer, to seek support for initiatives to be taken to tackle the threat posed by drug trafficking and drug-related crime particularly in the islands of the Eastern Caribbean. The joint letter called for a more co-ordinated Caribbean-wide approach to the fight against drugs under the framework of the United Nations International Drug Control Programme (UNDCP) and in co-operation with bodies such as the

---

[41] See The National Narcotics Intelligence Consumers Committee, NNICC, Report 1995, *The Supply of Illicit Drugs to the United States*, August 1996; Report of the EU Experts Group on *The Caribbean and the Drugs Problem*, April 1996; and also United Nations International Drug Control Programme, Report of the Regional Meeting on *Drug Control Co-operation in the Caribbean*, held at Bridgetown, Barbados, 15–17 May 1996.

Dublin Group, the Financial Action Task Force, Interpol and the World Customs Co-operation. The letter went on to request the Council and the Commission to examine what action the EU should take and to prepare a report as soon as possible. Financial contributions, according to the letter, could come both from the Community budget and directly from Member States.[42]

The Madrid European Council of 15/16 December 1995 reaffirmed the commitment at the EU level to launch new drugs control initiatives for both the Caribbean and Latin America. According to its conclusions, an international strategy for combatting drug abuse and drug trafficking should "be based on a comprehensive, co-ordinated approach designed to reduce drug supply and demand through bilateral co-operation between both regions".[43] For the purpose of preparing a report on proposals for action in both regions before April 1996, an *ad hoc* Working Party on Drugs was established.

4.7 EU-EC Experts Group Report

In view of this and also in preparation for a UNDCP-organised Caribbean regional meeting in Barbados in May 1996, an EU-EC Experts Group conducted a series of visits to countries within the Caribbean region between 12 February 1996 and 12 March 1996 to give them a clearer idea of the drugs problem in the region. The Experts Group worked closely with the EC offices and EU missions in the region and with DG VIII in Brussels. During this time the Experts Group also visited US experts in Miami, showing that, whilst this report was essentially an EU initiative, there was nonetheless real co-ordination with the US. Such co-ordination was necessary and useful as it managed to facilitate the possibility of "merging the EU recommendations with those of the US"[44] and also with those of other nations and international organisations attending the UNDCP Caribbean regional meeting in May 1996. The EU-EC Experts Group Report made a series of recommendations on wide-ranging areas covering law enforcement, drugs information and intelligence, harmonisation (or co-ordination) of legal and judicial systems in the region, money laundering, precursors, demand reduction and co-ordination of activities in general. Particular emphasis was placed on the importance of ensuring the active involvement of the Caribbean governments. The Report reiterated the need to enhance co-operation and co-ordination at all levels, i.e. between Caribbean countries,

---

[42] One can speculate as to the reasons behind and the timing of the Major-Chirac letter. Was the US for instance indirectly putting pressure on the EU, or at least some Member States with strong ties to the region, to share the burden of drug control measures?

[43] Presidency Conclusions, Madrid, 15, 16 December 1995, p. 18.

[44] USIS, Embassy of the United States of America (Belgium), Fact Sheet: EU-US Caribbean Counternarcotics Co-operation, White House Release of 16 December 1996, p. 2.

among third countries and among the myriad of drugs information/ intelligence systems already based in the region.

The feeling on the EU side is that the Experts Report greatly facilitated and influenced the proceedings of the UNDCP Regional meeting on Drugs Control Co-operation in the Caribbean, 15–17 May 1996. The UNDCP Regional Plan of Action that was adopted following the meeting reflects to a large degree many of the concerns and priority areas for action as outlined in the Report.

4.8 UNDCP Regional Meeting, Drugs Control Co-operation in the Caribbean, Barbados, 15–17 May 1996

What was evidently clear at this meeting was that there existed a strong political will to act in the region. This, it must be said, is largely due to the commitment of both the EU and the US. The EC delegation was led by the Commissioner for Justice and Home Affairs, Anita Gradin, and included, among others, Commission representatives from DG VIII, the Title VI Task Force within the General Secretariat, DG IB and various EC representatives in the Caribbean region. The Presidency of the Council and representatives from some EU Member States were also present (namely the UK, France, Spain, Germany, Netherlands, Italy and Greece). The US delegation was led by the Deputy Assistant Secretary of State for International Narcotics and Law Enforcement, Jonathan Winer. Also participating in the meeting were representatives from the Caribbean countries and a plethora of intergovernmental organisations, regional bodies and specialised agencies. Five working groups were established to address co-operation among National Drugs Control Councils, harmonisation of legislation, drug law enforcement co-operation, maritime co-operation and demand reduction. Following the conclusions of the five working groups, the outcome of the meeting was the adoption of an Action Plan for Drug Control Co-ordination and Co-operation in the Caribbean, as mentioned above, containing, in total, 68 recommendations.

The Action Plan has been, on occasions, referred to incorrectly as the joint EU-US Action Plan for the Caribbean. Whilst it is true that both the EU and the US were instrumental in preparing the ground for this agreement and will provide a sizeable portion of financial resources, it was, however, from the outset, made quite clear that this should be a multilateral initiative conducted in the framework of, and co-ordinated by the UNDCP. What is clear is that "EU-US co-operative efforts will assist Caribbean jurisdictions in implementing the Action Plan"[45] and that this will be carried out in co-ordination with "other donors" such as the UNDCP itself and the Organisation of American States/Commission Inter-americano para el control de Abuso de Drogas (DAS/CICAD).

[45] *Ibid* p. 2.

Whilst there was a high level of co-ordination between the US and the EU prior to and during the Barbados meeting, this does not mean that differences of opinion on methodology did not exist. The EU had shown a greater degree of interest in the development-related aspects[46] of drugs control co-operation whilst the US (along with some individual EU Member States) was more interested in participating in or contributing to law enforcement measures. This in principle should not prove to be too problematic as both parties' activities should complement each other. The EU perspective on drugs control co-operation differs slightly to that of the US. Some would view it as being less of a top-down approach than that of the US.[47] One example of where the different approaches may have led to a certain amount of tension between the two related to the "Ganja dilemma" as the EU-EC Experts Group Report put it. The Report had taken the view that Caribbean police and other law enforcement agencies were putting far too much time and money into the eradication of cannabis which could be better spent tackling other forms of drug-related crime. Whilst not suggesting that health risks associated with ganja abuse should be ignored altogether, the Report did feel that eradicating the drug would be difficult namely because the plant itself is easy to grow and thrives even in the most inaccessible of places and that there is a widespread acceptance in the Caribbean society of the use of the drug.

Most importantly, it was felt that the main threat to North America and Europe is the use of the Caribbean as a transshipment area for the trafficking of cocaine and marijuana originating from Latin America. Consequently, law enforcement efforts against the cultivation of ganja in the Caribbean should, according to the EU, be given a lower priority. This proved to be quite a sensitive issue for the US which had, after all, placed utmost importance on the promotion of law enforcement measures against the production and trafficking of any illicit drug and consequently viewed with suspicion the EU's approach which was hinting at the need to make a

---

[46]   This is not surprising seeing that within the Commission, DG VIII (Development) had taken the lead role in this area and in turn would be responsible for much of its implementation. Nicholas Dorn also argues that the EU approach to Latin American region differs from that of the US in that the former views the question primarily as a development issue whilst the latter considers it as first and foremost a security issue. See Dorn N. *Borderline Criminology: External Drug Policies of the EU* in Dorn N., Jepsen J. and Savona E. *European Drug Policies and Enforcement*, Macmillan Press, Britain, 1996, pp. 242–263.

[47]   During the course of the meeting, Justice and Home Affairs Commissioner Anita Gradin made the following remarks to a local newspaper: "What we really want is dialogue with the people and countries of the area to build up the fight against drugs" reflecting the "partner" image that the EU wanted to portray. Quoted in the Weekend Nation, Friday 17 May 1996.

distinction between "hard" and "soft" drugs.[48] This difference in approach was picked up on, perhaps rather unfortunately, by the local press during the UNDCP meeting.[49]

4.9 Implementation of the Caribbean Action Plan

Since the Florence European Summit of June 1996 the Commission has been examining ways in which to implement the proposals on the Caribbean. A working document, based on the proposals in the Council/Commission Report, presented at the Florence Summit, has been drawn up by the Commission along with those Member states that have greatest interest in the area. In order to facilitate the implementation of some of the more specific recommendations contained in the UNDCP Action Plan, it was considered appropriate to make a number of feasibility studies on a number of issues:

(1) *Maritime co-operation.* This study intends to assess the existing resource, equipment hardware of maritime law enforcement agencies with the aim of strengthening maritime co-operation in the region.
(2) *Intelligence communications.* The outcome of this study should be the development of an integrated intelligence communications network (police communications, computer systems etc.) for the Caribbean region.
(3) *Equipment and training.* Identification of training and equipment needs in the area of law enforcement.

These studies, which include the participation of US and Caribbean experts and in co-operation with some Member States (the UK, Netherlands and France) are funded by the Community, from both the drugs budget line and funds from Title VI TEU,[50] along with some bilateral French contributions. Further studies are to be launched in the areas of demand reduction, the fight against money laundering, regional forensic capabilities and precursor control.

---

[48] It is probably worth mentioning that, within the EU itself, there is still considerable disagreement among Member States whether or not to make the distinction between "hard" and "soft" drugs and national legislation differs accordingly.

[49] See article entitled "Focus drug war on cocaine" in The Weekend Nation, Friday 17 May 1996.

[50] Only a limited amount of funds in general have been allocated to Title VI activities owing to the highly sensitive nature of the subject matters dealt with in Third Pillar and the reluctance of Member States to accord full financial control over these areas to the Community framework. Thus the use of Title VI funds to partly finance feasibility studies on issues of drugs control is significant. On 14 October 1996, the Council adopted Decision 96/601/JHA (OJ No. L 268 of 19 October 1996) on measures implementing Article K1 TEU. This Decision allocates ECU 1 369 000 for the financing of projects covering co-operation with States engaged in structured dialogue with the EU, as well as Latin America and the Caribbean to combat drugs. The projects may, according to Article 2 of the Decision "take the form of training, the collection and exchange of information and experience, seminars, studies, publications or other operational measures in support of the European Union co-operation activities".

The Commission has made a financial commitment of 20 million Ecu. It is hoped that some individual Member States will make financial contributions amounting to approximately 3-5 million Ecu. However bilateral Member State contributions (mainly from the UK, France and the Netherlands and possibly also Spain) are difficult to gauge as it depends on Member States honouring political commitments. The US for its part for the 1997 fiscal year has pledged approximately 8 million US$. EC financial assistance shall cover mainly development-related drugs control issues whilst US contributions will go predominantly towards law enforcement measures (e.g. air/marine interdiction, etc.).

4.10 EU-US Co-ordination on Implementation of the Caribbean Action Plan

First and foremost, both the EU and the US work very closely with the UNDCP and keep it informed on a regular basis of progress on the implementation of the Plan. Furthermore, as in accordance with Recommendation No. 68 of the UNDCP Caribbean Action Plan an annual meeting should be held to evaluate progress in the implementation of various activities.

More specifically, at the level of the EU and US, a more structured form of co-operation has been established to ensure the highest possible level of co-ordination of drugs policies for the Caribbean region. EU experts and their US counterparts have for some time been meeting on quite a regular basis. On 24 and 25 October, in Washington, the Caribbean drugs co-operation initiative was discussed at a second meeting of the high level EC-US development assistance consultations which involved the Commission, US AID and the US State Department. At this meeting, a proposal was made to establish a joint EC-US working group dealing solely with the question of drugs in the ACP regions. This working group has since met to examine the state of progress of the implementation of the Caribbean Action Plan. The EC-EU has earmarked money laundering, training and judicial co-operation as possible areas for closer EC-US co-operation in the future.

The Commission is currently in the process of drawing up a table of projects, specifying, where necessary, areas subject to either Community funding or individual Member State funding. It is important to note that from the EU perspective, co-operation on drug control initiatives in the Caribbean region requires a considerable amount of co-ordination within the EU itself. The co-operation covers many areas that fall under the Third Pillar, where Member States more or less have the power to act where and how they wish, however other aspects fall under the First Pillar where the Institutions would play a lead role. Added to this will be additional participation (in terms of financing) by three or four individual Member states. It would be fair to say that the Commission has been given a considerable amount of leeway to co-ordinate the global EU approach and to represent the entirety of EU interests. This has required co-ordination within the Commission itself and with the Council. As said, drugs issues are spread right across the TEU. These issues can touch on many policy areas, and the competence to act may lie in several different sectors of the Commission. DG VIII on Development has probably taken the lead, as the initiative is very much linked to Development Policy. However, it would be difficult to act alone. The Title VI JHA Task Force in the Secretariat General has been very active logically as drug trafficking falls under Title VI of the TEU. A representative of the Commission JHA Task Force has been present at most of the meetings with the US. Other sections of the Commission that have been involved in some way include, among others, DG I (Relations with North America), DG IB (North-South co-operation), DG XXI (Customs and Indirect Taxation, responsible for precursors), DG XV (Internal Market and Financial Services - responsible for money laundering). On the Council side various working groups have been involved.

5. PROGRESS IN OTHER JHA AREAS–AN OVERVIEW

There is obviously a lot of progress that is hard to quantify. It is also a matter of interpretation. The establishment of structured dialogue is important and an increasing number of contacts from expert level right up to the ministerial level is having positive effects which invariably lead to an increased sense of mutual trust. The perception that success can only be measured by the number of legally binding texts that are signed between the two parties may be misguided. Neither side is at this stage looking for a harmonised EU-US approach on these issues. Harmonisation is not yet on the cards: rather, one should refer to the move towards greater interoperability[51] or the idea of "increasing integration and connectivity" as Deputy Assistant Secretary of State, Winer put it.[52] With this in mind the current balance sheet, excluding the areas of drug co-operation mentioned above, looks as follows:

(1) On asylum and immigration, some progress was made in terms of exchange of information. In April of 1996, EU officials visited southern US border sites. US officials were also involved in the CIS conference on

---

[51] This idea of interoperability is also currently being put forward as an alternative option at the EU level. The feeling within the EU is that full harmonisation among the 15 Member States would be a long drawn out and complicated process and probably much less desirable than, instead, the more practical-oriented approach of interoperability.

[52] Embassy of the United States of America, Belgium, press release on international crime: see note 19 *ante*.

migration.[53] The US has been further involved in the context of the EU working groups on asylum (CIREA) and immigration (CIREFI). This in practice means that, every so often, possibly once every Presidency, US representatives will be fully briefed right after the CIREA and CIREFI meetings. The US had been requesting greater participation for some time. This was finally achieved during the Irish Presidency in the second half of 1996.[54]

(2) On police co-operation, very little has happened on a formal level. However, possibilities do exist for the future. There is a provision in the Europol Convention (Article 42) allowing for regulated co-operation between Europol and third countries. The US is considering availing of this possibility once the Europol convention is ratified by all EU Member States and enters into force. The Europol Drugs Unit (EDU), in the Hague, which is seen as the precursor to the European Police Organisation, has been in operation since 1 January 1993 (Ministerial Agreement). Its role was formalised through a Joint Action of March 1995.[55] There is no provision, however, in the Joint Action for co-operation with third countries. There was, it seems, a proposal by the Italian Presidency to allow the US access to the data of the EDU[56] (possibly through a protocol); however, it appears this proposal has since been abandoned. For the time being co-operation between the EU and US will continue on the basis of *ad-hoc* informal contacts.

(3) There has thus far been no progress on attempts to secure EU participation in the International Law Enforcement Academy (ILEA) in Budapest which had been pinpointed as one of the priorities for EU-US co-operation in the NTA. The ILEA was set up in 1995 by the FBI in co-operation with the Hungarian Government, the aim of which was to train police officers from Central and Eastern European countries. Whereas individual EU Member States have already provided expertise and the EU Troïka ministers visited the Police Academy in April of 1996, there has thus far been no consensus among all Member States on some kind of formal EU participation.

(4) On extradition, the US in particular wanted to see some initiatives in this area but once again it is unclear whether both parties would like to see a formal agreement being adopted which might affect existing agreements.

The priorities for JHA co-operation in the near future shall include co-operation on combatting cybercrime, paedophilia, child pornography and

---

[53] See Senior Level Group Report to the EU-US Summit, 12 June 1996.

[54] Both CIREFI (Centre d'Information, de Recherche et d'Echange en Matière d'Asile (Centre for Information, Discussion and Exchange on Asylum)) and CIREA (Centre d'Information, de Recherche et d'Echange en Matière de Franchissement des Frontières et d'Immigration (Centre for Information, Discussion and Exchange on the Crossing of Frontiers and Immigration)) held a meeting with US experts in December 1996.

[55] Council, Joint Action concerning the Europol Drugs Unit on the basis of Article K.3.2(b) of the TEU, 10 March 1995, OJ No. L 62, 20 March 1995.

[56] This was reported in Statewatch Bulletin, Vol. 6 No. 1, January-February 1996.

international organised crime. This recent focus on the external dimension of JHA for the EU will be further taken into consideration when it comes to the drafting of legislation. An example is Article 42 of the Europol Convention, but one can also refer to provisions that have been included in more recent legal texts adopted by the Council.[57]

6. CONCLUSION

6.1 Weakness of the Third Pillar Structure and the Impact on Relations with Third Countries

JHA issues lie predominantly within the hybrid Third Pillar structure, which, whilst falling under the single institutional framework of the TEU (Article C TEU), is still very much intergovernmental. Its links with various provisions and policies within the EC Treaty make it difficult to co-ordinate externally. There are no clear guidelines and policy objectives are more often than not blurred. The role of the institutions in the Third Pillar is less than clear. Whilst it is difficult enough for third countries to negotiate on issues that fall within the EC Treaty, when these negotiations have to also include non-EC, TEU issues (e.g. Title V–CFSP, Title VI–JHA) there is a great deal of confusion as to who you are dealing with (the institutions or Member States), and how you are dealing with them (legal instruments, decision-making procedures). Miles Kahler's analysis of the EC's shortcomings in external economic relations could equally if not even more aptly apply to the difficulties that the EU faces in the fields of JHA:

> ... the regional entity, if it has a delegated external role, should be able to make, change, and implement credible bargains. This criterion of judgement–which has been the source of most criticisms of the EC, in turn implies clarity of competence, ability to co-ordinate internally, and reasonable efficiency in reaching a common position. If the competence of regional institutions *vis-à-vis* their members is blurred, non-members will have great difficulty in bargaining with the regional entity. An effective means of co-ordinating member governments as well as regional institutions implies the ability to reach a common position, to change that position, if necessary in the course of negotiation, and to indicate the means of implementation of any bargain reached.[58]

The confusion is understandable and the chances, thus, of the EU delivering on its promises are severely diluted. The point has already been made on the

---

[57] See for instance Joint Action introducing a programme of training exchanges and co-operation in the field of identity documents ("Sherlock"), OJ L287 8.11.96 p. 7, Article 7; Joint Action on a programme of incentives and exchanges for legal practitioners, ("Grotius"), OJ L287 8.11.96 p. 3, Article 8, para 4; and Joint Action providing a common programme of exchange and training of, and co-operation between, law enforcement authorities ("Oisin"), OJ L7 10.1.97 p. 5 Article 7 para 4.
[58] Kahler M. *Regional Futures and Transatlantic Economic Relations*, European Community Studies Association/Council on Foreign Relations Press, 1995, p. 28.

US side that negotiations on issues covered by the EC have been to a large degree more fruitful. This may boil down to a question of expectations, namely the idea, for instance, that with the EC "you know where you stand". However, even within the EC, negotiations can be tricky. When one is dealing with an issue that falls wholly within the competence of the EC, one still may find that the topic at hand is dispersed throughout various policies which will require internal co-ordination before the EC can negotiate with third parties.

The EU handling of the Caribbean initiative is surely a positive sign of how, when there is a convergence of interests among the Member States, within the institutions themselves, and between the EU and the US, progress can be achieved. The Caribbean initiative, as we have seen, was both a cross-pillar and cross-sectoral issue. It was cross-sectoral in a sense that it covered various sectors which are affected by or may contribute to drug control measures, i.e. development co-operation, trade policy, public health, customs, police co-operation, etc., and cross-pillar as it required the active participation of all three pillars of the TEU. The Commission was allowed to play an important co-ordinating role representing the EU interests, as many areas of the co-operation fell within the Community competence and thus the Commission had the right of initiative. In the areas of the Caribbean initiative that did not fall under the competence of the EC, but rather under the Third Pillar of the EU, the Council was obviously more active.

Whereas the Caribbean initiative is an example of progress that can be achieved between the US and the EU in JHA issues regardless of whether this involves the more intergovernmental Second and Third Pillars, it must be said that it is an isolated case in which there has been such a convergence of issues on all levels and an overriding desire to proceed. It is clear testament to the view that if the political will is there, the way will be found regardless of difficulties that may exist as a result of institutional, structural and legal complexities. The political momentum was indeed provided by the NTA; it would be hard to imagine such a high degree of co-operation if that political pressure did not exist. However, when the political will is not present among all EU Member States with regard to Third Pillar issues, structural and institutional weaknesses will highlight the EU's inability to overcome Member State divergences and, as a result, its inability to present a common approach *vis-à-vis* the US.

An important point, which should not be overlooked is that the European Community has the power to act by itself. Furthermore, for those areas that fall under its competence it can act at the international level and enter into contractual agreements with third countries/regions and organisations. The EC has legal personality[59] whilst the EU does not. The EU *per se* does not have the competence to act on its own, independently of the Member States.

---

[59]   See art 210 EC Treaty.

The institutional framework and structural make-up provided for in the TEU are lacking in this respect. The competence to pursue policies in the Third Pillar rests not with the EU but with the Member States and importantly the Third Pillar does not "deprive the Member States of their genuine tasks and powers in the areas of justice and home affairs".[60] Whereas the Council does take decisions on Third Pillar issues, it "cannot, according to the Treaty on European Union, act in the name of the Union and thereby create rights and obligations of the Union as such *vis-à-vis* third countries".[61]

If the Third Pillar, or aspects of the Third Pillar, were transferred to the First, they would then fall within the competence of the EC and the position of the EC *vis-à-vis* third countries in JHA areas would be greatly enhanced. This would facilitate enhanced co-operation from a practical point of view. The EC as one entity would be able to act far more effectively on the international scene in the fields of JHA. It would truly be an equal partner alongside the US. This of course is not likely to happen in the near future. A full incorporation of all fields of JHA would have enormous ramifications in view of the creation of a supranational state. Justice and Home Affairs are basic tenets of the nation state. They are inextricably linked to the concept of a national sovereignty. Whilst it is evidently clear that Member States are not ready for such a *saut quantitatif*, a transfer of some aspects of JHA may be envisaged.

6.2 Outcome of the 1996 Intergovernmental Conference on the Revision of the Treaties

In the context of the Intergovernmental Conference (IGC) negotiations on the revision of the Treaties, much time and effort has gone into looking at how Justice and Home Affairs can be dealt with more effectively and efficiently in the context of the EU. The outcome of these negotiations will be of considerable importance to the integration process and consequently will have an effect on transatlantic relations in the related areas. The US will be looking to see whether the institutional shortcomings of the EU can be rectified and the "internal EU debates with Member States about competence" resolved.

Whilst it may still be a little premature to talk about the creation of a European space of justice and security, progress at the IGC in the fields of JHA can be expected. In the Third Pillar, new areas may be added to the list of matters of common interest as provided for in Article K.1 TEU. The objectives of the Third Pillar may be further specified, the instruments and

---

[60]   Müller-Graff P. C. *The Legal Bases of the Third Pillar and its Position in the Framework of the Union Treaty* in Monar J. and Morgan R. *The Third Pillar of the European Union, Co-operation in the Fields of Justice and Home Affairs*, European Interuniversity Press, Bruges Conferences, No. 5, 1994, p. 33.

[61]   Epiney A. *Switzerland and the Third Pillar: Implications and Perspectives* in Bieber R. and Monar J. *Justice and Home Affairs in the European Union, the Development of the Third Pillar*, European Interuniversity Press, Bruges Conferences, No. 9, 1995, p. 369.

their legal status clarified, and the efficiency and effectiveness of the working procedures and structures improved. Community institutions such as the Commission, Court of Justice and European Parliament may be accorded a greater role. There is a strong likelihood that a new provision on co-operation with third countries will be included in the modified Third Pillar. Finally, there is much debate about the possibility of transferring some Third Pillar issues to the First, namely asylum and immigration, although it must be said that there is still a certain amount of reluctance among some Member States. The prospect of the whole of the Third Pillar being incorporated into the First is unlikely, to say the least.

The conclusion of the IGC and resultant modification of the Treaties[62] should at the very least ensure a greater degree of coherence, consistency and impetus in the EU-EC's treatment of Justice and Home Affairs both at an internal and external level. This will, in turn, enable further progress to be achieved between the EU and the US on the JHA aspects of the NTA. One cannot be more specific than this without entering into speculation. For the time being, it would be fair to say that with regard to EU-US co-operation in the fields of Justice and Home Affairs, the NTA has made some difference. The NTA has provided both sides with a political impetus to get things done. Whilst it has not resulted in a radical transformation in the forms of co-operation that existed prior to December 1995, it is seen by many of those technocrats who are involved as a political recognition that the work they were doing was indeed a priority, the clearest example being the Caribbean initiative. However, for the EU to deliver on its commitments (and meet US expectations), progress will have to continue, for the time being, on an issue-by-issue basis. The present set-up of the EU impedes the EU from committing itself to a comprehensive plan of action, with clear objectives to be complemented by concrete action, and a time frame within which such objectives must be achieved. If the EU is having so much difficulty in achieving this internally, there is even less hope for it to be any more successful in its relations with third countries in the fields of JHA.

---

[62]   It should be noted that, since the text of this article was written, the IGC has been concluded and the Treaty of Amsterdam has been signed. This Treaty modifies somewhat the structure of the Third Pillar and contains provisions on the transfer of some subjects (namely, free movement of persons, checks at external borders, asylum, immigration and judicial co-operation in civil matters) from the Third Pillar to the First.

Chapter 9

Defying a Global Challenge: Reflections About a Joint EU-US Venture Against Transnational Organised Crime[1]

Monica den Boer

1. INTRODUCTION

The co-operation between the United States and the European Union against crime and terrorism has had a long history. Previously, EC Member States were informally associated with other countries through the Trevi Group, in particular with the US, Canada, Norway and Morocco. These "friends of Trevi" were regularly consulted on law enforcement matters related to the fight against terrorism, drugs and serious crime.[2] Other co-operative frameworks which have encouraged transatlantic co-operation include the Financial Action Task Force (FATF), which mainly targets organised financial-economic crime such as money laundering, the International Criminal Police Organisation (Interpol), whose membership includes all EU Member States and the North American countries, and the World Customs Organisation (WCO), which covers relationships between the

---

[1]   It should be noted that, since the text of this chapter was written, there have been further developments in the area of EU co-operation in the field of justice and home affairs, e.g. concerning the High Level Group Action Plan on Organised Crime.

[2]   *Fortress Europe?*, September 1995, Circular Letter No. 37, p. 2; see also Van Outrive L. and Enhus E. *Internationale Politiesamenwerking – Europol*, Brussel, Centrum voor Politiestudies, 1994, p. 25; Van Ver Wel J. E. and Bruggeman W. *Europese Politiële Samenwerking. Internationale Gremia*, Brussels, Politieia, 1993, p. 44.

national customs administrations of over 130 countries and which works under the aegis of the 1976 Naples Convention.[3]

Criminal justice co-operation has been extended since the demise of Trevi in 1992. A new impulse has been given by the New Transatlantic Agenda (NTA), which was concluded in Madrid in December 1995. The Agenda comprises a number of intentional statements in response to "global challenges", which have been identified in the wake of the emergence of a multi-polar international political system.[4] Among these challenges are "the scourges of international crime, drug-trafficking and terrorism", but also illegal immigration and asylum. The EU and the US jointly commit themselves:

> to active, practical co-operation between the US and the future European Police Office, EUROPOL.

Furthermore, they will:

> jointly support and contribute to ongoing training programmes and institutions for crime-fighting officials in Central and Eastern Europe, Russia, Ukraine, other new independent states and other parts of the globe.[5]

The agenda that specifies these joint intentions is impressive, but rather open-ended.[6] Hence it may be difficult to assess in the future whether or not common goals have been achieved and to determine the rate of success of joint initiatives.

The transnational agenda on justice and home affairs issues has been formulated on the basis of a growing awareness that criminal justice is increasingly becoming a transnational enterprise. On the one hand, the target of transnational criminal justice activities covers a spectrum of criminal activities that has been identified as a global (crime) village. The arm of law enforcement initiatives therefore reaches further than ever: criminal investigation activities are staged in remote regions where illegal produce and illegitimate trade form the causal end of criminal activities at the other end of the world, often through liaison officers stationed at diplomatic posts. The growth of criminal justice as a transnational enterprise also receives frequent stimuli from international bureaucratic networks. Furthermore, the importance of flourishing transatlantic political and economic contacts for criminal justice should not be underestimated.

This chapter will probe the quality of criminal justice co-operation that has been in existence between the US and the EU Member States until now. The second part will look into the nature of the subject of this co-operation, namely international organised crime. The chapter concludes with a number of suggestions for the deepening of the criminal justice co-operation across the Atlantic.

---

3   Van Outrive L. and Enhus E. *Internationale Politiesamenwerking – Europol*, Brussel, Centrum voor Politiestudies, 1994, pp. 16, 35, 17.

4   Van Ham P. *The EC, Eastern Europe and European Unity. Discord, Collaboration and Integration since 1947*, London, Pinter, 1993, at p. 206. See the Appendix *post* where the NTA is set out in full.

5   *Agence Europe*, EUROPE Documents, No. 1970, Atlantic Document, No. 93, 12 January 1996, p. 3.

6   See *Responding to Global Challenges*, Chapter II of the Documents that were signed at the Transatlantic Summit between the EU and the US, see the Appendix, *post*, at p. 178.

2. THIRD PILLAR ISSUES AND THE TRANSATLANTIC RELATIONSHIP

The US has given plenty of signals that it would very much like to be more intensively involved in the EU activities in the field of Justice and Home Affairs co-operation. However, despite joint "progress in confronting global challenges of crime and disease and environmental degradation"[7], a sense of frustration in the US has become more than apparent. Its input in building the (mechanism of the) Third Pillar has been scant to say the least. Earl Anthony Wayne, who was a keynote speaker at the conference on "The New Framework of EU-US Relations" on 4 and 5 July 1996 in Brussels, said the following about Justice and Home Affairs co-operation:

> We ... lack progress on "Third Pillar" or home and justice issues. The United States is enthusiastic about building up our co-operative efforts against international crime and drug trafficking, but we have found the European Union institutionally less ready to move forward. There are internal EU debates with Member States about competence, and there is the need to establish internal EU practices in this area, which is, after all, a very new area for the EU under the Maastricht Treaty. We are encouraged by the progress we have made on the precursor chemical agreement and by our work together in preparation for the recent UNDCP workshop on counter-narcotics co-operation in the Caribbean. We are equally encouraged by the Irish government's decision to make the fight against crime and drugs one of the highest priorities of their presidency which began just three days ago.[8]

However, the transatlantic agenda should be extended, argues Wayne:

> But we can do more. For example, the US wants to co-operate with the EU in fighting crime in Central and Eastern Europe. As part of this effort, we hope to formalise, in the near future, full EU participation in the valuable contribution the Budapest International Law Enforcement Academy (ILEA) is making in democratic institution building in Central and Eastern Europe. As with CFSP, the Third Pillar decision-making structure is a topic of the IGC. The results of those deliberations will affect the extent to which we are able, together, to fulfill the goals of the NTA.[9]

Is there actually an added value to the Third Pillar? Wayne raised the almost painful question during the conference: "Does the existence of the Third Pillar actually make any difference at all?". It is a comforting thought that the Americans are not isolated in regarding the Third Pillar as too much of a Paper Tiger with little or no visible implementation. Even the responsible Commissioner, Ms Anita Gradin, confessed that the progress of the Third Pillar has been poor. She said:

---

[7] Wayne A. *The potential of the New Transatlantic partnership*, paper presented at the conference entitled "The New Framework of EU-US Relations", 4 and 5 July 1996, Brussels, p. 3 (mimeo).
[8] *Ibid* p. 5.
[9] *Ibid* p. 6.

... a higher level of unity on central issues would have been desirable .... The Commission
desires that co-operation becomes more effective. Today, it is too slow, there are too many
levels, and the requirement of unanimity makes it difficult to advance.[10]

Instead of regarding the Pillar on Justice and Home Affairs Co-operation as
a finished construction, it is better to characterise it as a process of "moving
towards".[11] Especially enlargement and the call for more transparency of the
decision-making process will put a heavy pressure on the moulding of this
field of co-operation. For the actors involved, it sometimes does not seem to
matter whether Third Pillar instruments are implemented and transformed
into tangible reality, which until now has been one of the greatest
shortcomings of the policy-making process in this field.

The considerable identity-crisis from which the Third Pillar suffers
certainly does not help to solidify its external image. The ambiguity with
which the US has ventilated some opinions about co-operation with the EU
has further contributed to the suppression of this image. On the one hand,
the US expresses its desire to be more seriously and systematically involved,
whilst on the other hand, it is rather sceptical about the effect that the Third
Pillar can possibly have on successful joint law enforcement initiatives
between the Member States of the EU.

Meanwhile, the "Big Brother" effect plays a role in the background as US
transnational policing activities are connoted with an involvement in the
national and international dimensions of politics.[12] At the same time, the EU
may be reluctant to draw in the US because it feels it cannot deliver. The
main reasons for this slack performance are seated in the intergovernmen-
talist character of the Third Pillar (unanimity) and the requirement of
subsidiarity. These are very much fundamental characteristics of a mixed
legal and political nature.

The intergovernmental character of the Third Pillar is a direct consequence
of the fact that internal security and criminal justice still belong to the
sovereignty of nation states. The EU therefore neither has a framework-
legislation in the field of criminal (procedure) law, nor a federalist law
enforcement agency. Despite striving for a European judicial space, the EU is
incapable of employing certain activities because it does not have criminal
law competences.[13] The EU Member States seem to first want to sort out
their mutual trouble concerning criminal law differences and contrasting

---

[10]   *Fortress Europe?*, September 1995, Circular Letter No. 37, p. 3.
[11]   Professor Michael Metcalf at the Round Table conference in Minneapolis-St. Paul, *"The Future of
Europe"*, May 1993.
[12]   "The Cold War vision of the United States as the world's policeman has yielded to a new post-Cold
War vision, one that more closely aligns the ordinary citizen's notion of policing with US involvement
in international politics". Nadelmann E. A. *Cops Across Borders. The Internationalisation of US
Criminal Law Enforcement*, University Park, Pennsylvania, Pennsylvania State University Press, 1993,
p. 476–477.
[13]   See Anderson M., Den Boer M., Cullen P., Gilmore W., Raab C. and Walker N. *Policing the
European Union. Theory, Law and Practice*. Oxford, Clarendon Press, 1995, Chapter 6 *The European
Union and Criminal Law*, pp. 181–217.

criminal policies by means of a stepwise, mostly bilateral approach. It is very much regretted by law enforcement agencies that criminals still flee across national borders because certain criminal justice concepts cannot be reversed, such as the freezing of assets or the temporary cancellation of the right to silence. It is very difficult, but also undesirable, to deal with the suspension of civil liberties at the supranational level. A federal policing system like the one that has existed for decades in the US, with a self-evident cross-border operational component, is as yet hard to imagine in the current intergovernmental climate that keeps Justice and Home Affairs co-operation in its grip.

The fact that the Third Pillar is intergovernmental implies that it is strongly influenced by the individual Member States. Approaches to criminal justice problems may diverge considerably. This means that it is very difficult to either harmonise or to operate *en bloc*, and furthermore, that a supranational body like the European police office cannot be formally allowed to use operational powers (apart from co-ordination and supervision of controlled deliveries). Instead, the Member States endeavour to achieve some form of interoperability, which is a far more modest aim than full legal harmonisation:

> interoperability allows for continued national differences while still achieving the necessary degree of complementarity for effective concerted action against transnational crime.[14]

Examples of the encouragement of interoperability are the secondment of liaison officers to diplomatic posts, the exchanges of magistrates, and the creation of resolutions on special investigation techniques such as witness protection.[15]

A further political hurdle is also implicit in the workings of the subsidiarity principle. This means that EU action is not required unless the interests of two or more Member States are being harmed as a consequence of the criminal activity.[16] The subsidiarity principle is coupled with the principle of proportionality, i.e. the crime must be serious and high-profile enough for an agency like the European Police Office to stage an investigation. The fear of competition with the traditional agents of internal security management,

---

[14] Williams P. and Savona E. U. T*he United Nations and Transnational Organised Crime*, Special Issue of the Transnational Organised Crime, Vol. 1, No. 1, Autumn 1995.

[15] E.g. *Droits et obligations des officiers de liaison*, Doc. 5459/96 EUROPOL 17, 19/20.03.1996, Conseil JAI (1909e pt. B 9c), Communication la Presse 5727/96 (Presse 63); Action commune (96/277/JAI) concernant un cadre d'échange de magistrats de liaison visant l'amélioration de la co-opération judiciaire entre les Etats membres de l'Union européenne, 22.04.1996 Conseil A.G. (1915e) pt. A 19, Communication la Presse 6561/96 Presse 98), JO L 105, du 27.04.96, pt. 1; OJC 97/C 10/01, *Council Resolution of 20 December 1996 on individuals who co-operate with the judicial process in the fight against international organised crime.*

[16] The crime to be investigated by the European Police Office must meet a number of subsidiarity criteria, namely that it concerns terrorism, unlawful drug trafficking and other forms of serious organised crime where there are factual indications that an organised criminal structure is involved and two or more Member States are affected by the forms of crime in question in such a way as to require a common approach by the Member States owing to scale, significance and consequences of the offences concerned". (Article 2.1, Convention on the Establishment of Europol).

i.e. the regional and national law enforcement agencies, is so large that the future European Police Office will only target serious international organised crime.

A certain feeling of incompetence on the side of the EU is also aroused by differentiated experiences: international organised crime manifests itself in many different shapes and sizes. The EU Member States have therefore neither been capable of painting an overall picture of its nature and threat, nor have they achieved the establishment of a common list of criteria to be used as a basis for an inventory of the activities of organised crime groups. Corruption forms an illustration of differentiated experiences: some Member States like Italy suffer from its endemic proportions, while in another Member State like the Netherlands corruption is still a relatively sporadic phenomenon. The absence of a common perception of organised crime within the international community can be a notorious obstacle in the process of legislative harmonisation.[17] There is as yet no common threat-assessment of organised crime in the European Union, although Europol's tasks include the provision of "strategic intelligence to assist with and promote the efficient and effective use of the resources available at national level for operational activities" and the preparation of "general situation reports".[18] In 1995, the Europol Drugs Unit already prepared a strategic report in the form of a comprehensive discussion document on criminal activities within the EU and threats posed by specific organised criminal groups.[19] The EU Member States have only recently decided to work on a joint directory of expertise on organised crime.[20]

---

[17]   Williams P. and Savona E. U. *The United Nations and Transnational Organised Crime*, Special Issue of the Transnational Organised Crime, Vol. 1, No. 1, Autumn 1995, p. 85: "A general agreement upon the essential concept and the use in all nations of similar, if not identical, types of criminalisation for members of criminal organisations can help slow the spread of organised crime and will facilitate legal co-operation, especially when it is based on the principle of dual criminality".

[18]   Article 3 (2.2) and 3 (2.3) of the Convention on the Establishment of Europol.

[19]   The report focused on Central and Eastern European criminal groups, Italian Mafia-type organisations, Nigerian criminal groups, Triad societies, Turkish criminal groups and former Yugoslavian criminal groups. Another strategic report looked at the threat posed by organised crime groups in the former Soviet Union and Central and Eastern Europe, and large scale money laundering emanating from the former Soviet Union into the EU. Furthermore, a "comprehensive overview of Drug Production and Drug Trafficking as it affects the European Union" was completed in the latter part of 1995; the report contained the Drug Seizure Statistics for 1994, Annual Report for 1995, Europol Drugs Unit, The Hague, April 1996, pp. 12–13.

[20]   *Joint Action of 29 November 1996 adopted by the Council on the basis of Article K.3 of the Treaty on European Union, concerning the creation and maintenance of a directory of specialised competences, skills and expertise in the fight against international organised crime, in order to facilitate law enforcement co-operation between the Member States of the European Union* (96/747/JHA), published in Official Journal of the European Communities, No L 342/2, 31 December 1996.

3. CO-OPERATION WITH THE US AT EU MEMBER STATE LEVEL

Even though the bilateral co-operation between the EU and the US in the field of Justice and Home Affairs is still a little bit on the thin side, there are several examples of a successful and influentual relationship between the US and the individual EU Member States. There are three criminal justice areas in which this relationship has proven to be particularly strong, namely police systems, (training in) police investigation techniques, and co-operative frameworks.

3.1 Police Systems

Numerous aspects of police systems currently existing in Europe have been inspired by the American model. One of these aspects is the enlargement of scale, which implies specialisation and centralisation of police tasks that are used to counter criminal activities with an infrequent occurrence, that have a high-profile character, or that can only be investigated with the help of special or expensive techniques that are not easily available to local (or even regional) police forces. Many EU Member States have seen the creation of umbrella-type police organisations. Examples are the creation of the National Criminal Intelligence Service in 1992 in the United Kingdom, the Algemene Politie Steun Dienst (General Police Support Service) in 1994 in Belgium, and the Landelijk Recherche Team (National Criminal Investigation Team, with executive powers) in 1995 in the Netherlands. The creation of some of these national units is both a side-effect of scale enlargement and an official requirement for the participation in the Europol Drugs Unit (EDU).

American inspiration can also be found in the area of federalism: Chancellor Kohl nurtured federalist ideas in relation to the creation of a European Police Office. He often employed the term "European FBI". Certainly this was not a mindless comparison, as some similarities can be found between the remit of the Federal Bureau of Investigation (FBI), which includes the gathering of domestic intelligence to fight terrorism and to fight organised crime, and the remit of the EDU-Europol. There are also some analogies between the Central Intelligence Agency (CIA) and EDU-Europol.

First of all, there is contextual analogy between the European and American law enforcement organisations. Both the CIA and the FBI were born out of the need to centralise intelligence, with the aim to position it with political leaders. This intelligence would not only be central, but also comprehensive, and not fragmentary and selective according to the need of sponsors. An important motivation for the creation of federal agencies was also the centralisation of resources. The contextual analogy lines up with the organisational analogy: the FBI, the CIA, EDU-Europol and several national criminal intelligence services are based on the need for a "central clearing house" with the aim to "synthesise all information".[21] There is also an analogy in legitimacy questions: both the CIA and EDU-Europol have enjoyed a gradual legitimisation process. The CIA was created on the basis of the National Security Act 1947. The Central Intelligence Agency Act 1949 provided enabling legislation for the CIA, i.e. provided details of operational competences. The legitimisation of EDU-Europol was also a phased process. It began with the Ministerial Agreement on the Establishment of the Europol Drugs Unit (Copenhagen, 2 June 1993). A Joint Action of 10 March 1995 extended the remit of the infant organisation beyond drugs trafficking and associated money laundering to vehicle theft, the smuggling of nuclear materials and illegal immigration networks. Whilst waiting for ratification of the Convention on the Establishment of Europol, which was signed on 26 July 1995, its mandate was widened to trade in human beings by means of a joint action (23 October 1996). It could be argued that Europol's legal basis is less substantial than that of the CIA, as the extension of its mandate by means of joint actions was not approved by a democratic power (national parliaments or European Parliament). Finally, there is some similarity in the thematic focus of the two organisations: the CIA concentrates on the fight against terrorism, but also drug-trafficking and nuclear proliferation. Drug-trafficking activities and the smuggling of nuclear substances are also subjects included in the itinerary of EDU-Europol, and after ratification of the Convention on the Establishment of Europol, terrorism will be added to this list.

The similarities between EDU-Europol and the CIA are, however, outweighed by the differences. The historical context in which the CIA was created differs greatly from the context in which EDU-Europol was created. It was only when it was decided after World War II to dismantle the Office of Strategic Services (OSS) that an effective US intelligence system became indispensable. The CIA was created in the Cold War period. It was meant to be a wartime agency, whereas EDU-Europol has been set up in peacetime. Furthermore, the type of intelligence collected by the two is different: the CIA has always focused on foreign, political intelligence, while EDU-Europol will focus on domestic and criminal intelligence. This implies that EDU-Europol is less of an instrument used by politicians, but more a practical instrument at the service of criminal intelligence agencies based in EU Member States. The final difference is that the CIA is a more responsive organisation than EDU-Europol: the CIA acts on request of the National Security Council, whereas Europol takes its own initiative and will then report back to the European Council.

---

[21]   Darling A. B. *The Central Intelligence Agency. An Instrument of Government to 1950*, University Park and London, Pennsylvania State University Press, 1990 (in Introduction to Chapter 1).

Despite the flirt that some European politicians have had with the federalist component in European policing it is obvious that the US federal system cannot simply be transposed to the EU. Especially cross-border policing can have negative aspects when the criminal justice system is not quite ready. When the FBI began to target organised crime, the decentralisation of the American policing system, the fragmentation of the jurisdiction and the decentralisation of criminal prosecution posed some real problems to cross-border policing activities[22]:

> While organised crime syndicates operate regionally, nationally, and even internationally, local prosecutors do not have authority to follow leads and witnesses across local boundary lines.[23]

It makes sense therefore not to glorify the American system, but to learn from its experiences. The experience demonstrates that suitable legislation has to be in place in the EU Member States before effective cross-border investigations can be staged (e.g. criminalisation of the membership of a criminal organisation; anti-money-laundering regulations and confiscation rules).[24] The advantages of a federal system should not be lost sight of however. It could aim at an avoidance of jurisdictional fragmentation and at the institutional arrangement of accountability at a supranational (supra-state) level. Even though the debate has started in Europe, for instance, evolving around the creation of a European judicial space and the introduction of a European Prosecution Service, no genuine solutions have yet been found. Certain forms of US policing cannot be transplanted to the European situation: North American regional co-operation against drugs cannot be the same as EU regional co-operation against drugs as the EU does not have a Drugs Enforcement Agency (DEA) type organisation with cross-border police powers.[25]

3.2 Covert Policing Activities

Traditional law enforcement techniques are insufficiently effective to combat organised crime. The involvement of intelligence agencies and the employment of covert policing methods has become part and parcel of criminal justice strategies against organised crime and drug trafficking.

---

[22] Jacobs J. *The Failures of American Law Enforcement in Combatting Organised Crime*, in Fijnaut C. and Jacobs J. *Organised Crime and its Containment. A Transatlantic Initiative*, Kluwer Law International, 1991, pp. 121–133, at pp. 121, 122.

[23] *Ibid* at p. 121.

[24] For a reflection on the usage of American experiences in the European Union, see Fijnaut C. and Verbruggen F. *The Eagle has not landed yet. The Federalisation of Criminal Investigation: Precedents and Comparisons*, in Den Boer M. *Undercover Policing and Accountability from an International Perspective*, European Institute of Public Administration, Maastricht, 1997, pp. 129-141.

[25] The DEA was set up to prevent corrupt linkages between the FBI and the local police forces. At the same time however, the DEA has primarily dealt with international narcotics matters.

A range of covert, proactive and/or undercover policing activities that are currently employed in Europe have been modelled upon American practices, notably through FBI-training modules on covert policing. One often speaks of the "Americanisation" of European drug enforcement[26], which applies to ways of acquiring evidence (e.g. through front stores or protected witnesses), the usage of covert techniques and the performance of forfeiture and confiscation on criminal assets.[27] Nadelmann gives three changes in the European criminal justice environments that paved the path for the "Americanisation" of police investigation techniques. The first change was institutional. As mentioned above, many police systems in Europe experienced an enlargement of scale, which implied centralisation and specialisation. By the end of the 1980's, most European police agencies had units that were specialised in drug trafficking. There was also an operational change, which concerns the importation of investigative techniques with the increase of US drug enforcement activities in Europe: these included:

> "buy and bust" tactics and more extensive undercover operations, "controlled delivery" of illicit drug consignments, various forms of non-telephonic electronic surveillance, and offers of reduced charges or immunity from prosecution to know drug dealers to "flip" them into becoming informants.[28]

Covert investigation techniques were initially regarded as illegal, but with the intensification of anti-drug trafficking efforts these techniques have become more acceptable. Most EU Member States have guidelines for the regulation of covert policing methods[29], but there have also been law enforcement failures which gave rise to parliamentary inquiries and criminal trials.[30] Nadelmann may therefore be a little too optimistic when he relates the "Americanisation" of investigation techniques in Europe to a legal

---

[26]   Nadelmann E. A. *The DEA in Europe*, in Fijnaut C. and Marx G.T. *Undercover. Police Surveillance in a Comparative Perspective*. The Hague, London, Boston, Kluwer Law International, 1995, pp. 269–289, at p. 272.

[27]   Nadelmann E. A. *Cops Across Borders. The Internationalisation of US Criminal Law Enforcement*, University Park, Pennsylvania, Pennsylvania State University Press, 1993, p. 194.

[28]   *Ibid* at p. 270.

[29]   See, for instance, Gropp W. *Besondere Ermittlungsmaßnahmen zur Bekämpfung der Organisierten Kriminalität*, Freiburg I. Breisgau, Max Plank Institut für ausländisches und internationales Strafrecht, 1993; Tak P.J.P., Hommes E G. A., Manunza E. R., en C.F. Mulder, *De normering van bijzondere opsporingsmethoden in buitenlandse rechtsstelsels. Een onderzoek naar de regeling en het gebruik van bijzondere opsporingsmethoden in de pro-actieve en re-actieve fase in Denemarken, Duitsland, Frankrijk, Italië en Noorwegen*. Nijmegen, 1995; Enquêtecommissie opsporingsmethoden, *Inzake opsporing*, Bijlage V, Opsporingsmethoden, Chapter 11 ("Rechtsvergelijkend perspectief opsporingsmethoden"), pp. 455–524.

[30]   For instance, a parliamentary inquiry was held in Belgium (1988-1990) to investigate the organisation of the fight against criminal groups and terrorism after the country experienced the case of a corrupt Gendarmerie officer (François) and after Belgian law enforcement agencies failed to identify and arrest the members of a violent criminal organisation (Bende van Nijvel). In the Netherlands, after a difficult trial in 1979 against two DEA officers who had infiltrated the Dutch drugs scene, there was the collapse of the Interregional Investigation Squad, causing the resignation of two Ministers and giving rise to the installation of a Parliamentary Inquiry (1995–1996), chaired by Mr. Maarten van Traa.

authorisation.[31] Despite a growing legal, political and public acceptance of covert policing, legal rules in the form of laws remain largely absent. Germany is the country with the most extensive array of legal rules; the Netherlands will introduce legislation in the near future.

3.3 Co-operative Frameworks

Criminal justice co-operation between the US and EU Member States is primarily organised on a bilateral or multilateral basis. A complicated web of agreements exists, and often these agreements can be seen as complementary to one another.[32]

The most successful example of bilateral co-operation is the secondment of US liaison officers to Europe, who have tasks varying from the investigation of Interpol-type queries, strategic analyses and dealing with questions relating to the operational support in the field of surveillance and undercover policing activities.[33] The DEA[34] and other internationally active American law enforcement organisations have quite a few postings to different Member States of the EU.[35]

In its overseas capacity, the US Drug Enforcement Administration plays a unique role in international politics. As a transnational organisation, it is a hybrid of a national police agency and an international law enforcement organisation. It represents the interests of one nation and its agents abroad are responsible to the ambassador, yet it has a mandate and a mission effectively authorised by international conventions and the United Nations. Like most agencies with representatives in US embassies abroad, its principal role is one of liaison. But unlike virtually all other agencies except the CIA and the military's investigative divisions, its agents are "operational" in most of the countries where they

[31] Nadelmann E. A. *Cops Across Borders. The Internationalisation of US Criminal Law Enforcement*, University Park, Pennsylvania, Pennsylvania State University Press, 1993, p. 271.
[32] Williams P. and Savona E. U. *The United Nations and Transnational Organised Crime*, Special Issue of the Transnational Organised Crime, Vol. 1, No. 1, Autumn 1995, p. 87.
[33] Enquêtecommissie opsporingsmethoden, *Inzake opsporing*, Chapter 10: "Internationale Opsporing", Bijlage V, Opsporingsmethoden, p. 452.
[34] Nadelmann E. A. *Cops Across Borders. The Internationalisation of US Criminal Law Enforcement*, University Park, Pennsylvania, Pennsylvania State University Press, 1993, p. 129.
[35] A few years ago, there were US liaison officers in the United Kingdom (London), Greece (Athens), Germany (Bonn and Frankfurt), Belgium (Brussels, also covering Luxembourg), France (Paris and Marseilles), Italy (Milan and Rome), Spain (Madrid), Portugal (Lisboa), The Netherlands (The Hague) and Denmark (Copenhagen). Source: Project Team Europol, *The Position of Europol within the Framework of European Co-operation, Member State Institutions, European Information Systems, International Organisations and Agencies*, 1993, p. 16.
      Nadelmann speaks of an "expansion": "A few indications of the pace of the expansion can be found in the personnel statistics. Between 1967 and 1991, the number of US drug enforcement agencies stationed abroad rose from about 12 in eight foreign cities to about 300 in more than seventy foreign locations. ... Between 1979 and 1990, the number of attorneys in the Criminal Division's Office of International Affairs rose from 4 to 40. During the same period, the US national central bureau of Interpol, based in the Justice Department, increased its staff from 6 to 110, its budget from $125,000 to $6,000,000, and the number of law enforcement agencies represented from 1 to 16". Nadelmann E. A. *Cops Across Borders. The Internationalisation of US Criminal Law Enforcement*, University Park, Pennsylvania, Pennsylvania State University Press, 1993, p. 3.

are stationed, they cultivate and pay informants, conduct undercover operations, and become directly involved in the activities of their local counterparts. The DEA's principal objective, broadly stated, is to stem the flow of drugs to the United States, yet it has devoted considerable efforts to assisting foreign law enforcement agencies in countering drug trafficking that has left little or no impact on the United States.

To take the Netherlands as an example: toward the end of the 1970's Canada, Sweden and the US had seconded liaison officers to this country. Currently there are 15 US liaison officers stationed in the Netherlands: five from the DEA, three from the US Customs Service, and two officers from the FBI (the latter are stationed in Brussels). The activities of American (DEA) liaison officers on foreign territory have often been met with scepticism, mainly because some of their investigations took place outside the knowledge and supervision of the local authorities. In a rich and informative study of American cross-border activities in Europe, Nadelmann claims that DEA agents "had devised means of circumventing the civil law restrictions on undercover operations and the use and recruitment of informants in Europe (and Latin America)".[36] From a survey that was conducted by the Dutch Parliamentary Inquiry Committee into Undercover Policing it could be established that many police officers and lawyers do not trust the DEA very much. The Committee could however not find much evidence of the DEA's wrongdoing. The relationship with the DEA improved considerably after some initial incidents and after the issuing of the Guidelines with regard to stationing liaison-officers in the Netherlands.[37] Also important to highlight are the networks between liaison officers abroad. There is the example of the Foreign Anti-Narcotics Committee which arose from a group of liaison officers stationed in Islamabad from the Netherlands, the US, France, Germany, Norway, Italy, Australia and Canada.[38]

Another example of bilateral co-operation is the existence of joint task forces, which can be very successful, as is the case with a task force that was set up between the US and Italy. The DEA focuses at the federal level on the national and international distribution and trafficking of all kinds of illicit drugs, and it increases its law enforcement activity by initiating and supporting task forces.[39] Other examples of bilateral co-operative frameworks are the well-known Mutual Legal Assistance Treaties (MLATs)[40], mostly covering the obtaining of evidence and witnesses or extradition; bilateral diplomatic contacts, mostly through embassies; and the Memoranda of Understanding (MoUs) which are usually signed in relation to specific

---

[36]   Nadelmann E. A. *Cops Across Borders. The Internationalisation of US Criminal Law Enforcement*, University Park, Pennsylvania, Pennsylvania State University Press, 1993, p. xviii.

[37]   Enquêtecommissie opsporingsmethoden, *Inzake opsporing*, Chapter 10, "Internationale Opsporing", Bijlage V, Opsporingsmethoden, pp. 451–452.

[38]   *Ibid* at p. 448.

[39]   Project Team Europol, 1993, p. 15.

[40]   Nadelmann E. A. *Cops Across Borders. The Internationalisation of US Criminal Law Enforcement*, University Park, Pennsylvania, Pennsylvania State University Press, 1993, pp. 324–341.

cases and which may contain the conditions for the employment of an American informer or infiltrator on foreign territory.

Well-known authors like Williams and Savona, who have done extensive research on the fight against organised crime, see certain advantages in bilateral forms of co-operation, especially when they are undertaken by states with "similar preoccupations and approaches".[41] However, bilateral agreements can become unpopular in the weaker of two countries when there is an imbalance of power between the two co-operating states. Bilateral agreements can also be rather ad hoc, which causes inefficiencies, a lack of co-ordination and overlap, and can be time-consuming, which is especially difficult for smaller states. Moreover, Williams and Savona[42] suspect that bilateral forms of co-operation are more prone to sabotage by transnational criminal organisations: "The Colombian cartels for example, did everything possible to disrupt bilateral co-operation between Colombia and the United States". But bilateral co-operation agreements are also viewed positively, especially because they are tailor-made to respond to specific needs and objectives and because they draw a strong commitment or rather precisely oriented obligation from the two participating states. Bilateral agreements are co-operative in nature, reflecting states' recognition of mutual interests in crime control as well as principles of reciprocity and comity.[43]

Meanwhile, multilateral frameworks are regarded as potential catalysts for the conclusion of smaller bilateral agreements.[44] Examples of multilateral co-operation between the US and some EU Member States are the Police Working Group on Terrorism and the International Police Working Group on Undercover Policing. Although it may be difficult to achieve consensus between a larger group of participating states, a wide involvement of foreign governments may also have its charm: multilateral agreements are relatively cost-effective for smaller states, and are less likely to be a target for criminal groups.[45]

Co-operation is also possible at an organisational level, such as for instance between the future Europol and international organisations or bodies governed by public law. Article 42. 2 of the Convention on the Establishment of Europol concerns relations with third States and third bodies.[46] In the future, Europol may request these third States and

---

[41] Williams P. and Savona E. U. *The United Nations and Transnational Organised Crime*, Special Issue of the Transnational Organised Crime, Vol. 1, No. 1, Autumn 1995, p. 87.

[42] *Ibid* at p. 146.

[43] Nadelmann E. A. *Cops Across Borders. The Internationalisation of US Criminal Law Enforcement*, University Park, Pennsylvania, Pennsylvania State University Press, 1993, p. 472.

[44] *Ibid* at p. 10.

[45] Williams P. and Savona E. U. *The United Nations and Transnational Organised Crime*, Special Issue of the Transnational Organised Crime, Vol. 1, No. 1, Autumn 1995, p. 148.

[46] Convention on the Establishment of Europol, Article 42.2. states: "Insofar as is required for the performance of the tasks described in Article 3, Europol may also establish and maintain relations with third States and third bodies within the meaning of Article 10 (4), points 4, 5, 6 and 7. Having obtained the opinion of the Management Board, the Council, acting unanimously in accordance with

third bodies to forward relevant information. There will also be a direct relationship between Europol and US Federal Law Enforcement Agencies, like the DEA and the FBI:

> It is essential therefore that EDU-EUROPOL establishes and maintains links with US representatives of the appropriate services, in relation to illegal drug trafficking and other forms of drugs criminality. In the post Convention phase a relationship with DEA at both the working and the strategic level has to be created in order to exchange the necessary information.[47]

From the aforementioned examples of criminal justice co-operation between the US and the EU, it emerges that most co-operation is very pragmatic and case-oriented in nature. The War on Drugs has undoubtedly acted as the most important vehicle for the promotion of transnational policing efforts. At the beginning of the eighties the US had a US$ 42 million fund allocated to worldwide drug policing.[48]

> Between 1981 and 1990 the federal government increased its drug budget by nearly 800 per cent. In 1990 it spent US$ 9,483.2 billion on the DEA, border policing, international programmes, research, treatment, drug education, on everything that relates to drug control except prisons.[49]

But the transposition of the War on Drugs to Europe has had several problematic aspects. Anti-drug trafficking efforts usually take place in an environment which is loaded with sovereignty problems: each Member State has its own solution to the drugs problem, even though the Member States have agreed to endeavour to approximate their laws and practices in the field of drug trafficking.[50] Moreover, there are a few senior law enforcement officials in the Member States who have already declared that the War on Drugs will never be won. Work continues however on the joint task forces, such as in the Caribbean.

However, if the EU does not involve the Americans on a formal basis, and if the US does not get the opportunity to be actively engaged in a debate and negotiations, bilateral and multilateral co-operation will intensify considerably.

(Cont.)
the procedure laid down in Title VI of the Treaty on European Union, shall draw up rules governing the relations referred to in the first sentence .. ". The third States and third bodies referred to above are specified only as "third States; international organisations and their subordinate bodies governed by public law; other bodies governed by public law which are based on an agreement between two or more States, and the International Criminal Police Organisation Interpol". Bunyan comments upon this Article that "The Council here empowers itself to draw up and agree the rules governing relations with "third states" and "third bodies" (Bunyan T. *The Europol Convention*, A Statewatch Publication, 1995, p. 10).

47   Project Team Europol, 1993, p. 17.
48   Bagley B. *Colombia and the War on Drugs*, Foreign Affairs, Vol 67, pt. 1, 1988, p. 80.
49   The figure for 1981 was US$ 1,230.7 billion. Source: DEA. From: De Grazia J. *DEA. The War Against Drugs*, London, BBC Books, 1991.
50   "Joint Action of 17 December 1996 adopted by the Council on the basis of Article K.3 of the Treaty on European Union concerning the approximation of the laws and practices of the Member States of the European Union to combat drug addiction and to prevent and combat illegal drug trafficking" (96/750/ JHA), published in Official Journal of the European Communities, No L 342/6, 31 December 1996.

This intensification could precisely result in a situation the EU wanted to counter when it created a European Police Office, namely lack of co-ordination and multiplication of efforts. But except from the loss of rationalisation, there will be an encouragement of old and forlorn practices, such as the uncontrolled and unsupervised staging of law enforcement operations by the DEA on the territory of EU Member States. Such an undesirable scenario stands in sharp contrast with measures currently undertaken by individual Member States to increase the legality and improve the co-ordination of (international) covert policing activities.

4. TRANSNATIONAL ORGANISED CRIME: COMMON THREAT OR GLOBAL CHALLENGE?

Although there is a common discourse between the EU and the US in the way post-Cold War security dangers are appreciated, there are also some considerable differences. Bigo[51] observes that in the US, the discourse concerning security dangers very quickly focused on the fight against drugs[52], the possible militarisation of the frontier with Mexico, and the future role of the US in the world. The mafia, more or less directed by the Colombian drug cartels, assumed global proportions and replaced the USSR as principal enemy: (imported) crime replaced the Soviet soldier. Even though this discourse also prevailed in Europe, the difference was that in Europe it was amplified by the topic of immigration from Central and East Europe and the countries of the Maghreb, as well as by the fear that the abolition of internal border controls would lead to an influx of asylum seekers. In other words, the motor that has propelled the security discourse in Europe has thrived much more strongly on the security deficit resulting from the abolition of border controls.

Whether or not organised crime should indeed be regarded as a dominant security danger depends on how one defines the problem. Some perceive organised crime as a global phenomenon with an in-built capacity to destabilise security orders. This perception becomes apparent in the context of the drugs problem which is seen as a major threat to whole macro-regions in the world, such as Latin America and South-East Asia. Others regard illegal activities as a natural component of a global socio-economic infrastructure. The emerging global village finds a large part of its origin in

---

[51] Bigo D. *Polices en réseaux. L'expérience européenne*, Paris, Presses de Sciences Po, 1996, pp. 259–260.

[52] See Enquêtecommissie opsporingsmethoden, *Inzake opsporing*, Chapter 11, "Rechtsvergelijkend perspectief opsporingsmethoden", p. 505; Goldstock R. *Organised Crime and Anti-Organised Crime Efforts in the United States: an Overview*, in Fijnaut C. and Jacobs J. *Organised Crime and its Containment. A Transatlantic Initiative*, Deventer/Boston, Kluwer Law and Taxation Publishers, 1991, p. 7.

network structures: migration, combined with improved means of transport and communication, make it possible to link up home and host economies.[53] On the other hand, the analysis and assessment of organised crime phenomena can also be "de-globalised", in the sense that these activities are often strongly associated with certain local opportunities[54] that present themselves. An incentive for organised criminal activities may be provided by distinctive differences in economic wealth and criminal justice sanctions. Local market demands can be an added rationale for setting up an illicit business or trade relationship. It is clear that for organised crime to thrive, the local infrastructure, such as the presence of a port, tourism or commerce, can be a crucial element. Naturally the concepts of a global village and local opportunities can be fused, like Williams and Savona have done when they talk of a "global-local-nexus".[55]

The similarities between the internal security threats to the US and the EU should be acknowledged, but not exaggerated. An analysis of transnational organised crime leads to the almost disappointing conclusion that there is "a similarity in its variety", as Professor Williams said at the conference. There are indeed strongly diverging criminal patterns. An example of this divergence is the phenomenon of racketeering: in Europe there is hardly any evidence that trade unions and the building industry are a target for racketeering activities such as in New York.[56] Furthermore, geographical proximity determines to a large extent whether or not a criminal organisation is perceived as an internal security danger:

> The Chinese Triads have expanded in Europe, and the Colombian cartels have put out their tentacles in Latin and Central America, while the Russian criminal organisations have extended their activities to other countries of the Commonwealth of Independent States and to the countries of Eastern Europe. The process of internationalisation that allows these well-established groups to operate in areas of the world far away from their traditional location originally began within the region.[57]

At the level of the region, policies and mechanisms can be developed to prevent the growth of regionally active criminal groups. Especially when

---

[53] For an analysis of drug smuggling activities in Surinamese, Moroccan and Turkish communities that have settled in the Netherlands, see: Bovenkerk F. and Fijnaut C. *Georganiseerde criminaliteit in Nederland: Over allochtone en buitenlandse criminele groepen*, Bijlage VIII, Deel I, Enquêtecommissie opsporingsmethoden, Tweede Kamer, Vergaderjaar 1995–1996, pp. 59–227. For an analysis of Turkish criminal organisations, see Williams P. *Transnational Criminal Organisations and International Security*, Survival, Vol. 36, No. 1, Spring 1994, pp. 96–113, pp. 104–105.

[54] See note 13 supra, pp. 21–26.

[55] Williams P. and Savona E. U. *The United Nations and Transnational Organised Crime*, Special Issue of the Transnational Organised Crime, Vol. 1, No. 1, Autumn 1995, p. 76; Williams P. *Transnational Criminal Organisations: Strategic Alliances*, The Washington Quarterly, Vol. 18, No. 1, Winter 1995, pp. 57–72, at p. 61.

[56] See for instance Marx G. T. *When the Guards Guard Themselves: Undercover Tactics Turned Inward*, in Fijnaut C. and Marx G. T. *Undercover. Police Surveillance in Comparative Perspective*, Deventer, Kluwer Law International, 1995, at p. 222.

[57] Williams P. and Savona E. U. *The United Nations and Transnational Organised Crime*, Special Issue of the Transnational Organised Crime, Vol. 1, No. 1, Autumn 1995, p. 126.

looking at the Caribbean[58] and the Andean countries, there are common regional concerns, such as the money laundering activities in Aruba and the production of precursor materials in Latin America. Interestingly, this is where internal and external security concerns meet: the cross-roads of Justice and Home Affairs and Common Foreign and Security issues allow for an alternative perspective on formal and informal co-operative frameworks. Within this realm, some forms of co-operation in the field of the fight against drugs are to take place between the EU and the Andean Pact states (Colombia, Peru, Bolivia, Venezuela and Ecuador).[59] It should be pointed out, however, that the EU has a less exclusive focus on Latin America as a drugs-producing region than the US. In fact a lot of attention is given to illegal drugs production in and drug trafficking from East Asia and Morocco. EU Member States have, as Bigo[60] observes, a much more inverse look at the drugs problem, and this has therefore functioned as one of the prime motives for the establishment of regionalised forms of international police co-operation (i.e. the creation of the European Police Office).

5. TACKLING TRANSNATIONAL ORGANISED CRIME: JOINT STRATEGIES

Thus far it has been established that traditional (reactive, control-oriented) law enforcement is rather handicapped in its fight against organised crime, which has made covert policing activities a great deal more attractive. At the same time, many authorities acknowledge the darker aspects of undercover policing: it is risky, expensive, not always succesful in getting a case to trial, and generally minimally accountable. Hence, there should be a more serious plea in favour of preventive measures, setting preventive goals and removing opportunities for transnational organised crime groups.[61] This may assist in the immunisation of weak governments or infrastructures that have been prone to exploitation and misuse by criminal organisations. An example of a joint EU-US strategy in the preventive sphere is the promotion of morally sound governance in Central and East European countries, with a view to minimising opportunities for corruption. As Williams says: "weak states provide a flourishing ground for organised crime".

Secondly, the US and the EU could jointly work with drugs-producing

---

58   The Dutch islands, for instance, had become known as tax havens. See Nadelmann E. A. *Cops Across Borders. The Internationalisation of US Criminal Law Enforcement*, University Park, Pennsylvania, Pennsylvania State University Press, 1993, p. 349.

59   *Fortress Europe?*, September 1995, Circular Letter No. 37, p. 2.

60   Bigo D. *Polices en réseaux. L'expérience européenne*, Paris, Presses Sciences des Politiques, 1996, pp. 285–286.

61   Williams P. and Savona E. U. *The United Nations and Transnational Organised Crime*, Special Issue of the Transnational Organised Crime, Vol. 1, No. 1, Autumn 1995, pp. 11, 43.

countries, not necessarily only by means of a repressive approach, but also by diverting local economies (e.g. Bolivia) towards the production of alternative commodities. These efforts can be strengthened by the development of horizontal programmes (on drugs) like the 1995 Madrid Declaration. This underlines simultaneously that a lot of co-operation against drugs is a joint subject of Justice and Home Affairs Co-operation and Common Foreign and Security Policy.

Looking at the global potential of organised crime and its capacity to undermine regional security orders, the US and EU could assume a shared role in security politics and in the world community. In the context of the New Transatlantic Partnership, some progress has been made in:

> ... confronting global challenges of crime and disease and environmental degradation ...
> In our joint fight against crime and drug trafficking, we are nearing the conclusion of a
> chemical precursors agreement which would prevent illicit shipments of chemicals used in
> the manufacture of illegal drugs.[62]

Furthermore, there should be a continuous exchange of law enforcement experiences and joint training activities. This need for training, which is the major instrument for co-operation and learning to understand each other's practices, is also inspired by a cost-benefit balance: co-operation of this kind saves cost and effort. In the past, there has already been quite a considerable experience with the information about innovative investigation techniques, such as the buy and bust technique, which was introduced in Europe via FBI-training. New techniques, such the employment of administrative law methods (e.g. through the verification of licences) in the fight against organised crime. Methods like these have to a certain extent evolved in the EU through the activities of the Anti-Fraud Unit of the European Commission. In addition, there is also a strong argument for a joint evaluation of the effectiveness of law enforcement techniques, such as the effectiveness of computer-matching in the fight against organised crime and undercover infiltration in so-called ethnic organised crime groups.[63] There are numerous lessons to be learnt in law enforcement, and also these could be approached from a joint perspective. For instance, how to avoid interagency competition and conflict; how to build in checks and balances in order to prevent intelligence gathering institutions from reaching beyond their constitutional remit; how to avoid corruptive links between federal and local law enforcement agencies; how to build a solid criminal justice framework for cross-border policing activities; how to guarantee continuous expertise in law enforcement organisations? The US has considerable experience with the judicial and democratic accountability of law enforcement agencies that investigate organised crime: if the EU will ever be ready for the design of a European judicial space and a European Prosecution Service, it may warmly welcome some wise suggestions from across the Atlantic.

---

[62]   Wayne A. *The potential of the New Transatlantic Partnership*, paper presented at the conference *The New Framework of EU-US Relations*, 4, 5 July 1996, Brussels at p. 3.
[63]   Williams P. and Savona E. U. *The United Nations and Transnational Organised Crime*, Special Issue of the Transnational Organised Crime, Vol. 1, No. 1, Autumn 1995, p. 10.

Chapter 10

Asylum: Experiences, Problems and Management Techniques in the European Union

Kay Hailbronner

1. INTRODUCTION

This chapter will outline the European asylum policy, as illustrated by the Commission to the Council of the European Parliament, which focuses on control and prevention of illegal immigration, and by the European Council Plan of Action, which gives priority to the harmonisation of substantive asylum law. Comparison shall be made, and an overview given, to the asylum situation in the United States which is in dire need of additional resources, administrative streamlining and other reforms to prevent the system backlogging, and which, it is submitted, is at present open to fraud and abuse. Considerable attention is given to streamlining the asylum procedure to remedy the system's shortcomings and the filing of unfounded asylum claims. There exists the necessity for an objective general assessment under the concept of the safe country of origin and for its extension and diversification. Concerning the safe third country concept, important questions are raised concerning the criteria to be employed in determining safety and of the burden shifting to countries which may be ill equipped to deal with asylum seekers. The Resolution on Burden Sharing of 25 September 1995 attempts to address these problems. However there is no real decision-making process nor exact determination of criteria: these are left to the individual Member States.

2. EUROPEAN ASYLUM POLICY

Within the Member States of the European Union, a number of measures and proposals on the national, as well as on the European level have been submitted or enacted to render asylum manageable. According to a Communication from the Commission to the Council and the European Parliament of 23 February 1994[1] the Commission attaches primary importance to the control of migration flows to the EU and prevention of illegal immigration. The Commission report mentions the following points:

(1) Improving procedures for the exchange of information on routes and carriers and the taking of appropriate follow-up measures of a preventive nature.
(2) Adoption and implementation of the revised draft Convention on the Crossing of External Borders.
(3) Development of measures designed to identify persons illegally resident in the Community focussing in particular on combatting illegal employment.
(4) Definition of minimum standards for the treatment of those who have been found to be in an irregular situation.
(5) Development of guidelines on repatriation policies concerning particularly vulnerable groups, such as unaccompanied minors.
(6) Approximation of schemes for the voluntary repatriation of illegal immigrants and intensification of co-operation between Member States in order to facilitate repatriation in appropriate cases and extension of this co-operation to relevant third countries.
(7) Conclusion of re-admission agreements with relevant third countries and making the necessary linkage between these agreements and corresponding external agreements of the Community and examination of the consequences of such re-admission agreements for certain relevant countries of origin or transit.[2]

Relating to the question of international protection for convention refugees and "humanitarian refugees" the Commission considers streamlining procedures to be an essential step to manage refugee movements as well as a new protection concept such as temporary protection for persons in need of protection. The following items are identified as part of a European refugee policy:

(1) Implementation of the Plan of Action approved by the European Council in December 1993 in regard to:
   (a) harmonised application of the definition of refugees in accordance with Article 1A of the Geneva Convention;

[1]   COM (94) 23 final.
[2]   COM (94) 42 *seq.*

(b) development of minimum standards for fair and efficient asylum procedures.
(2) The elaboration of a Convention on manifestly unfounded asylum applications and the implementation of the third host country principle.
(3) Harmonisation of policies concerning those who cannot be admitted as refugees, but whom Member States would nevertheless not require to return to their country of origin in view of the general prevailing situation in that country.
(4) Harmonisation of the schemes for temporary protection.
(5) Development of a monitoring system for absorption capacities and creation of a mechanism which would make it possible to support Member States who are willing to assist other Member States faced with mass influx situations; similarly to support projects of Member States or third transit countries faced suddenly with new pressures.[3]

The Commission refers to the European Council Plan of Action approved in December 1993.[4] The Council, representing the governments of the EU's states, has decided to give priority to the following subjects:

In the field of harmonisation of substantive asylum law,
(1) unambiguous conditions for determining that applications for asylum are clearly unjustified;
(2) definition and harmonised application of the principle of first host country;
(3) common assessment of the situation in countries of origin with a view both to admission and expulsion;
(4) harmonised application of the definition of a refugee as given in Article 1A of the Geneva Convention.

In addition, there is general agreement that the aims of asylum and immigration policy are to be included in external relations with third states. Therefore, the Council has decided to establish common principles to be included in bilateral or multilateral agreements on readmission or return. A link of asylum policy of the Union in the area of return and repatriation with external relations is also envisaged in association, and co-operation agreements of the EU with third states.[5]

Comparing the Commission's and the Council's proposals on a European asylum policy, most progress seems to have been achieved in the area of migration control and the restriction of access of asylum-seekers by special procedures for manifestly unfounded or abusive asylum claims. These procedures are also applicable to persons arriving via a safe third country or a safe country of origin. A co-ordinated restrictive policy in the field of

---

[3] COM (94) 42 *seq.*
[4] Doc. 10655/93 of 2 December 1993.
[5] For a discussion of Return Agreements see Reermann *Return Agreements*, in Hailbronner K., Martin D. and Motomura H. *Immigration Admissions*, Berghahn Books (Providence) 1997, pp. 121-145.

border control, visa requirements, and carrier sanctions is considered as necessary to render asylum manageable.

A second major field of action concerns the introduction of asylum policy into external relations (return, re-admission and repatriation) starting with a return agreement of the Schengen states with Poland of January 1993.[6]

Thirdly, a new technique of rendering asylum manageable has been the emphasis on regional and local protection and the extension of the first host country concept beyond the limits of the EU.

On 30 November and 1 December 1992 Immigration Ministers have passed various conclusions and recommendations which are not binding but are recommended for incorporation into national law by a specified date[7]. The most important of these resolutions concerns a procedure on manifestly unfounded applications for asylum.[8] In addition, a conclusion on countries in which there is generally no serious risk of persecution has been passed. Finally, the resolution on a harmonised approach to questions concerning host third countries relates to the safe third country concept. A decision establishing a clearing house sets the framework for an exchange of information and compilation of documentation on all matters relating to asylum.

In 1995, a resolution on minimum guarantees for asylum procedures was passed. Member States have declared that they will take account of these principles in the case of all proposals for changes to their national legislation. In addition, Member States will strive to bring their national legislation into line with these principles by 1 January 1996. In conjunction with the Commission and in consultation with the United Nation High Commissioner for Refugees (UNHCR), they will periodically review the operation of these principles and consider whether any additional measures are necessary. Finally, a Joint Position of 4 March 1996 contains on the basis of Article K.3 of the Treaty on European Union a harmonised definition of the term "refugee" in Article 1 of the Geneva Convention. The Joint Position provides for "guidelines" which shall be notified to the administrative bodies which are requested to take them as a basis without prejudice to Member States' "case law on asylum matters and their relevant constitutional positions". The Joint Position shall not bind the legislative authorities or affect decisions of the judicial authorities of the Member States.[9]

Within the EU the Dublin Convention determining the State responsible for examining applications for asylum lodged in one of the Member States entered into force only on 1 September 1997, after a very long ratification process.[10] A similar system as the Dublin Agreement concerning the

---

6   *Ibid.*
7   For a survey of conventions, resolutions, recommendations, decisions and conclusions until July 1995 see E. Guild *The Developing Migration and Asylum Policies of the European Union*, The Hague/London/Boston, 1996.
8   See Section 4.2 *post, et seq.*
9   See Official Journal of the European Communities No. L 63/2, 13 March 1996.
10   Official Journal of the European Communities No. C 254/1, 19 August 1997; No. L 242/1, 4 September 1997.

determination of the competent asylum state is contained in the Schengen Implementation Agreement between Benelux States, the Federal Republic of Germany and France of 19 June 1990.[11] The Schengen Implementation Agreement became operative on 26 March 1995.[12]

To what extent recently introduced legal and administrative concepts have been "successful" is a matter of very controversial debate. There are as yet no precise assessments on the basis of the resolutions and conclusions of the EU Immigration Ministers, since Member States have only begun to adapt their national law to these principles. In Germany, the amendment of the Basic Law (Constitution) modelled according to the principles recommended by EU Immigration Ministers,[13] has substantially contributed to a calming down of an extremely emotional debate. In 1996, approximately 123,000 asylum-seekers were registered. The reduction in numbers is basically attributed to a streamlining of the procedure, the "safe third country clause" and a relatively strict deportation and return policy.

The new instruments envisaged by national laws and recommendations of EU Immigration Ministers have provoked criticism from refugee advocates circles and scholars. In striking contrast to a broad acceptance by the public, the "fortress Europe" slogan has become the most common criticism. It is argued that Western European asylum policy is basically restrictive, establishing a "cordon sanitaire" preventing entry into Western Europe by safe third country clauses and other barriers like visa requirements and carrier sanctions.[14]

3. A COMPARATIVE OVERVIEW OF THE UNITED STATES

For a Western European observer the present US asylum situation shows some similar features to the Western European situation in 1989. Asylum claims in 1993 rose to 150,000, well above the expected number. The asylum system is frequently characterised as "increasingly fair but decreasingly timely".[15] Without additional resources, administrative streamlining and other reforms the US asylum programme is expected to fall further and

---

[11] Bundesgesetzblatt 1993, II, p. 1010.

[12] Spain and Portugal have joined the Agreement; it is expected that Italy, Greece and Austria, as well as Denmark, Finland and Sweden will also join the system once all technical requirements are met.

[13] For a survey of the German legislation see Hailbronner K. *Asylum Law Reform in the German Constitution*, 9 American University, Journal of International Law and Policy, 1994, p. 159; Zimmermann A. *Asylum Law in the Federal Republic of Germany in the Context of International Law*, 53 Zeitschrift für ausländisches öffentliches Recht und Völkerrecht, 1993, p. 49.

[14] For a critical survey see Hathaway J. C. *Harmonising for whom? The Devolution of Refugee Protection in the Era of European Economic Integration*, 26 Cornell Int L.J., 1993, p. 719; Joly D. *The Porous Dam: European Harmonisation of Asylum in the 90's*, 6 IJRL, 1994, p. 159.

[15] Beyer G. A. *Reforming Affirmative Asylum Processing in the United States: Challenges and Opportunities*, Loyola Law School, 19 February 1994.

further behind. The number of unadjusted cases has continued to grow from 114,000 in April 1991 to 354,000 by January 1994. Overburdened, the system is considered to provide ample opportunities for fraud and abuse. Migrants with little or no legitimate fear of persecution are claiming asylum primarily to gain entry into the US. Very similar to the previous German system, increasing numbers of others are using the asylum system to get into the "work authorised backlog".[16]

There is general agreement that the fundamental reform of the asylum system is overdue. The Justice Department and the INS in 1994[17] announced asylum reforms intended to:

(1) Reduce spurious and abusive claims by "boilerplate" petitions (virtual carbon copy applications inadequate to support a claim) to the claimants for more detail, and by providing for possible fines and criminal prosecution of persons who prepare such applications.
(2) Reform regulations so that asylum-seekers who have passed through a "safe country of transit" could be denied asylum and returned to that safe country if the US had a reciprocal agreement for return.

Among the administrative matters to curb the growing number of asylum applications interdictions at sea in combination with external examination procedures have marked a new stage in the asylum policy. The US has followed a zig-zag path in its treatment of "Haitian boat people". On 16 June 1994, the US announced that henceforth Haitians picked up at sea and seeking asylum would be eligible to present to US asylum officers on board US ships evidence that they face persecution in Haiti. As a result, over 11,627 Haitians were picked up by the US Coast Guard by 6 July: many hoped that they would be granted refugee status and allowed to go to the US. Those turned down, about 70 per cent of those requesting asylum, continue to be returned to Haiti. Clinton changed the policy on 5 July. After that date, Haitians picked up at sea were sent to the US base at Guantanamo Bay, Cuba, to present their case for asylum. If they were deemed in need of safe haven, they were sent to safe haven camps, but not to the US. Most nearby Caribbean nations refused to provide safe haven for Haitians. After the Clinton administration stopped shipboard hearings for refugees in mid-July, the number of Haitians picked up by the Coast Guard dramatically dropped.[18]

With regard to Cuba, in August 1994 a 28-year-old policy was reversed. Henceforth, persons from the island nation heading for the US on rafts and small boats are to be treated as illegal aliens, detained in centres outside the US, and not permitted to enter the US unless they can satisfy the criteria for

[16]   *Ibid.*
[17]   See Legomsky *The New Techniques for Managing High-Volume Systems* in Hailbronner, Martin, Motomura (ed) *Immigration Controls*, Providence, Oxford, 1998, p. 117.
[18]   Migration News, August 1994, Vol. 1, No. 7, p. 1.

refugee or immigrant status individually. After the policy change on August 19, 1994, some 18,000 Cubans were picked up at sea and taken to safe haven at the US naval base in Guantanamo Bay, Cuba. There are already almost 15,000 Haitians at Guantanamo. On August 24, the US announced plans to expand the tent camps at Guantanamo to hold up to 40,000 Cubans there. Panama and Honduras promised to take up to 15,000 Cubans for up to six months. Cubans taken to Guantanamo will not be admitted to the US unless they qualify individually for refugee or immigrant status.[19]

In Congress three proposals for major immigration reforms and various individual bills dealing with illegal immigration have been introduced. The administration announced in July 1994 a legislative package including a special expedited exclusion procedure for bogus asylum applicants arriving at ports of entry. This proposal, however, was apparently dropped, since the number of bogus applications coming through JFK airport has been reduced substantially.

In September 1996 the Congress approved a bill aimed at reducing illegal immigration and reducing access of legal immigrants to welfare. The Immigration Control and Financial Responsibility Act of 1996 provides for stronger border enforcement, bringing the total number of border patrol agents from 5,175 in 1996 to almost 10,000 by the year 2000. Secondly, it introduced a pilot telephone verification programme to enable employers to verify the status of newly hired workers. Thirdly, the bill imposed restrictions on the access of legal immigrants to welfare benefits. Non-US citizens will be barred from Food Stamp assistance and Supplemental Security Income by the welfare law enacted in August 1996. It is however left to states to decide whether to permit legal immigrants to participate in Medicaid for the poor. To make it less likely that immigrants will request welfare assistance after their arrival, US sponsors will have to have higher incomes.[20]

4. STREAMLINING PROCEDURE

4.1 General Remarks

The need for a faster and more efficient asylum procedure is generally acknowledged. The delay in the traditional asylum system led almost inevitably to an abuse of the system. The bigger the backlog, the longer the average asylum procedure, the greater the expectation to make use of the asylum procedure to achieve some kind of residence status which would not be available under normal immigration rules. Once a certain time has passed it becomes increasingly difficult to enforce negative asylum

---

[19]   Migration News, Vol. 1, No. 8 of September 1994 p. 1.
[20]   See Migration News, Vol. 3, No. 10 of October 1996.

decisions. The system has great difficulty in sending anyone home.[21] There are different opinions on the evaluation of recognition rates. Even the most careful commentators, however, would not dispute that a large majority of asylum-seekers do not have valid reasons to apply for asylum.

One of the main reasons for the failure of the system lies in its judicially orientated approach and the disregard of the political and discretionary elements of the decision-making process. In addition, the particularities of the interests involved in an asylum procedure are neglected. Asylum-seekers are frequently interested in a delay of the procedure, particularly if the chance is increased to qualify for a legalisation programme or some other kind of residential status.

Increasing substantially the staff of adjudicators and immigration judges is an essential instrument of reducing the average time of procedure.[22] There may also be a need of sanctions against lawyers or representatives who engage in "frivolous behaviour", although in the German legal system the attempt to draw a line between frivolous and creative would be doomed to failure.

The task to find out whether somebody has a well-founded fear of persecution under different political and social conditions in a remote country cannot be dealt with under the same rules as a right to build a house or operate a business. In the absence of witnesses and documentary proof it is frequently a matter of intelligence and legal advice whether an asylum claim turns out to be successful. The impossibility in many cases to enter into a thorough examination procedure of a purported danger of persecution calls for a stronger role of discretionary and even political elements in the decision-making process. This is not to deny that individual expertise and special training are to play an essential role in the decision-making process. It should be recognised however that a system of extensive administrative and judicial review is not necessarily contributing to more justice. Even if one accepts the assumption that judicial review is contributing to the protection of bona fide refugees, the costs of such a system are too high if it leads to a virtual non-enforcement of immigration law. Therefore, preference should be given to a system of specially trained adjudicators deciding in one single procedure on asylum claims as well as any other temporary or permanent right of residence. Judicial review should be open within a certain time limit and be restricted to legal issues. Suspensive effects of a remedy cannot always be considered as necessary if an asylum claim has been determined as manifestly unfounded or abusive.

A second element of traditional asylum procedure is its focus upon the individual situation of an asylum-seeker. The individual case-by-case determination seems to be a logical consequence of the individual persecution

---

[21]   Martin D. *Reforming Asylum Adjudication: On Navigating the Coast of Bohemia*, 138 U.Pa.L. Rev.1247 at p. 1377.

[22]   In Germany the staff of the Bundesamt has been raised from 2,900 in February 1993 to 4,400 in January 1994.

requirement under the Geneva Convention. In reality, however, the decision-making process is frequently focused upon certain categories of cases and the likelihood of political persecution of a special group of applicants. The question may be raised whether a group-decision process, made publicly known and used as a precedent in individual asylum procedures, may not contribute substantially to distinguish in a shorter procedure between bona fide asylum-seekers and those filing manifestly unfounded asylum claims. Experience shows that in many cases members of certain ethnic groups, for example, the Roma and Sinti in Eastern European states, are submitting similar claims relating to the danger of political persecution; it seems to be unnecessary to examine those claims in thousands of individual cases. A group-decision element may of course work both ways. A positive determination may contribute as a pull factor for everybody belonging to a certain group. Most governments will not be inclined to issue such an invitation to all members of a group. Therefore, governments insisted that only on the basis of an individual examination process can asylum be granted. In spite of these objections, general assessments of the political situation in a given country relating to a certain ethnic or religious group may contribute in preventing unfounded asylum claims. A beginning in this direction has been made with the safe country of origin concept (see Section 4.3 *post*).

A third element of traditional asylum procedure has been its focus upon provisional rights of asylum-seekers amounting to a temporary right of residence based on a filing of an asylum claim, procedural rights and social privileges like a right to work and to claim social benefits. It is clear that a provisional right of residence is necessary to effectively pursue an asylum claim. The question however has to be answered to what extent effective implementation of immigration legislation gains priority over the right of provisional residence during the asylum procedure. Execution of negative asylum decisions is frequently impossible due to a lack of documents and other reasons once a certain period of time has lapsed. It is therefore necessary to draw distinctions between different types of asylum claims and the public and private interests involved. In the type of cases discussed in the following section, when immediate deportation after a administrative procedure by trained adjudicators has taken place, it may well be acceptable to reconcile conflicting interests of immigration control and individual protection needs.

4.2 Special Procedures in Case of Manifestly Unfounded or Abusive Asylum Claims

EU Immigration Ministers passed in November-December 1992 in London a Resolution on manifestly unfounded asylum applications. The Resolution provides that an application for asylum shall be regarded as manifestly unfounded if it clearly raises no substantive issue under the Geneva Convention for one of the following reasons:

(1) There is clearly no substance to the applicant's claim to fear persecution in his/her own country; or
(2) the claim is based on a deliberate deception or is an abuse of an asylum procedure.

Furthermore, an application for asylum may not be subject to determination when it falls under the provision of the resolution on host third countries (see Section 5 *post*). The accelerated procedure does not envisage to include necessarily full examination at every level of the procedure. It also provides for the possibility that Member States may operate admissibility procedures under which applications may be rejected quickly on objective grounds.

Member States will aim to reach initial decisions on applications which fall under the Resolution as soon as possible and at the latest within one month and to complete any appeal or review procedures as soon as possible. Appeal or review procedures may be more simplified than those generally available in the case of other rejected asylum applications. A decision to refuse an asylum application will be taken by a competent authority at the appropriate level fully qualified in asylum or refugee matters. The applicant should be given the opportunity for a personal interview with a qualified official. Every Member State will ensure that the applicant whose application is refused leaves Community territory, unless he/she is given permission to enter or remain in other grounds.

Under the Resolution the claim is considered to be manifestly unfounded particularly for the following reasons:

(1) The grounds of the application are outside the scope of the Geneva Convention.
(2) The application is totally lacking in substance.
(3) The application is manifestly lacking in any credibility; the story is inconsistent, contradictory or fundamentally improbable.

Member States may consider an application as manifestly unfounded for asylum-seekers from a special geographical area where effective protection is readily available for an individual in another part of his/her own country to which it would be reasonable to expect him/her to go. A consultation mechanism is provided for on the application of this paragraph.

As deliberate deception or abuse of asylum procedures the Resolution describes the following cases in which the applicant has without reasonable explanation:

(1) based the application on a false identity or forged or counterfeit documents which he has maintained are genuine when questioned about them, deliberately made false representations about his claim either orally or in writing, after applying for asylum;

(2) in bad faith destroyed, damaged or disposed of any passport, other document or ticket relevant to his claim, either in order to establish a false identity for the purpose of his asylum application or to make the consideration of his application more difficult;

(3) deliberately failed to reveal that he has previously lodged an application in one or more countries, particularly when false identities are used;

(4) having had ample earlier opportunity to submit an asylum application, submitted the application in order to forestall an impending expulsion measure;

(5) flagrantly failed to comply with substantive obligations imposed by national rules relating to asylum procedures;

(6) submitted an application in one of the Member States, having had his application previously rejected in another country following an examination comprising adequate procedural guarantees and in accordance with the Geneva Convention on the Status of Refugees. To this effect, contacts between Member States and third countries would, when necessary, be made through UNHCR.

The factors mentioned are indications of bad faith and justify consideration of a case under accelerated procedures. But according to the Resolution they cannot in themselves outweigh a well-founded fear of persecution under Article 1 of the Geneva Convention and none of them carries any greater weight than any other.

The Resolution does not define the procedural rights in an accelerated procedure. At the Brussels meeting of the European Council in November 1994, a consensus was achieved on the rights of asylum-seekers in the procedure, judicial remedies and the suspensive effect of remedies. Every asylum application is examined by a specialised authority fully competent in asylum and refugee matters and deciding on the basis of objectivity and neutrality. The asylum-seeker must have a chance to present the individual circumstances of his/her case in a personal hearing. He/she may consult with a lawyer and must be informed about his/her rights and remedies. As a rule, he/she has a right of provisional residence until his/her asylum claim has been decided upon.

In principle the possibility to file a remedy within an appropriate time is also recognised. The right of provisional residence during the review procedure however is limited. Restrictions are possible under national law, and under specified circumstances. As a minimum standard the asylum-seeker is to be given the right to ask for a stay of the deportation with a court or an independent review authority. Additional restrictions are envisaged for manifestly unfounded asylum claims and for the examination of claims of asylum-seekers entering from safe third countries. The right of judicial review can be restricted to cases of manifestly unfounded asylum claims if an independent executive authority of higher level confirms the negative decision and its immediate execution.

Generally speaking, the introduction of special procedures for manifestly unfounded or abusive claims can be considered as an effective instrument to prevent the overburdening of the system. The crucial issue is the fairness and accuracy of the procedure and the reasonableness of the criteria used. A common criticism is that some of the criteria are hardly sufficient to allow for a decision on the legitimacy of an asylum claim. The Immigration Ministers' Resolution makes clear that the criteria used are not replacing an examination of the claim of well-founded fear of persecution. Accelerated procedures are not necessarily based on a negative *prima facie* assessment of an asylum claim but on the need to effectively sanction certain types of behaviour like the use of false documents or the failure to co-operate in the asylum procedure. An asylum-seeker may well be forced to use falsified passports. There is however no convincing reason to conceal identity or use falsified documents when questioned by immigration authorities. As a consequence, firm practices will contribute to the elimination of established abuse practices that have for a long time been used to escape rejection or deportation.

One may even go one step further and ask whether the list of criteria should not be extended to other cases where an urgent resolution of the claims considered is necessary. A need for an accelerated procedure arises particularly if the applicant has committed a serious offence, or if he/she is to be considered as a danger to public security. The EU Immigration Ministers' Resolution makes clear that national provisions of Member States for considering such cases under accelerated provisions are not affected although they are not included explicitly in the Resolution.

It may also be considered as an abuse of asylum if an asylum-seeker files an asylum application a long time after he entered the country. Frequently asylum applications are filed as a reaction to expulsion or deportation or to enforce a prolongation of stay. In theory, there is no reason why an asylum-seeker should not be obliged to present within a certain time limit the reasons for an asylum claim. It may however be very difficult in practice to find out when an asylum-seeker has entered the country. In addition, it is frequently argued that time prescriptions are of no use since asylum-seekers must not be returned to a country in which they face persecution. Both arguments are not altogether convincing. It is true that a sanctioning of such requirements seems to be difficult. However, one alternative could be the general use of accelerated procedures if an asylum-seeker does not file an asylum claim within a prescribed time limit.

4.3 The Safe Country of Origin Concept

Within the EU no agreement can yet be reached on a common European decision-making process for the purpose of designating safe countries of origin. The Immigration Ministers' meeting, in December 1992, did not reject the idea as such; the Resolution on manifestly unfounded applications for asylum includes a reference to the concept of countries in which there is in general no serious risk for persecution. It is left to each Member State, however, to decide which countries qualify on the basis of those elements set out in the conclusions. Member States have an interest in reaching common assessment of certain countries in this context, although every Member State will consider the claims of all applicants from such countries, and any specific individual factors presented by the applicant that might outweigh a general presumption.

According to the conclusions of the Immigration Ministers, a safe country of origin is defined as that "which can be clearly shown, in an objective and verifiable way, normally not to generate refugees or where it can be clearly shown, in an objective and verifiable way, that circumstances which might in the past have justified recourse to the 1951 Convention have ceased to exist".[23] This is intended to assist Member States in establishing a harmonised approach to applications from nationals of countries which produce a high proportion of clearly unfounded applications, and to reduce pressure on asylum determination systems. An appropriate framework of information exchange on relevant national decisions is envisioned.

Member States will take into account of the following elements in any assessment of the general risk of persecution in a particular country:

(a) Previous numbers of refugees and recognition rates. It is necessary to look at the recognition rates for asylum applicants from the country in question who have come to Member States in recent years. Obviously, a situation may change and historically low recognition rates need not continue following (for example) a violent coup. But in the absence of any significant change in the country it is reasonable to assume that low recognition rates will continue and that the country tends not to produce refugees.

(b) Observance of human rights. It is necessary to consider the formal obligations undertaken by a country in adhering to international human rights instruments and in its domestic law and how in practice it meets those obligations. The latter is clearly more important and adherence or non-adherence to a particular instrument cannot in itself result in consideration as a country in which there is generally no serious risk of persecution. It should be recognised that a pattern of breaches of human rights may be exclusively linked to a particular group within a country's population or to a particular area of the country. The readiness of the country concerned to allow monitoring by Non-governmental Organisations (NGO) of their human rights observance is also relevant in judging how seriously a country takes its human rights obligations.

(c) Democratic institutions. The existence of one or more specific institutions cannot be a *sine qua non* but consideration should be given to democratic processes, elections, political pluralism and freedom of expression and thought. Particular attention should be paid to the availability and effectiveness of legal avenues of protection and redress.

(d) Stability. Taking into account the above-mentioned elements, an assessment must be made of the prospect for dramatic change in the immediate future. Any view formed must be reviewed over time in the light of events.[24]

---

[23]   Report from Immigration Ministers to the European Council Meeting in Maastricht, Doc. WGI 930, p. 38.
[24]   European Communities, The Council, Doc. 10579/92, IMMIG 2, Annex C to Annex II.

The conclusions of the Immigration Ministers explicitly provide that an assessment by an individual Member State of a country as one in which there is generally no serious risk of persecution should not automatically result in the refusal of all asylum applications from its nationals, or their exclusion from individualised determination procedures. A Member State may choose to use such an assessment in channelling cases into accelerated procedures as described in the Resolution on manifestly unfounded applications.

The safe country of origin concept is criticised as a denial of the right to be judged on an individual case-by-case basis and as an unacceptable restriction of the geographical scope of the Geneva Convention. These objections are unfounded. The concept of countries of origin does not provide for an automatic rejection of asylum claims but only for a refutable presumption of safety and acceleration of individual procedure.

It has been doubted, however, whether the system can be of any practical effect, since the bulk of asylum-seekers come from countries in which a general assessment of safety seems to be difficult to make. However, experience in Germany as well as in other European countries shows that the concept as a whole has functioned efficiently. The number of applicants from countries determined as safe countries of origin has dropped substantially. The concept, however, has met some difficulties concerning the evidence required to refute the presumption of safety.

Administrative courts have frequently requested that authorities thoroughly examine assertions of individual persecution, in spite of the general presumption of safety of a country of origin. A chamber of the German Constitutional Court has upheld this interpretation of the law, holding in preliminary injunction proceedings that the individual right of asylum, maintained in Article 16a(1) of the Basic Law, implies an individual's right to present concrete assertions of individual persecution which an administrative court will have to examine.[25]

To make the concept efficient, it could be extended and diversified. Rather than making a general assessment about the safety of a country of origin, a general assessment could be made relating to the safety of special ethnic or religious groups within a certain country or a particular region within a specified country or region. Alternative possibilities of protection within a country of origin or a specified region or internationally controlled zone could also be included in a more general evaluation of safety.

Any general assessment of safety provokes the question of fairness and individual justice. There is a danger that for political reasons a third state is determined as a safe country of origin. This danger, however, can be reduced substantially by the establishment of an objective assessment procedure and the

---

[25]   See decision of 22 July 1993, Neue Zeitschrift für Verwaltungsrecht, Beilage 1/93 zu Heft 8/93, p. 1; in its decisions of 14 May, 1996, the Constitutional Court has confirmed the constitutionality of the presumption of safety of a country of origin and of the safe third country clause (Decisions of the Constitutional Court Vol. 94, p. 115 *et seq* and p. 49 *et seq*).

participation of advisory committees in the determination progress. In addition, the legitimacy of a decision could be greatly increased by international corporation. Within the EU, common assessment procedures are envisaged but not yet established. The conclusions only refer to the "goal to reach common assessment of certain countries that are of particular interest in this context".

The resolution on manifestly unfounded asylum applications also leaves it to every Member State to decide whether a country is one in which there is in general terms no serious risk of persecution. In deciding, however, whether a country is one in which there is no serious risk of persecution, Member States are obliged to take into account the elements which are set out in the conclusions of EU ministers. Member States will nevertheless consider the individual claims of all applicants from such countries and any specific indications presented by the applicant which might outweigh a general presumption.

4.4 Pre-screening or Summary Exclusion Procedure

In general, the pre-screening procedure in order to find out whether a category of asylum-seekers should be admitted to the asylum procedure has turned out to be of little value in rendering asylum more manageable. The main purpose of such procedure is to dispose quickly of manifestly unfounded or abusive asylum claims. If the concept is to be effective, border or police authorities, generally not sufficiently trained to evaluate asylum claims, would have to decide on the spot on the admission of asylum-seekers to the asylum procedure. In order to correct the danger of erroneous decisions inherent in such a procedure, the possibility of judicial or at least administrative review can not be excluded altogether. This in effect might easily lead to a procedure within the procedure. It makes more sense to decide in a general accelerated procedure on the merits of an asylum claim rather than concentrate upon admission to the asylum procedure.

There may, however, be a need for special procedures at ports of entry to prevent entry and possible disappearance of asylum-seekers. Frequently, asylum-seekers arriving at air or seaports destroy their travel documents in order to prevent rejection or deportation.

The rapidly growing number of asylum-seekers arriving at airports led to the inclusion of a special airport procedure in cases where asylum applicants from safe countries of origin arrive via an international flight. Under Section 18a of the German asylum procedure law of 27 July 1993, the Federal Office for the Recognition of Refugees must carry out the asylum proceedings before the applicant enters the country. The same procedure applies to aliens requesting asylum at the airport who are unable to establish their identity with a valid passport or other documentation.

The authorities accommodate the asylum-seeker at the airport during the proceedings and the asylum-seeker is not allowed to leave the transit area. He or she may apply for a provisional legal protection within three days of a

Federal Office decision rejecting the application. The administrative court must rule on such an appeal within 14 days, and, if it fails to do so within this time-frame, the government must allow the alien to enter the country. This rule also applies when the Federal Office for the Recognition of Refugees has not taken a decision on the asylum application within two days after the applicant lodges his or her application.

Within the EU the Resolution on minimum standards of asylum procedures provides for a special procedure at ports of entry to find out whether an asylum claim is manifestly unfounded. During the procedure the asylum-seeker is not rejected but can be detained. In case of a manifestly unfounded application the asylum-seeker is refused entry. Suspensive effect of remedies may be excluded. In this case, refusal to grant entry must be authorised by the immigration minister or a central authority. The same rules are to apply in case of asylum applications of asylum-seekers entering via a safe third state.

5. THE SAFE THIRD COUNTRY CONCEPT

The EU Immigration Ministers' Resolution on host third countries emphasises the need for a concerted response in dealing with the safe country concept. The Resolution on manifestly unfounded applications for asylum refers to a concept of host third country. Without prejudice to the Dublin Convention, an application for asylum, according to the Resolution, may not be subject to determination by a Member State under the 1951 Convention when it falls within the provisions of the resolution on host third countries. That resolution in turn incorporates the following procedural principles:

(a) The formal identification of a host third country in principle precedes the substantive examination of the application for asylum and its justification.
(b) The principle of the host third country is to be applied to all applicants for asylum, irrespective of whether or not they may be regarded as refugees.
(c) Thus, if there is a host third country, the application for refugee status may not be examined and the asylum applicant may be sent to that country.
(d) If the asylum applicant cannot in practice be sent to a host third country, the provisions of the Dublin Convention will apply.
(e) Member State retains the right, for humanitarian reasons, not to remove the asylum applicant to a host third country.

The Resolution outlines some fundamental requirements determining a host third country:

(a) In those third countries, the life or freedom of the asylum applicant must not be threatened, within the meaning of Article 33 of the Geneva Convention.
(b) The asylum applicant must not be exposed to torture or inhuman or degrading treatment in the third country.
(c) It must either be the case that the asylum applicant has already been granted protection

in the third country or has had an opportunity, at the border or within the territory of the third country, to make contact with that country's authorities in order to seek their protection, before approaching the Member State in which he is applying for asylum, or that there is clear evidence of his admissibility to a third country.

(d) The asylum applicant must be afforded effective protection in the host third country against *refoulement*, within the meaning of the Geneva Convention.

If two or more countries fulfil the above conditions, the Member States may expel the asylum applicant to one of those third countries. Member States will take into account, on the basis in particular of the information available from the UNHCR, known practice in the third countries, especially with regard to the principle of *non-refoulement*.[26] It is not clear whether the Immigration Ministers' Resolutions require a determination in each individual case. It does not anticipate an assessment whether the fundamental requirements of the resolution concerning safety are fulfilled in "each individual case", but an individual assessment may refer either to an individual application or to an individual country assessment. The resolution on manifestly unfounded applications supports the second interpretation, by allowing that applications for asylum "may not be subject to determination by a Member State of refugee status ... when it falls within the provisions of the Resolution on host third countries". In addition, the Resolution on host third countries provides, that "if there is a host third country, the application for refugee status may not be examined, and the asylum applicant may be sent to that country".

The basic rationale of the concept of a safe third country is the idea that an asylum-seeker disposing of alternative ways of finding protection is not in a situation of urgent need of protection. In 1989 the UNHCR Executive Committee passed a resolution on irregular movements of asylum-seekers and refugees.[27] Asylum-seekers in general therefore are not expected to move on once they have found protection in a third country.

Theoretically, there is no convincing argument against an extension of the concept of alternative protection, provided an asylum-seeker is safe from persecution and will not be returned to a persecuting country. As the German Constitutional Court has pointed out, asylum has basically been intended to provide immediate relief from urgent inescapable danger.[28] An asylum-seeker disposing of alternative ways of getting protection either internally, or in a third country, is not in the same situation as an asylum-seeker facing persecution if returned or rejected.

The principle that an asylum-seeker may choose his or her country of asylum application on the basis of economic or social considerations runs counter to any longer term strategy for coping with world-wide refugee movements, so far as it may encourage migration of the best qualified, to the

---

[26]   European Communities, The Council, Doc. 10579/92 IMMIG 2, Annex B to Annex II.
[27]   Res. No. 58 (XL) 1989.
[28]   Decisions of the Bundesverfassungsgericht Vol. 74, p. 49.

detriment of local development. In addition, the changes for a durable solution may be considerably increased if refugees remain in a culturally and socially familiar environment in neighbouring areas, instead of being encouraged to migrate to Western Europe for economic and welfare reasons.

Garvey argues that the "problem becomes more manageable the more it is treated as a problem of relations and obligations amongst states. The essential need is to articulate inter-state obligations as the basic foundation for international refugee protection".[29] Therefore, "the aim should be a solution in the country of first asylum".[30] This in turn, calls for a truly international and geo-politically representative authority: "In exchange, refugees would not have the liberty to seek asylum in the State of their choice, but would rather be afforded protection within a culturally, racially, politically or otherwise affiliated State".[31]

The effective use of limited financial resources also supports an approach to an international distribution of refugees based on both objective and humanitarian criteria, rather than relying primarily on an asylum-seeker's free choice. Objective criteria include chances for durable solutions, the possibility of economic and social integration, efficient use of financial resources, and the prospect of achieving long-term aims of refugee policy. The high costs spent on asylum applicants in Western Europe could be used more efficiently in other countries where asylum-seekers find protection, or could have found protection, and where they may be returned to without danger of persecution or *refoulement*.

There are some weaknesses in the concept. The question arises as to who will decide about safety and what criteria can be used in determining safety. Secondly, the problem of burden-shifting to countries which may be ill equipped to deal with asylum-seekers arises. A safe third country concept must, with some reliability, exclude "refugee in orbit" situations as well as irregular movements of asylum-seekers.

Within the EU, the Dublin Convention has established a regional system of exclusive responsibility. Even if recognition standards vary among the Western European countries adhering to the system, the acceptability of successive application, or "free choice", should be abandoned in favour of the principle that every asylum-seeker in need of protection should have the chance to file an application in the region of Europe that is politically homogeneous and which subscribes to common basic standards of protection.

Although there are yet unresolved issues relating to a harmonisation of recognition standards and equitable burden-sharing, a concept of a safe

---

[29]   Garvey, 26 Harvard International Law Journal, 1985, p. 483.
[30]   Köfner *Migrationen aus der Dritten Welt*, pp. 119, 122.
[31]   Hathaway, Harvard International Law Journal, 31 (1990), pp. 129, 182; see also Coles, *Changing Perspectives of Refugee Law and Policy*, Geneva, 23-24 May 1991, pp. 11, 13; *ibid., Solutions to the Problem of Refugees and the Protection of Refugees*, 1989, p. 314.

country of asylum can already be said to apply between European States, on the basis of a system of international arrangements determining responsibility. The Dublin Convention is itself premised on the assumption that all EU Member States constitute safe countries of asylum, and this assumption should be extended to other European countries fulfilling certain common standards.

Experience with the application of the concept beyond the EU shows that legitimate objections will be overcome if certain conditions are met. The application of the concept outside the EU does not necessarily lead to a "fortress Europe". First, there is still a large number of asylum-seekers making their way to their preferred country of destination. Safe third countries are necessarily linked to Return Agreements. As a rule, these agreements require the proof that the asylum-seeker has entered illegally to that country within a certain time limit. Evidence of the travel route and the identity of an asylum-seeker is frequently not available; international agreements are therefore urgently needed.

As to the unilateral burden shifting, the experience with Poland, the Czech Republic and some other Eastern European states shows that so far very few asylum-seekers have in fact chosen to file asylum applications in those countries. Nevertheless, there may be an increasing burden for those countries which has to be distributed among the European countries. Therefore, corporation agreements are needed providing for administrative and financial help. In a long-term perspective, in addition to economic and administrative corporation, legal harmonisation in asylum matters should be included in the treaty network of the EU with these countries.

6. TEMPORARY PROTECTION AND REGIONAL APPROACHES

Temporary protection and regional approaches can be a useful technique to render asylum manageable provided that its provisional character is strictly maintained and that temporary protection does not develop into a kind of subsidiary asylum.

There is clearly a need to grant temporary protection to persons trying to escape war or civil war or general violence. The solution to the problem cannot be found however in an enlarged refugee definition.

Temporary protection evolved when it became apparent that the Geneva system of 1951 was not fit to cope with large refugee movements. The refugee definition laid down in the Geneva Convention did not fully take into account that beyond the traditional political refugee type there were other people in need of some kind of protection. The Geneva system had developed in practice an established right of political refugees to be granted permanent residence and equal treatment and eventually naturalisation although, deliberately, an individual right of asylum was not included in the Convention.

Entry and reception under rules established to implement the Geneva Convention did generally result in permanent residence. Existing regulations did not provide for a sufficient precaution of refugee protection turning into immigration. The duties arising from the Geneva Convention, in particular relating to the economic and social rights of convention refugees, are supporting this trend. The rights granted under the convention and the legal status of convention refugees are in principle based on the assumption of an unlimited period of protection. This system is hardly suitable to grant protection on a more flexible and temporary basis. There is no need to grant protection for refugees escaping violence and civil war if the circumstances giving cause to flight have changed. Receiving states reacted by either accommodating these persons into the traditional pattern of refugee procedure, or by leaving them in an uncertain status of deportable aliens tolerated on a insecure legal basis. Both solutions proved to be unsatisfactory.

It seems that only very little progress has been achieved on the European level with regard to the admission and residence of persons on a temporary basis. During the Balkan crisis EU Immigration Ministers passed two Resolutions, one of 25 September 1995 concerning burden sharing with regard to the admission and residence of displaced persons on a temporary basis,[32] another one on an alert and emergency procedure for burden sharing with regard to the admission and residence of displaced persons on a temporary basis of 4 March 1996.[33]

The Resolution on burden sharing of 25 September 1995 applies to persons whom Member States are prepared to admit on a temporary basis under appropriate conditions in the event of armed conflict or civil war, including those persons who have already left their region of origin to go to one of the Member States. The Resolution provides that a harmonised action can be taken in case of a mass influx of displaced persons into the territory of the Member States or in case of a strong probability that the Member States may soon have to cope with such an influx. In addition, a burden-sharing mechanism is envisaged taking into account a number of factors as criteria for a distribution, in particular the contribution which each Member State is making to the prevention or the solution of a crisis, in particular by the supply of military resources, as well as all economic, social and political factors which may affect the capacity of a Member State to admit an increased number of displaced persons under satisfactory conditions. The Resolution however does not provide for a specific procedure for burden-sharing in case of a mass influx. Harmonised action

[32]   Official Journal No. C 262 of October 7, 1995, p. 1.
[33]   Official Journal No. L 63 of March 13, 1996, p. 10.

is only envisaged as a possible common action which is not obligatory upon the Member States of the EU.

The Council Decision of 4 March 1996 introduces an alert and emergency procedure in order to implement the principles laid down in the Resolution in cases of emergency. A procedure can be initiated by either the presidency, a Member State or the Commission. The Co-ordinating Committee under Article K.4 TEU may deal in an urgent meeting with all aspects of an emergent situation, including the drawing up of a plan for admission requirement and an indication by each Member State of the number of persons who will be admitted pursuant to the Council Resolution of 25 September 1995. It is up to the Committee to decide whether a situation requiring a concerted action exists. The Committee may adopt a proposal which will be submitted to the Council for approval. An approval of a plan however does not contain binding obligations of the Member States.

The Resolutions were passed by the Council, despite the difficulty in reaching a consensus on burden-sharing within the EU. It is obvious that the system elaborated does not contain an obligatory mechanism for burden-sharing in case of a mass influx of refugees.[34] There is no real decision-making process on burden-sharing. It is still up to the Member States to indicate the number of persons who will be admitted and when they will be admitted. In addition, there is no exact determination of criteria for burden-sharing. The Resolution only enumerates possible factors leaving it to the Member States to decide on the relative importance and priority of these factors. It has therefore rightly been observed that a coherent legal system on the admission of displaced persons is still missing.[35]

---

[34] Compare Kerber K. *Presentation in the Conference on Refugee Rights and Realities*, University of Nottingham, 30 November 1996, Workshop Harmonisation of European Policy on Asylum and Refugees.
[35] *Ibid.*

Chapter 11

Asylum: Experiences, Problems and Management Techniques in the United States[1]

Stephen H. Legomsky

1. INTRODUCTION

Nowhere in the world is asylum a more pressing issue than in Europe and North America. Many of the American problems, and some of the proposed solutions, have counterparts in the Member States of the European Union. On both sides of the Atlantic, asylum issues have generated intense, often emotional debate. That is not surprising, because almost all the options entail sacrifices of important interests. At the substantive level, one must balance the humanitarian relief of suffering and the promotion of international human rights against real or perceived limits on the absorptive capacity of the receiving nation. At the procedural level, the need for fair and accurate adjudication of enormously important individual interests collides with the benefits of speed, efficiency, and conservation of finite adjudicative resources. Principled decision-making and a thoughtful weighing of the competing interests are the ideal prescription. Regrettably, domestic politics and the desires of elected officials to appear "tough on immigration" have tended to drive much of the discussion.

All sides will surely agree that the ideal outcome would be the elimination of the root causes of forced migration. National and international efforts to eradicate poverty, war, and human rights violations, therefore, must

---

[1] For a fuller treatment of the issues discussed here, see Legomsky S. H. *The New Techniques for Managing High-Volume Asylum Claims*, 81 Iowa L. Rev. 671, 1996.

obviously continue. On the assumption that these and other evils will never be obliterated entirely, however, after-the-fact responses will remain critical. The aim should be to develop procedures that adequately accommodate the competing interests of fair, accurate decision-making and efficient use of government resources.

2. CURRENT UNITED STATES PRACTICE

In the United States, a "refugee" must have a "a well-founded fear of persecution on account of race, religion, nationality, membership in a particular social group, or political opinion".[2] By statute, the Attorney General or his or her delegates may grant asylum to any refugee.[3] One who receives asylum may remain in the US at least temporarily, and ordinarily permanently.[4]

In contrast, the slightly weaker remedy of *non-refoulement* is mandated both by US statutory law[5] and by the leading United Nations Refugee Convention.[6] It prohibits the US and other signatory states from returning or deporting a refugee to the country of persecution, but it permits deportation to a safe third country.

To apply for asylum, an alien must be in US territory.[7] The procedures vary. When the asylum-seeker is at a port of entry, seeking admission, the application is decided by an immigration judge in a quasi-formal "removal hearing" subject to the new summary exclusion procedure discussed in section 4 below. Either the alien or the Immigration and Naturalisation Service (INS) may appeal the decision of the immigration judge to an administrative tribunal called the Board of Immigration Appeals (BIA). If the BIA denies the claim, the alien may obtain judicial review.[8]

If the alien has already entered the US (either after a temporary admission or by evading inspection), and the INS has instituted removal proceedings, then the asylum application is decided in those proceedings. Again the adjudicator will be an immigration judge, and again both BIA review and judicial review will generally be possible.[9]

If removal proceedings have not yet commenced, the alien may take the initiative by filing an asylum application with the INS. Approximately 90 per

---

2   8 USC § 1101 (a)(42).
3   8 USC § 1158.
4   8 USC §§ 1158, 1159.
5   8 USC § 1251 (b)(3).
6   UN Convention Relating to the Status of Refugees, 28 July 1951, 189 UNTS 137, art. 1.A.2, as amended by UN Protocol Relating to the Status of Refugees, 31 January 1967, 19 UST 6223, 606 UNTS 267, TIAS No. 6577, art. I.
7   8 USC § 1158.
8   Legomsky S. H. *The New Techniques for Managing High-Volume Asylum Claims*, 81 Iowa L. Rev. 671 1996, pp. 672–673.
9   *Ibid.*

cent of all asylum claims originate in this way. The alien will then be interviewed by a specialised INS "asylum officer". Under new procedures implemented by the INS in January 1995, the asylum officer quickly grants the application if it is clearly approvable; otherwise, the asylum officer refers the application to an immigration judge, who decides it during removal proceedings. At that point, the procedures described in the preceding paragraph become operative.[10]

3. THE PROBLEMS

Prominent among the problems that plague the asylum processes of the major refugee-receiving countries is the lack of political will to safeguard adequately the vital human interests at stake. False negatives, by definition in this context, are potentially life-threatening. Yet, in the major refugee-receiving countries of Western Europe and North America, public sentiment has driven elected officials to emphasise ways of discouraging the filing of asylum claims and reducing the processing times for those cases that are filed. Rather than merely lament that reality, refugee advocates must acknowledge it, evaluate critically the positive and negative effects of the reforms recently adopted or proposed, and search for ways to enhance the speed and efficiency of the process without undue loss of accuracy. The approaches recently considered or implemented in the US will be considered.

4. THE REFORMS

In fiscal year 1995 the INS achieved impressive increases in asylum dispositions, mostly through a combination of more adjudicators and more dispositions per adjudicator. The latter phenomenon is generally attributed to the new INS grant-or-refer procedure discussed earlier, a procedure that has enabled INS asylum officers to skip some of the steps that would be more vital if a negative decision resulted in a final denial. At the same time, the number of filings dropped substantially, possibly because of a simultaneous INS decision to delay, for up to 180 days, permission for the applicant to work. The combination sharply reversed the previous pattern of growing backlogs.[11]

One technique for discouraging asylum claims has been the interdiction of Haitian, and more recently Cuban, vessels on the high seas. Under one variant, all passengers, refugees and non-refugees alike, were intercepted and

[10]   *Ibid* at p. 673.
[11]   *Ibid* at pp. 673–674.

returned to the country of origin (Haiti). Under a less radical variant, those passengers who claimed to be refugees were given at least some opportunity, albeit limited, to convince the INS that their claims were plausible enough to warrant full asylum hearings. Elsewhere this interdiction has been criticised,[12] and because it is not yet a strategy embraced ambitiously in Europe,[13] it will merely be noted here.

The US has not adopted either the safe country of origin or the safe third country limitations now more established in Europe. Those strategies too remain controversial, as recent writings attest.[14]

One suggestion, embodied in legislation now pending before Congress, is to require asylum claimants to file their applications within a prescribed time after arriving in the US. That, it is submitted, would be unwise. As others have pointed out,[15] the persons most likely to suffer from time limits are those applicants whose claims are genuine. They are the people whose filings are most likely to be delayed by trauma, by the need to find housing, food, employment, and other necessities of life, by the difficulty of securing counsel, and by the amount of effort that the preparation of a serious application requires. The frivolous claim, which can be prepared in minutes, would not be deterred. Nor, as argued previously, is the return of a genuine refugee to his or her persecutors an appropriate sanction even for the refugee who is at fault for procrastinating.[16]

Over the years, Congress and the INS have also considered, and to some extent adopted, a range of strategies designed to discourage asylum claims by removing some of the interim benefits that applicants might otherwise attain. Already mentioned is the January 1995 decision by the INS to delay employment authorisation for six months. Detention pending resolution of the claim falls under this same heading and, in the US, is more common in deportation cases than in exclusion cases.[17] There is ample reason to think that some such approaches, especially delaying work authorisation, can be effective,[18] but study is needed to assess the degree of economic hardship that the denial of work authorisation has produced. Detention, too, might well significantly dampen the incentive to file unfounded claims. The disadvantages,

12   *Ibid* at pp. 676–678; see also Legomsky S. H. *The Haitian Interdiction Programme, Human Rights, and the Role of Judicial Protection*, 2 Int L.J. Refugee Law, Special Issue, Oxford University Press, 1990, p. 181.

13   Italy's interdiction of Albanian vessels has been an important exception.

14   See generally Hailbronner K. *The Concept of "Safe Country" and Expeditious Asylum Procedures: A Western European Perspective*, 5 Int L. J., Refugee Law 31, 1993; Legomsky S. H. *The New Techniques for Managing High-Volume Asylum Claims*, 81 Iowa L. Rev. 671 1996, pp. 678–682.

15   For an especially effective criticism, see Schrag P. G. *Don't Gut Political Asylum*, Washington Post, 12 November 1995, at C7; see also Legomsky S. H. *The New Techniques for Managing High-Volume Asylum Claims*, 81 Iowa L. Rev. 671 1996, pp. 684–685.

16   Legomsky S. H. *The New Techniques for Managing High-Volume Asylum Claims*, 81 Iowa L. Rev. 671 1996, p. 685. Congress has now established a one-year time limit: 8 U.S.C. § 1158 (a)(2)(b).

17   See *ibid* at pp. 685–686.

18   Asylum applications dropped dramatically once that change was implemented. See *One Year Later: Asylum Claims Drop by 57%*, 73 Interpreter Releases 45, 45–47, 1996.

however, include the enormous expense, the possible deterrence of genuine claims, and the hardship that prolonged confinement can cause for those genuine refugees who apply despite the prospect of detention. Additionally, since INS detention facilities are rarely located in urban settings, detention effectively shuts off access to counsel for most of the detainees.[19]

The INS in 1994 considered imposing a fee for filing an asylum application. The idea was that the fees collected would raise revenue that could then be used to hire additional adjudicators. The premise was that users of government services should pay for these services rather than shift the cost to the public. In the face of strong opposition, the INS eventually withdrew the proposal. Part of the resistance was philosophical. The very idea of requiring payment for protection from persecution was, to many, objectionable. Philosophy aside, almost all agreed that any fee system would have to allow waivers for those unable to pay, and the prospect of a whole new bureaucracy to adjudicate requests for fee waivers was daunting.[20]

Yet another set of strategies is to impose sanctions when claims are found to be legally frivolous. Under one variant, the sanctions are incurred by the lawyer or other representative who prepared the application. Those types of sanctions are now specifically authorised,[21] though it is not clear how often that authority is exercised. In addition, Congress has now permanently disqualified from all immigration benefits, any alien found to have filed a frivolous application for asylum. The harshness of such an approach becomes apparent when one considers that the most likely occasion for a rejected applicant to seek US immigration benefits later in life is marriage or some other close family relationship. Moreover, especially when an application is prepared by counsel, it is far from obvious that the claimant, who might well be unfamiliar with the US legal system or even the English language, is at fault at all.[22]

Last-in-first-out is another means by which the INS attempts to discourage unfounded applications. With a large backlog, deciding cases in the order in which they are filed would mean that each applicant could anticipate a long delay before his or her case is finally decided. By deciding the most recently filed cases first, the INS hopes to dampen the incentive to apply for asylum just to achieve delay. The downside, of course, is that the more senior claimants are left in limbo, possibly for many years.[23]

Expedited removal, enacted as part of a larger anti-terrorism bill in 1996, is another strategy aimed both at discouraging asylum claims in the first place and shortening the processing times for some of the claims that are filed

---

[19] See Legomsky S. H. *The New Techniques for Managing High-Volume Asylum Claims*, 81 Iowa L. Rev. 671 1996, pp. 685–686.

[20] *Ibid* at pp. 688–689.

[21] 8 CFR § 292.3 (a)(15).

[22] See generally Legomsky S. H. *The New Techniques for Managing High-Volume Asylum Claims*, 81 Iowa L. Rev. 671 1996, pp. 689–690. See also 8 U.S.C. § 1158 (d)(6).

[23] *Ibid* at p. 692.

nonetheless. Those aliens who appear at ports of entry without documents, or with documents that the immigration inspector suspects are fraudulent, are summarily excluded. If they apply for asylum, the INS will assign a specialised asylum officer to interview them promptly and to remove quickly those found not to have presented "credible" claims, defined to require, a "significant possibility" of eligibility for asylum. This strategy affects only that small proportion of asylum claimants who apply at ports of entry; the gain, therefore, is minor. For reasons discussed elsewhere,[24] however, the procedure creates risks of erroneous denials for those claimants who do apply at ports of entry.

Searching for ways to shorten the procedure by eliminating those ingredients whose benefits are only marginal might well be productive. The January 1995 INS reforms took this approach. Eliminated were "notices of intent to deny," which had given applicants a chance to respond to tentative concerns of asylum officers, and written statements of the reasons for denial. If the asylum officers' decisions were final, the deletion of those steps would be more serious, but in a world where the only consequence of non-approval is referral to another adjudicator, the losses might indeed be marginal.[25] Whether the grant-or-refer procedure will prove useful is another question; on that, the verdict is still out. For the most part, the large stack of referrals still awaits adjudication by immigration judges and, for those cases that are appealed, the BIA.

When all is said and done, the most effective reform would be to attack the backlog with a dramatic infusion of new adjudicative resources, both to enable genuine refugees to proceed with their lives and to reduce the delay that the INS believes spurs unfounded claims. To be fair, Congress has recently appropriated the funds to implement precisely such an expansion. Whether the expansion will be sizeable enough remains to be seen.[26]

5. CONCLUSION

In the US, as is true around the world, the debate on asylum reform has been polarised. Preferences for particular responses inevitably reflect people's views as to the severity of the various problems. For those whose principal concern is with the humanitarian relief of suffering and the strenuous promotion of international human rights, the first priority in the present context is to assure the fairness and accuracy of the process, even if this

---

[24]   *Ibid* at pp. 693–695. See also 8 U.S.C. § 1225 (b)(1)(B)(v).
[25]   *Ibid* at p. 698.
[26]   *Ibid* at pp. 701–703; see also Legomsky S. H. *Reforming the Asylum Process: An Ambitious Proposal for Adequate Staffing, in Immigration Law: United States and International Perspectives on Asylum and Refugee Status*, American University Journal, Int. Law & Policy and Loyola L.A. Int. & Comp. Law J., 1994.

requires significant government expense, and even if the resulting process permits some number of undeserving applicants to succeed. For those whose principal concerns are the fiscal expense and the abuse of the system, the first priority is likely to be the deterrence of unfounded claims and the speedy processing of all claims. It is all a matter of perceptions, values, and goals.

PART IV

CONCLUSIONS

Chapter 12

EU-US Relations and the "NTA Approach": Challenges, Chances and Conditions for Success

Jörg Monar

1. INTRODUCTION

If two political actors use forcefully positive terminology in their relations this indicates more often than not growing problems and uneasiness rather than a healthy state of their relationship. The terminology of the texts adopted by the European Union and the United States in December 1995, with its emphasis on a "new agenda" and a comprehensive "action programme", is so forcefully activist that it creates suspicions about this apparent certificate of health of EU-US relations. These are increased by the fact that this is already the second time in the 1990's that leaders on both sides of the Atlantic felt it necessary to give bilateral relations a dynamising injection of solemnly affirmed common aims and principles. Although more limited in scope and much more vague in its content, the Transatlantic Declaration of 1990 was clearly similar to the "New Transatlantic Agenda" (NTA) of 1995[1] in its search for political reassurance and firm common ground. In spite of the positive rhetoric surrounding its adoption the NTA is the result of continuing concerns about a possible drifting apart of the EU and the US, concerns which have been growing rather than receding during the 1990's.

This background of nagging doubts about a possible erosion of the transatlantic partnership raises two questions. Firstly, to what extent the

---

[1]   See the Appendix *post* where the NTA and the Joint Action Plan are set out in full.

governments on both sides have actually reason to be concerned about the risks of erosion of the EU-US relationship on the threshold to the next century. Secondly, the question arises as to whether and under which conditions the NTA can provide an effective response to these challenges, rather than being only another declaratory attempt at bringing new life into the transatlantic partnership.

2. THE RISKS OF EROSION

The recurrent debate about the state and the future of transatlantic relations might at times appear as a form of political hypochondria to observers from third countries. After all there is no manifest crisis in EU-US relations and the intensity and scope of transatlantic contacts and co-operation still far exceeds that of any other bilateral relation of the US and the EU. Yet there are a number of risks of erosion which are clearly not imaginary and must be regarded as major challenges to the transatlantic partnership.

One of these is linked to that central pillar of the post-war political order that was (and still is) the transatlantic security partnership. For four decades it dominated transatlantic relations to such an extent that the change and the relative decline of the security rationale after the end of the Cold War seemed rather suddenly to put into question the entire relationship between the EU and the US. This perception did, of course, not correspond to reality. The transatlantic partnership with its plethora of historical and cultural links, shared values, and common economic and political interests had always been more than the security relationship within the NATO framework. Yet perceptions are a powerful and often slowly changing reality in politics, and as the end of the century approaches transatlantic relations are still overshadowed by an obsession with the only relative decline of the importance of the security partnership. This often tends to artificially narrow the horizon of the transatlantic political debate and to detract from the efforts put into other areas of co-operation. The security partnership, though still important, will clearly never again be the same as before 1989.[2] Those who continue to regard it as the central rationale of EU-US relations and see its changing nature as a sign of crisis risk to absorb transatlantic relations in an area which instead of any prospect for maintaining or restoring the "old" pre-1989 partnership offers huge scope for growing and potentially very damaging frustration and disappointments.

Of even greater importance for the future of EU-US relations are the changes in geopolitical orientation which are becoming increasingly apparent on both sides of the Atlantic. Since the 1970's there were recurrent fears in Europe that the US might increasingly turn its attention away from Europe

---

[2]   See Chapter 4 *ante.*

to Asia and the Pacific and Central and South America as apparently very promising zones of economic interest and political influence. Little happened during the 1970's and 1980's to fully justify these fears. Yet during the last years a number of major developments such as the signing of the North American Free Trade Area (NAFTA) and Asia-Pacific Economic Co-operation (APEC) agreements, the Miami Free Trade Area of the Americas (FTAA) summit and the drastic reduction of North American troop strengths in Europe provided hard evidence for a process of geopolitical reorientation in the US. There are also a number of internal indicators for a change of perspective such as the decreasing European presence in American universities.[3] All this has not led to a dramatic reversal of US foreign policy priorities and is unlikely to do so in the foreseeable future. But the process of reorientation is likely to continue and will have an impact on transatlantic relations because it is based on powerful political and economic realities such as the relative decline of the security problems in Europe after the of the Cold War and the growing importance of the Asia-Pacific region and of the Americas for the US economy.

European analysts have not failed to point to the risks of a growing geopolitical reorientation of the US. Yet they are often less clear about the fact that the EU is also undergoing a process of reorientation in its external relations. Since 1989 the European Commission and the Member States have made an unprecedented effort to intensify their political and economic relations with nearly all countries in their wider geographical neighbourhood. The prospect of accession opened to several Central and Eastern European Countries, the European Agreements which have been concluded with most of them, the PHARE programme (Poland and Hungary Action for Restructuring of the Economy), the Euro-Mediterranean partnership launched at Barcelona in November 1995 and the entry into force of the customs union with Turkey at the beginning of 1996 englobe areas of proximity of at least twice the geographical size of the present EU. The declared aim of this comprehensive effort is the political stabilisation of the wider Europe and the Mediterranean. Yet it obviously serves major political and economic interests of the EU and reflects new priorities which are certainly no less important on the EU's external agenda than those which led the US Government to sign the NAFTA and APEC agreements.[4] Although this process of consolidating and expanding regional zones of political and economic interests is unlikely to lead to any direct conflicts of interests between the EU and the US, it can contribute to different priorities and approaches of both sides when it comes to addressing international problems within these wider "zones of interest". That this can cause some degree of

---

[3]   See Nelson M. *Bridging the Atlantic. Domestic Politics and Euro-American Relations*, Centre for European Policy Reform, London, 1997, pp. 12–13.

[4]   On the economic aspects of this reorientation see Krenzler H. G. *A New Transatlantic Agenda*, European Foreign Affairs Review 1, 1996, pp. 13–14.

transatlantic friction is shown by the examples of Cuba, where the US clearly regard the EU's position as less than helpful, and of the Middle East, where the EU seems often enough concerned about the repercussions of US support for Israel on the EU's Mediterranean policy.

Whatever form geopolitical reorientation might take in regional and global terms, it does not mean that the EU and the US will necessarily drift apart. Yet it means that the importance traditionally given to transatlantic relations on the external agenda of both sides will face greater competition by other major foreign policy and economic interests. A re-balancing of geopolitical interests and priorities will inevitably take place both in the EU and the US. It will be reinforced by other long-term factors such as the weakening effect large scale immigration from other parts of the world into the US will have on cultural links with Europe. In this situation the priority attached to EU-US relations cannot any longer be taken for granted but needs to be underpinned by a strong new rationale of co-operation. This can be provided neither by the old concept of the security partnership nor by the much praised commonality of values. Much of the common set of "Western" values which during the Cold War formed a sort of close ideological bond between the two sides of the Atlantic has by now lost the character of a political platform it formerly possessed when threatened by the Soviet empire. If the EU and the US fail to find substantial common ground beyond these and other traditional icons of their relations, then the ongoing geopolitical reorientation may well lead to a substantial downgrading of the priority given so far to the transatlantic partnership.

Another element of concern should be the continuing strain of trade frictions. This is not a new problem, and so far trade disputes have never led to a serious deterioration in transatlantic relations. Yet it has to be said that neither the Transatlantic Declaration of 1990 nor the compromises achieved in the Uruguay Round nor the NTA have so far led to a significant reduction of trade related conflicts. 1996 and 1997 even saw a series of particularly bitter disputes such as those over the exterritorial effects of the 1996 Helms-Burton and d'Amato Acts and the proposed merger of Boeing and McDonnell while both sides still continued to struggle over a number of long dragging points of contention like the EU market regime for bananas and the import of American hormone treated meat. Even after the recent reforms of EU and US agricultural policies (MacSharry and FAIR) there is still considerable potential for the re-emergence of major conflicts in this area, especially if there is a significant decline of agricultural commodity prices.[5] The different attitudes on both sides of the Atlantic as regards the acceptance of genetically modified food is likely to create a whole range of new points of conflict in transatlantic trade relations.

It is quite possible that in the future the fall-out of major trade friction

---

[5]   See Chapter 7 *ante*.

might be more harmful to political relations between both sides than in the past. There are clear indications that American citizens in the 1990's attach as much priority as ever to their economic situation, and the pressure on the US administration to use trade policy instruments to further the interests of the US economy has been mounting.[6] With most of the economies of the EU Member States going through a painful process of adaption to the pressures of globalisation the European side is also more than ever on its guard as regards its external trade interests. Since 1995 the EU has not only adopted a wide set of new strategic guidelines on access to foreign markets and other key issues, it has also substantially improved its trade policy instruments by refining the criteria for their use and simplifying procedures. While this cannot be taken as a sign for an "arms race" in trade instruments it is certainly an indication of a toughening stance of the EU in external economic relations.

Transatlantic differences over trade could be exasperated by different approaches to economic policy in general. The recent electoral victories of parties of the left in Italy, France and the United Kingdom, the ineffectual efforts of the German Government to reform the German tax and welfare system during 1996/97 and the growing public criticism of the Economic and Monetary Union (EMU) motivated austerity measures introduced in countries like Belgium, France and Italy can be taken as indications that most European citizens are not prepared to follow the American model of deregulation, labour market flexibility, low taxation and strict limitation of social welfare. Whatever consequences this may have for economic developments in Europe and the EMU project, it will also have an impact on transatlantic trade relations. Positions adopted by the US administration on issues affecting European economic interests, the controversy over the Boeing-McDonnell merger can be taken as an example, can easily appear as attempts to impose the rules of the American economic model on a Europe which is struggling to preserve as far as possible the social market economy system which became predominant from the 1960's. This could lead to much sharper defensive reactions than in the past. New tensions could also arise from the EMU: should the Euro be able to establish itself as a successful international reserve currency, the US could find it much more difficult to finance their balance of payments deficits through Dollar exports. All this means that there is a potential for increasingly hard trade conflicts, and with some of the "old" transatlantic ties being in a process of transition or even of losing their binding force these could for the first time become really divisive at the political level.

A final risk of erosion for the transatlantic relationship lies in the structural weaknesses of the EU as a partner of the US in international relations. In the area of external economic relations the EU appears normally

---

[6] See on this point Heuser B. *Transatlantic Relations, Sharing ideals and costs*, Pinter, London, 1996, pp. 79–81.

as a cohesive and effective negotiating partner because of the communitarised powers and procedures under the Common Commercial Policy. Yet even in this area particular national interests of Member States can seriously disturb, if not derail, the negotiation process. The French threats in the final phase of the Uruguay Round to block the envisaged compromise on agriculture is just one example of many. In addition, the need for the Commission to seek approval by the Member States in the framework of the relevant Council bodies for any change to its original negotiating mandate often leads to delays in negotiations on trade matters. If this is at times already exasperating for the US administration the situation is clearly much worse as regards foreign and security policy. In the framework of the EU's "Common Foreign and Security Policy" (CFSP) the predominance of the unanimity rule, the absence of supranational powers, cumbersome decision-making procedures, the lack of effective instruments and the rotating Presidency all reduce the EU's effectiveness as an actor on the international stage. With decisions normally being taken only on the basis of the least common denominator, an endemic exposure to the conflicting short-term interests of Member States, and prone to be absorbed by consultation and co-operation procedures rather than by concrete results, the CFSP is far from providing a real counterpart to the unitary actor that is the US. The only very limited reforms of CFSP introduced by the new EU Treaty of Amsterdam of June 1997 are unlikely to bring dramatic changes in this respect, although some elements, such as the new treaty making possibilities provided for under the CFSP and justice and home affairs "pillars" of the EU, could ease the process of transatlantic co-operation.[7]

There are two risks for EU-US relations which result from the continuing structural weaknesses of the EU. One is that the EU will continue to simply fail to deliver substantial and consistent action within reasonable time when the US most expects it. This has happened on more than one occasion during the crisis in former Yugoslavia, although it must be said that the positions adopted by the US were also not always very helpful from the EU's point of view. There are also other fields outside of classic matters of foreign policy, such as justice and home affairs, where doubts can be expressed about the EU's actual structural capacity to be an effective partner of the US as regards potential common action.[8] While this "only" reduces the transatlantic partnership's capacity for joint policy formulation and action, American frustration over the EU's continuing disabilities, the second risk, could have even more serious consequences. It has always been and will always be a temptation for the US administration to draw the greatest possible advantage for US policy from the internal divisions and the weaknesses of the EU and to try to impose its own priorities and political guidelines rather than to seek

---

[7]   See Monar J. *The European Union's foreign affairs system after the Treaty of Amsterdam: A "strengthened capacity for external action?"*, European Foreign Affairs Review 4, 1997, pp. 413–436.
[8]   See Chapter 8 *ante*.

a real compromise with a disunited and often apparently incapacitated partner. The US have certainly good chances of getting their way on these occasions, but the inevitable consequence is considerable ill-feeling amongst at least some of the EU Member States about this sort of "leadership". The doubts expressed by the US Government about the EU's appointment of a "Special Envoy" to the Middle East Peace Process in October 1996[9] and the way in which the US concept of NATO enlargement came to prevail at the Madrid summit of July 1997 are cases in point. Although US frustration over the Europeans' slowness and disunity is understandable, there can also be little doubt that any increasing signs of American high-handedness and exploitation of inner-EU divisions on issues of primary relevance to Europe could do lasting damage to transatlantic relations.

3. THE RESPONSE OF THE NTA: AN EXTENDED AND EQUAL PARTNERSHIP BASED ON COMMON ACTION

Taken together the negative factors mentioned above clearly constitute a powerful reason for the governments on both sides of the Atlantic to search for new common ground and a revised rationale for the transatlantic partnership. The NTA is certainly a response to these concerns, but, and this is the second question, can it be regarded as an effective one? At the time of writing it is not yet possible to answer this question by looking only at the concrete results achieved so far. Too many initiatives are still in a rather early stage of implementation. Yet there are enough elements in the NTA's general approach and the steps taken so far in its implementation to suggest that the NTA indeed offers a promising blueprint for the future development of EU-US relations. Four of these are of particular importance for the future of the transatlantic partnership and offer real chances for its successful transformation and development.

The first element is a new rationale of transatlantic co-operation. Instead of mainly affirming general principles and strengthening procedures, as the Transatlantic Declaration of 1990 did, the NTA and the Joint EU-US Action Plan linked to it combine the definition of common approaches with concrete aims for common action. The concrete commitments entered in respect to assistance co-ordination with regard to Central and Eastern Europe, the New Independent States (NIS) and the Middle East, the "Transatlantic Market-place" project, the "Transatlantic Business Dialogue" (TABD) and the extensive provisions on co-operation in the fight against organised crime, terrorism and drug trafficking, these and most of the other elements of the

---

[9]   See Chapter 4 *ante*.

NTA form parts of a new partnership concept based on common action rather than the affirmation of general principles and traditional partnership. As already pointed out, EU-US relations must find a new rationale going beyond pre-1989 concepts such the centrality of the security partnership and the binding force of the commonality of values. The NTA, although it does not formulate it as such, provides for a new rationale: common action in a wide range of policy areas with more or less clearly defined concrete aims which are based on a new assessment of common global interests. This emphasis on common action is reinforced by the half-yearly updating or new definition of priorities for the partnership by the Transatlantic Summits on the basis of recommendations submitted by the joint Senior Level Group (SLG). Since the adoption of the NTA there have already been a number of successful common actions by both sides on concrete issues, which demonstrates the potential that the transatlantic partnership has in this respect. One noteworthy example is EU-US co-operation in the fight against drugs: both sides did not only step up joint counternarcotics actions in the Caribbean, where the EU is participating in a regional marine interdiction programme, but they were also able, after difficult negotiations, to conclude on 28 May 1997 the Agreement on Chemical Precursors which can be an effective instrument in curbing the diversion of chemicals used in the manufacture of illicit drugs.

The second positive element is the extension of the scope of transatlantic co-operation. The NTA extends the areas identified for common action of the EU and the US well beyond traditional co-operation on foreign and security policy and economic issues.[10] This applies, in particular, to the areas of justice and home affairs where EU-US co-operation had been very limited before the NTA.[11] Yet there are also a number of other fields in which the NTA establishes structured co-operation for the first time. One example is the dialogue on macroeconomic issues provided for by the NTA, an area which had still been completely left out by the Transatlantic Declaration of 1990. The NTA has also introduced new elements in well established bilateral areas of co-operation. The reduction and elimination of barriers hindering the flow of goods, services and capital between the EU and the US has been a major issue in transatlantic relations for many years. With the "Transatlantic Marketplace" project the NTA has effectively widened the scope of bilateral co-operation on this issue. Although the original deadline of end of January 1997 was missed, the conclusion in June 1997 of the Mutual Recognition Agreement on product testing, inspections and other procedures proved that both are willing and able to make progress towards this ambitious project even in areas of particular complexity. The innovative elements in existing areas of co-operation also extend to the multilateral sphere: the commitments entered in respect to co-operation within the World Trade Organisation

---

10   See Chapters 1, 2 *ante*.
11   See Chapters 8, 9 *ante*.

(WTO), for instance, go further than in previous texts. Although these have not prevented the recent conflicts over trade issues mentioned earlier, they have contributed to the successful conclusion of the Information Technology Agreement and the Basic Telecommunication Services Agreement during the first months of 1997 and have helped to make substantial progress on the Financial Services Agreement during the second half of 1997. EU-US co-operation also proved to be instrumental in ensuring the success of the Organisation for Economic Co-operation and Development (OECD) negotiations during 1997 on a comprehensive anti-bribery convention. The extension of the scope of co-operation can put transatlantic relations on a more solid basis because it reduces their vulnerability to friction over individual issues. This is particularly true for the area of trade relations where there is a continuing risk that even a conflict over a single category of products could turn into a wider trade war with serious political consequences.

The third positive element of the NTA is that it is based on the concept of a full and equal global partnership of the EU and the US. As pointed out earlier, the transatlantic partnership could be severely affected by US attempts to impose American aims and priorities on foreign and security policy issues either as part of a general approach or in reaction to the often exasperating structural weaknesses on the EU side. The NTA avoids this danger by basing the goals for common action on full equality between both sides both as regards the balance of interests and the commitments. There are certainly points in the NTA which reflect more American than European interests, such as the commitment to support the Korean Peninsula Energy Development Organisation (KEDO). Conversely there are others, such as co-operation on relations with Turkey and on the Cyprus problem, which are of greater relevance to the EU than the US. It is true that in practice transatlantic co-operation still sometimes falls short of the principle of equality. Recent cases in point are American "leadership" in the decision-making process on NATO enlargement and EU dissatisfaction with US financial participation in the joint reconstruction effort in former Yugoslavia. Yet the NTA itself clearly makes a convincing model for an equal EU-US partnership in all areas of co-operation and provides a blueprint for a sound balance of global interests and commitments.

The fourth and final positive element contained in the NTA is the emphasis placed on the non-governmental side of EU-US relations. In order to avoid the above-mentioned risks of geopolitical reorientation intense co-operation at the level of governments alone will not be sufficient. Long-term support by public opinion and major socio-economic actors also needs to be secured. The establishment of the TABD is a significant move in this respect. Business co-operation, it is true, had got well underway before the NTA as the conference of business leaders in Seville in November 1995 had shown. Yet the NTA and the Joint Action Plan have considerably strengthened the influences of business networks in transatlantic relations, and recommendations of the TABD have played a key role in bringing about the final compromise on the Mutual Recognition Agreement of June 1997.[12] The establishment of the "Transatlantic Social Dialogue" (TASD) by European and American trade union movements in May 1997[13] illustrates how successful interaction between one major group of non-governmental actors on both sides can have "spill-over" effects on other groups. Yet the NTA also emphasises the need of building bridges between the people on both sides of the Atlantic. The Transatlantic Conference of 5–6 May 1997 has identified a number of successful initiatives which have already been undertaken in the areas of electronic exchange, civil society, education, culture, youth and economic co-operation, pointing to the importance of close co-operation of public and private players.[14] A whole range of new proposals for strengthening "people-to-people" links been generated, some of which, such as the "Transatlantic Information Exchange Service" (TAIES) providing Internet links between a wide range of US and EU groups, are already in the process of implementation. In this respect the NTA has also been able to effectively broaden the framework of transatlantic relations.

4. CONDITIONS FOR THE LONG-TERM SUCCESS OF THE "NTA APPROACH"

The four positive elements of the NTA which have been identified above can serve as guiding lines for a successful further transformation and development of transatlantic relations. Yet the long-term success of what may be called the "NTA approach" will also depend on a number of other conditions.

One of these is early conflict prevention. Especially in the sphere of trade, both the EU and the US often continue to confront the other side with the accomplished fact of an adopted controversial position or even action. Taking into account the many consultation mechanisms in place this is surprising. Both sides need to make additional efforts to involve the other in the decision-making process on measures likely to be contentious as early as possible. Even if the measure cannot be avoided early consultation and negotiation can help to reduce ill-feeling and overreaction. Both the achievements and the failures of EU-US co-operation in the Middle East peace process[15] show how important early and comprehensive consultation and co-ordination are. Since conflicts on trade issues are often linked to

---

12   This was formally acknowledged in the Senior Level Group Report to the EU-US Summit in The Hague on 28 May 1997.

13   See Europe No. 6972, 12, 13 May 1997, p. 11.

14   See "*Transatlantic Conference Concluding Statement and Recommendations*", Washington DC, 6 May 1997.

15   See Chapter 4 *ante.*

controversial legislation, a greater involvement of parliaments in the transatlantic process, to which the NTA makes only a rather short reference, could also make a useful contribution to early conflict prevention. Mutual consultation in the early stages of drafting regulations, to which both sides committed themselves in December 1997[16], could also prevent major tensions at a later stage.

Another condition is pragmatism. The EU and the US are, and will continue to be partners with fundamentally different internal structures, a whole range of different political and economic interests and subject to different influences from within and without. As a result no side can expect the other always to attach the same importance to issues on the common agenda and to make the same input in consultation and common action. Differences in the speed and the degree of the reaction to each other's concerns should not immediately be taken as a sign of lack of commitment to the partnership, or even a "crisis" in transatlantic relations. but as an inevitable matter-of-fact consequence of relations between two major international actors. As the example of EU-US co-operation in the framework of the UN shows[17], tolerance and sensitivity to the problems each other has in policy formulation are necessary parts of a pragmatic approach avoiding undue touchiness and unrealistic expectations which can only reduce the potential for common positions and action. The US, for instance, will continue to need a good deal of pragmatic sensitivity to the complexities of the internal EU decision-making process which the EU largely failed to reform during the 1996–97 Intergovernmental Conference.

Openness towards third parties is also an important condition for success. The EU-US partnership must always be seen as part of the international relations system and increasing global interdependence. Not only can the transatlantic partnership be enriched by associating other countries with certain initiatives but an exclusively transatlantic approach to certain issues may also be sub-optimal and even counterproductive. There may be some distinct advantages: for instance, in enlarging the so far purely bilateral Transatlantic Free Trade Area (TAFTA) project at least partially to a trilateral dimension involving Japan as the biggest other single trade partner of both the US and the EU.[18] The prospective enlargement of both NATO and the EU calls anyway for a broadened understanding of the scope of "transatlantic" relations.

The final condition for long-term success which should be mentioned here is the ability of both sides to learn from each other's experiences. The US and the EU not only share a huge number of internal and external problems and challenges they will have to face at the turn of the century, each of them also

---

[16] See the Joint Statement on "*Regulatory Co-operation: Promoting trade while facilitating consumer protection*", 5 December 1997.
[17] See Chapter 5 *ante*.
[18] See Chapter 6 *ante*.

possesses a wealth of experience with these problems and, often enough, also a wealth of strategies to solve them. As the case of asylum policies in the EU and the US shows[19], both sides could learn from the successes and failures of their respective policies in areas which are of major concern to both of them. A more systematic sharing of experiences and know-how on a variety of policy-making issues would have the additional benefit of increasing sensitivity to the values, institutional mechanisms and particular problems influencing decision-making on the other side of the Atlantic. The creation of issue-oriented discussion fora (like the "Transatlantic Conference" of May 1997) bringing together governmental and non-governmental actors, greater support for comparative research, the involvement of experts from the other side in decision-making on certain issues could all make a useful contribution to this sort of transatlantic learning process.

The NTA has established an innovative and substantial framework for the future of EU-US relations. This responds to a real need because there are, as pointed out, some real risks of erosion which cloud the sky of the transatlantic relationship. As the next century approaches transatlantic relations are still struggling with the consequences of the end of the Cold War. Comprehensive change is inevitable, and the NTA provides a constructive and promising agenda for the transformation of the EU-US partnership. Yet the framework set by the NTA still needs to be filled out. The first two years have already brought concrete results, but they have also shown that the NTA alone is no remedy to any new or existing difficulties in EU-US relations. It can only provide a sound framework for the continuous effort of co-operation which is needed to maintain and develop the quality of the transatlantic relationship. However laborious this effort may sometimes be, it is essential for the strengthening of both sides' confidence and ability to meet the challenges of a rapidly changing world whenever and wherever necessary by an effective common response.

---

[19]   See Chapters 10, 11 *ante*.

APPENDIX

THE NEW TRANSATLANTIC AGENDA[1]

CONTENTS

---

[1] Adopted on 3 December 1995.

THE NEW TRANSATLANTIC AGENDA

We, the United States of America and the European Union, affirm our conviction that the ties which bind our people are as strong today as they have been for the past half century. For over fifty years, the transatlantic partnership has been the leading force for peace and prosperity for ourselves and for the world. Together, we helped transform adversaries into allies and dictatorships into democracies. Together, we built institutions and patterns of co-operation that ensured our security and economic strength. These are epic achievements.

Today we face new challenges at home and abroad. To meet them, we must further strengthen and adapt the partnership that has served us so well. Domestic challenges are not an excuse to turn inward; we can learn from each other's experiences and build new transatlantic bridges. We must first of all seize the opportunity presented by Europe's historic transformation to consolidate democracy and free-market economies throughout the continent.

We share a common strategic vision of Europe's future security. Together, we have charted a course for ensuring continuing peace in Europe into the next century. We are committed to the construction of a new European security architecture in which the North Atlantic Treaty Organisation, the European Union, the Western European Union, the Organisation for Security and Co-operation in Europe and the Council of Europe have complementary and mutually reinforcing roles to play.

We reaffirm the indivisibility of transatlantic security. NATO remains, for its members, the centrepiece of transatlantic security, providing the indispensable link between North America and Europe. Further adaptation of the Alliance's political and military structures to reflect both the full spectrum of its roles and the development of the emerging European Security and Defence Identity will strengthen the European pillar of the Alliance.

As to the accession of new members to NATO and to the EU, these processes, autonomous but complementary, should contribute significantly to the extension of security, stability and prosperity in the whole of Europe. Furthering the work of Partnership for Peace and the North Atlantic Co-operation Council and establishing a security partnership between NATO and Russia and between NATO and Ukraine will lead to unprecedented co-operation on security issues.

We are strengthening the OSCE so that it can fulfil its potential to prevent destabilising regional conflicts and advance the prospect of peace, security, prosperity, and democracy for all.

Increasingly, our common security is further enhanced by strengthening and reaffirming the ties between the European Union and the United States within the existing network of relationships which join us together.

Our economic relationship sustains our security and increases our prosperity. We share the largest two-way trade and investment relationship in the world. We bear a special responsibility to lead multilateral efforts towards a more open world system of trade and investment. Our co-operation has made possible every global trade agreement, from the Kennedy Round to the Uruguay Round. Through the G-7, we work to stimulate global growth. And at the Organisation for Economic Co-operation and Development, we are developing strategies to overcome structural unemployment and adapt to demographic change.

We are determined to create a New Transatlantic Marketplace, which will expand trade and investment opportunities and multiply jobs on both sides of the Atlantic. This initiative will also contribute to the dynamism of the global economy.

At the threshold of a new century, there is a new world to shape – full of opportunities but with challenges no less critical than those faced by previous generations. These challenges can be met and opportunities fully realised only by the whole international community working together. We will work with others bilaterally, at the United Nations and in other multilateral fora.

We are determined to reinforce our political and economic partnership as a powerful force for good in the world. To this end, we will build on the extensive consultations established by the 1990 Transatlantic Declaration and the conclusions of our June 1995 Summit and move to common action.

Today we adopt a New Transatlantic Agenda based on a Framework for Action with four major goals:

1. Promoting peace and stability, democracy and development around the world.
   Together, we will work for an increasingly stable and prosperous Europe; foster democracy and economic reform in Central and Eastern Europe as well as in Russia, Ukraine and other new independent states; secure peace in the Middle East; advance human rights; promote non-proliferation and co-operate on development and humanitarian assistance.
2. Responding to global challenges.
   Together, we will fight international crime, drug-trafficking and terrorism; address the needs of refugees and displaced persons; protect the environment and combat disease.
3. Contributing to the expansion of world trade and closer economic relations.
   Together, we will strengthen the multilateral trading system and take concrete, practical steps to promote closer economic relations between us.
4. Building bridges across the Atlantic.
   Together, we will work with our business people, scientists, educators and others to improve communication and to ensure that future generations remain as committed as we are to developing a full and equal partnership.

Within this Framework, we have developed an extensive Joint EU-US Action Plan. We will give special priority between now and our next Summit to the following actions:

I. PROMOTING PEACE AND STABILITY, DEMOCRACY AND DEVELOPMENT AROUND THE WORLD

- We pledge to work boldly and rapidly, together and with other partners, to implement the peace, to assist recovery of the war-ravaged regions of the former Yugoslavia and to support economic and political reform and new democratic institutions. We will co-operate to ensure: (1) respect for human rights, for the rights of minorities and for the rights of refugees and displaced persons, in particular the right of return; (2) respect for the work of the War Crimes Tribunal, established by the United Nations Security Council, in order to ensure international criminal accountability; (3) the establishment of a framework for free and fair elections in Bosnia-Herzegovina as soon as conditions permit and (4) the implementation of the agreed process for arms control, disarmament and confidence-building measures. While continuing to provide humanitarian assistance, we will contribute to the task of reconstruction, subject to the implementation of the provisions of the peace settlement plan, in the context of the widest possible burden-sharing with other donors and taking advantage of the experience of international institutions, of the European Commission and of all relevant bilateral donors in the co-ordination mechanism.
- We will support the countries of Central and Eastern Europe in their efforts to restructure their economies and strengthen their democratic and market institutions. Their commitment to democratic systems of government, respect for minorities, human rights, market oriented economies and good relations with neighbours will facilitate their integration into our institutions. We are taking steps to intensify our co-operation aimed at sharing information, co-ordinating assistance programmes and developing common actions, protecting the environment and securing the safety of their nuclear power stations.
- We are determined to reinforce our co-operation to consolidate democracy and stability in Russia, Ukraine and other new independent states. We are committed to working with them in strengthening democratic institutions and market reforms, in protecting the environment, in securing the safety of their nuclear power stations and in promoting their integration into the international economy. An enduring and stable security framework for Europe must include these nations. We intend to continue building a close partnership with a democratic Russia. An independent, democratic, stable

and nuclear weapons-free Ukraine will contribute to security and stability in Europe; we will co-operate to support Ukraine's democratic and economic reforms.

- We will support the Turkish Government's efforts to strengthen democracy and advance economic reforms in order to promote Turkey's further integration into the transatlantic community.
- We will work towards a resolution of the Cyprus question, taking into account the prospective accession of Cyprus to the European Union. We will support the UN Secretary General's Mission of Good Offices and encourage dialogue between and with the Cypriot communities.
- We reaffirm our commitment to the achievement of a just, lasting and comprehensive peace in the Middle East. We will build on the recent successes in the Peace Process, including the bold steps taken by Jordan and Israel, through concerted efforts to support agreements already concluded and to expand the circle of peace. Noting the important milestone reached with the signing of the Israeli-Palestinian Interim Agreement, we will play an active role at the Conference for Economic Assistance to the Palestinians, will support the Palestinian elections and will work ambitiously to improve the access we both give to products from the West Bank and the Gaza Strip. We will encourage and support the regional parties in implementing the conclusions of the Amman Summit. We will also continue our efforts to promote peace between Israel, Lebanon and Syria. We will actively seek the dismantling of the Arab boycott of Israel.
- We pledge to work together more closely in our preventive and crisis diplomacy; to respond effectively to humanitarian emergencies; to promote sustainable development and the building of democratic societies; and to support human rights.
- We have agreed to co-ordinate, co-operate and act jointly in development and humanitarian assistance activities. To this end, we will establish a High-Level Consultative Group to review progress of existing efforts, to assess policies and priorities and to identify projects and regions for the further strengthening of co-operation.
- We will increase co-operation in developing a blueprint for UN economic and social reform. We will co-operate to find urgently needed solutions to the financial crisis of the UN system. We are determined to keep our commitments, including our financial obligations. At the same time, the UN must direct its resources to the highest priorities and must reform in order to meet its fundamental goals.
- We will provide support to the Korean Peninsula Energy Development Organisation (KEDO), underscoring our shared desire to resolve important proliferation challenges throughout the world.

II. RESPONDING TO GLOBAL CHALLENGES

- We are determined to take new steps in our common battle against the scourges of international crime, drug trafficking and terrorism. We commit ourselves to active, practical co-operation between the US and the future European Police Office, EUROPOL. We will jointly support and contribute to ongoing training programmes and institutions for crime-fighting officials in Central and Eastern Europe, Russia, Ukraine, other new independent states and other parts of the globe.
- We will work together to strengthen multilateral efforts to protect the global environment and to develop environmental policy strategies for sustainable world-wide growth. We will co-ordinate our negotiating positions on major global environmental issues, such as climate change, ozone layer depletion, persistent organic pollutants, desertification and erosion and contaminated soils. We are undertaking co-ordinated initiatives to disseminate environmental technologies and to reduce the public health risks from hazardous substances, in particular from exposure to lead. We will strengthen our bilateral co-operation on chemicals, biotechnology and air pollution issues.
- We are committed to develop and implement an effective global early warning system and response network for new and re-emerging communicable diseases such as AIDS and the Ebola virus, and to increase training and professional exchanges in this area. Together, we call on other nations to join us in more effectively combating such diseases.

III. CONTRIBUTING TO THE EXPANSION OF WORLD TRADE AND CLOSER ECONOMIC RELATIONS

- We have a special responsibility to strengthen the multilateral trading system, to support the World Trade Organisation and to lead the way in opening markets to trade and investment.
- We will contribute to the expansion of world trade by fully implementing our Uruguay Round commitments, work for the completion of the unfinished business by the agreed timetables and encourage a successful and substantive outcome for the Singapore WTO Ministerial Meeting in December 1996. In this context we will explore the possibility of agreeing on a mutually satisfactory package of tariff reductions on industrial products, and we will consider which, if any, Uruguay Round obligations on tariffs can be implemented on an accelerated basis. In view of the importance of the information society, we are launching a specific exercise in order to attempt to conclude an information technology agreement.

- We will work together for the successful conclusion of a Multilateral Agreement on Investment at the OECD that espouses strong principles on international investment liberalisation and protection. Meanwhile, we will work to develop discussion of the issue with our partners at the WTO. We will address in appropriate fora problems where trade intersects with concerns for the environment, internationally recognised labour standards and competition policy. We will co-operate in creating additional trading opportunities, bilaterally and throughout the world, in conformity with our WTO commitments.
- Without detracting from our co-operation in multilateral fora, we will create a New Transatlantic Marketplace by progressively reducing or eliminating barriers that hinder the flow of goods, services and capital between us. We will carry out a joint study on ways of facilitating trade in goods and services and further reducing or eliminating tariff and non-tariff barriers.
- We will strengthen regulatory co-operation, in particular by encouraging regulatory agencies to give a high priority to co-operation with their respective transatlantic counterparts, so as to address technical and non-tariff barriers to trade resulting from divergent regulatory processes. We aim to conclude an agreement on mutual recognition of conformity assessment (which includes certification and testing procedures) for certain sectors as soon as possible. We will continue the ongoing work in several sectors and identify others for further work.
- We will endeavour to conclude by the end of 1996 a customs co-operation and mutual assistance agreement between the European Community and the US.
- To allow our people to take full advantage of newly developed information technology and services, we will work toward the realisation of a Transatlantic Information Society.
- Given the overarching importance of job creation, we pledge to co-operate in the follow-up to the Detroit Jobs Conference and to the G-7 Summit initiative. We look forward to further co-operation in the run up to the G-7 Jobs Conference in France, at the next G-7 Summit in the Summer of 1996 and in other fora such as the OECD. We will establish a joint working group on employment and labour-related issues.

IV. BUILDING BRIDGES ACROSS THE ATLANTIC

- We recognise the need to strengthen and broaden public support for our partnership. To that end, we will seek to deepen the commercial, social, cultural, scientific and educational ties among our people. We pledge to nurture in present and future generations the mutual understanding and sense of shared purpose that has been the hallmark of the post-war period.

- We will not be able to achieve these ambitious goals without the backing of our respective business communities. We will support, and encourage the development of, the transatlantic business relationship, as an integral part of our wider efforts to strengthen our bilateral dialogue. The successful conference of EU and US business leaders which took place in Seville on 10/11 November 1995 was an important step in this direction. A number of its recommendations have already been incorporated into our Action Plan and we will consider concrete follow-up to others.
- We will actively work to reach a new comprehensive EC-US science and technology co-operation agreement by 1997.
- We believe that the recent EC/US Agreement on Co-operation in Education and Vocational Training can act as a catalyst for a broad spectrum of innovative co-operative activities of direct benefit to students and teachers. We will examine ways to increase private support for educational exchanges, including scholarship and internship programmes. We will work to introduce new technologies into classrooms, linking educational establishments in the EU with those in the US and will encourage teaching of each other's languages, history and culture.

Parliamentary Links

We attach great importance to enhanced parliamentary links. We will consult parliamentary leaders on both sides of the Atlantic regarding consultative mechanisms, including those building on existing institutions, to discuss matters related to our transatlantic partnership.

Implementing our Agenda

The New Transatlantic Agenda is a comprehensive statement of the many areas for our common action and co-operation. We have entrusted the Senior Level Group to oversee work on this Agenda and particularly the priority actions we have identified. We will use our regular Summits to measure progress and to update and revise our priorities.

For the last fifty years, the transatlantic relationship has been central to the security and prosperity of our people. Our aspirations for the future must surpass our achievements in the past.

JOINT EU-US ACTION PLAN[1]

CONTENTS

[1] Adopted on 3 December 1995.

JOINT EU-US ACTION PLAN

This Action Plan for expanding and deepening EU-US relations reflects a framework with four shared goals:

- Promoting peace and stability, democracy and development around the world;
- Responding to global challenges;
- Contributing to the expansion of world trade and closer economic relations;
- Building bridges across the Atlantic.

I. PROMOTING PEACE AND STABILITY, DEMOCRACY AND DEVELOPMENT AROUND THE WORLD

We attach the highest importance to perfecting a new transatlantic community reflecting our joint interest in promoting stability and prosperity throughout the whole continent of Europe, based on the principles of democracy and free markets. We will co-operate both jointly and multi-laterally to resolve tensions, support civil societies, and promote market reforms.

Our partnership is also global. We accept our responsibility to act jointly to resolve conflicts in troubled areas, to engage in preventive diplomacy together, to co-ordinate our assistance efforts, to deal with humanitarian needs and to help build in developing nations the capacity for economic growth and self-sufficiency. In this global partnership we are guided by the firm belief that the strengthening of democratic institutions and respect for human rights are essential to stability, prosperity, and development.

1.   Working Together for a Stable and Prosperous Europe

a) Peace and reconstruction in the former Yugoslavia

We pledge to work boldly and rapidly, together and with other partners, to implement the peace, to assist recovery of the war-ravaged regions of the former Yugoslavia and to support economic and political reform and new democratic institutions.

We will co-operate to ensure: (1) respect for human rights, for the rights of minorities and for the rights of refugees and displaced persons, in particular the right of return; (2) respect for the work of the War Crimes Tribunal, established by the United Nations Security Council, in order to ensure international criminal accountability; (3) the establishment of a framework for free and fair elections in Bosnia-Herzegovina as soon as conditions permit; and (4) the implementation of the agreed process for arms control, disarmament and confidence-building measures.

While continuing to provide humanitarian assistance, we will contribute to the task of reconstruction, subject to the implementation of the provisions of the peace settlement plan, in the context of the widest possible burden-sharing with other donors and taking advantage of the experience of international institutions, of the European Commission and of all relevant bilateral donors in the co-ordination mechanism.

We will continue to support the BosnianCroat Federation.

b) Central and Eastern European countries

We will reinforce existing dialogue and co-operation on consolidating democracy, stability and the transition to market economies in Central and Eastern Europe. To this end, we will hold annual high-level consultations.

We will co-operate in support of the structural and microeconomic reforms in the countries of Central and Eastern Europe with a view to their integration into international political and economic institutions. We will continue to consult on ongoing technical assistance efforts to develop their financial systems and capital markets. We are fostering the creation of the legal and judicial infrastructure necessary in these countries to support expanded trade and investment.

We will pursue assistance co-operation on the spot in beneficiary countries via regular and intensified contacts between US missions and Commission Delegations, including assistance co-ordination meetings in selected capitals.

We will co-operate in helping the countries of Central and Eastern Europe to address their environmental problems by identifying joint projects consistent with the Lucerne Environmental Plan of Action, supporting the Budapest Regional Environmental Centre and building on proposals from the October 1995 Sofia Ministerial.

We will work together to promote economic reform in the countries participating in the Partners in Transition programme at the OECD, to facilitate their acceptance of OECD obligations and encourage their early accession. We will support the OECD's outreach efforts to the other Central and Eastern European countries seeking a closer relationship with the OECD.

c) Russia, Ukraine and other new independent states

We will reinforce existing dialogue and co-operation on consolidating democracy, stability and the transition to market economies in Russia, Ukraine and other new independent states (NIS). To this end, we will hold annual high-level consultations.

We will co-ordinate activities in support of the integration of Russia, Ukraine and other NIS in the global economy.

We will also reinforce the existing co-ordination relationship including technical assistance and enhanced on the spot co-ordination.

We will:

- consider complementary initiatives such as: legal advice for reforms, tax reform, banking sector reform, human resource development, privatisation and post-privatisation activities, small and medium-sized enterprise development and democracy-building;
- intensify co-operation on projects aimed at protecting the environment in the fields endorsed by the Sofia Conference. In addition, we agree to take steps to establish an institution similar to the Budapest Regional Environmental Centre within the NIS.

We will continue to improve co-ordination on food assistance, using the successful co-ordination in the Caucasus as a practical example on which to build in future.

d) Turkey

We will support the Turkish Government's efforts to strengthen democracy and advance economic reforms in order to promote Turkey's further integration into the transatlantic community.

e) Cyprus

We will work towards a resolution of the Cyprus question, taking into account the prospective accession of Cyprus to the European Union. We will support the UN Secretary General's Mission of Good Offices and encourage dialogue between and with the Cypriot communities.

2. Promoting the Middle East Peace Process

We will work together to make peace, stability and prosperity in the Middle East become a reality.
   To this end, we will:

– continue our support for Palestinian self-government and economic development;
– support the Palestinian elections which should contribute to the Palestinian democratic development;
– play an active role at the Conference for Economic Assistance to the Palestinians;
– work ambitiously to improve the access we both give to products from the West Bank and the Gaza Strip;
– encourage Jordanians, Palestinians, Israelis and Egyptians to establish comprehensive free trade agreements among themselves;
– support the regional parties in their efforts to establish road links, electricity grids, gas pipelines and other joint infrastructures necessary to foster regional trade and investments;
– encourage and, as appropriate, support the regional parties in implementing the conclusions of the Amman Summit.

In addition, we will:

– continue our efforts to promote peace between Israel, Lebanon and Syria;
– actively seek the dismantling of the Arab boycott of Israel.

3. Sharing Responsibility in Other Regions of the World

We will strengthen our joint efforts in preventative diplomacy, attacking the root causes of crisis and conflict, and will facilitate the movement from relief to long-term development.
   We will:

– jointly assess the regional dimensions of the conflicts in Rwanda and in Burundi, jointly identify and plan for transitional priorities and support African led regional initiatives to deal with these conflicts;
– support and participate in the UN/OAU sponsored Conference on the Great Lakes region;
– foster peace and economic reconstruction in Angola and Mozambique;
– take strong and appropriate steps to promote the rapid restoration of civilian democratic rule in Nigeria;
– intensify consultations in the field and deepen our policy dialogue, including our support for the consolidation of democratic institutions in El Salvador and Nicaragua;

- support the peace process in Guatemala and the implementation of agreements among the parties;
- help Haiti to strengthen democracy and the rule of law by improving the effectiveness of its judicial system;
- promote democracy, economic reforms and human rights in Cuba;
- support smooth, successful transitions for Hong Kong and Macao in 1997 and 1999 respectively under the terms of the 1984 Sino-British and 1987 Sino-Portuguese Joint Declarations;
- work together to reduce the risk of regional conflict over the Korean peninsula, Taiwan and the South China Sea;
- reinforce our joint efforts to further the process of democratic reform in Burma;
- continue jointly to support the development of human rights and democratic practices in Cambodia; and
- continue to offer our strong support to the UN Secretary General in his efforts to find a lasting and just solution to the question of East Timor.

4.   Development Co-operation and Humanitarian Assistance

We have agreed to co-ordinate, co-operate and act jointly in development and humanitarian assistance activities.

To this end, we will establish a High-Level Consultative Group on Development Co-operation and Humanitarian Assistance to review progress of existing efforts, to assess policies and priorities and to identify projects and regions for the further strengthening of co-operation. This group will complement and reinforce existing co-ordination arrangements. The following areas for action have already been identified:

a) Development co-operation

We will:

- co-ordinate policies on democracy and civil society, on health and population, on development co-operation within the framework of international institutions and organisations and on food security;
- develop a joint food security strategy in a number of selected countries;
- co-ordinate our support for sustainable development and economic reform in the context of political liberalisation in the Special Programme for Africa, co-operate in the Horn of Africa Initiative and on approaches *vis-à-vis* Southern Africa (including discussions with the Southern Africa Development Community, the Common Market for Eastern and Southern Africa and the exploration of opportunities for collaborative long-term assessments);
- co-ordinate assistance policies to promote the participation of women at all levels.

b) *Humanitarian assistance*

We will:

- co-operate in improving the effectiveness of international humanitarian relief agencies, such as the United Nations High Commission for Refugees, the World Food Programme and the United Nations Department of Humanitarian Affairs, and in our planning and implementation of relief and reconstruction activities;
- consider joint missions whenever possible, starting in Northern Iraq, Liberia and Angola, and hold early consultations on security in refugee camps as well as on the use of military assets in humanitarian actions;
- work towards greater complementarity by extending operational co-ordination to include the planning phase, continuing and improving European Community-US operational information sharing on humanitarian assistance, appointing EC-US humanitarian focal points on both sides of the Atlantic; and improving staff relations by exchange of staff and mutual training of officials administering humanitarian aid.

5.   Human Rights and Democracy

We will:

- consult (bilaterally and within the framework of the relevant bodies of the UN, particularly the UN Commission on Human Rights) on countries where there is serious violation of human rights, in order to co-ordinate policies and, as appropriate, to develop joint initiatives;
- support jointly UN human rights activities, reinforcing the office of the UN High Commissioner on Human Rights and the Centre for Human Rights and following up UN conferences on human rights;
- ensure greater integration of the OSCE human dimension into conflict prevention and the daily activities of OSCE (both regular meetings/contacts and missions on the ground);
- work to expand legal rights for women and to increase women's equal participation in decision-making processes, building on commitments made at the Fourth World Conference on Women in Beijing;
- aim at strengthening civics education in order to nurture the culture of democracy and, to that end, explore the possibility of EU participation in developing the coalition of public figures, educators, and private sector representatives established at the CIVITAS conference in Prague in June 1995.

6.   Co-operation in International Organisations

We will increase co-operation in developing a blueprint for UN economic and social reform including better co-ordination of UN activities, review and adjustment of agencies' mandates and adoption of more efficient management techniques with a more transparent and accountable Secretariat. We will co-operate to find urgently needed solutions to the financial crisis of the UN system.

We are determined to keep our commitments, including our financial obligations. At the same time, the UN must direct its resources to the highest priorities and must reform in order to meet its fundamental goals.

We will co-operate to improve coherence in international economic organisations' activities, encouraging them to strengthen co-ordination between themselves and reduce overlap (e.g. between UN economic bodies, WTO, Bretton Woods institutions, OECD).

We will strengthen co-ordination in the OSCE framework, including conflict prevention/crisis management, confidence and security-building measures, and the economic dimension.

We will co-operate on global fisheries issues, in particular on the follow-up to the results of the UN Conference on Straddling Fish Stocks and Highly Migratory Fish Stocks.

7.   Non-proliferation, International Disarmament and Arms Transfers

We will work together to promote Nuclear Non-proliferation Treaty adherence by non-parties to the Treaty. We will co-ordinate actions to encourage non-adherents to act in accordance with the principle of non-proliferation.

We will combine our efforts to conclude in the Geneva Conference on Disarmament, in 1996, an effective, verifiable and universally applicable comprehensive Test Ban Treaty. We will undertake joint efforts for immediate negotiations on a Fissile Material Cut-Off Treaty.

We will co-ordinate on the prudent extension of the Missile Technology Control Regime to non-participating countries in order to control the spread of missile technology.

We will co-operate with a view to revising the 1972 Convention on Biological Weapons in order to promote new measures to increase its effectiveness. We will work to counter the proliferation of chemical and biological weapons.

We will support international efforts to curtail the use and proliferation of antipersonnel landmines (APLs). We will co-operate for a successful outcome of the Review Conference of the 1980 Convention on Prohibition and Restrictions on the Use of Certain Conventional Weapons, especially on the provisions relating to landmines. We will co-operate on the possible establishment of controls on the production, stockpiling and transfer of APLs.

We will continue efforts to establish a new multilateral arrangement for export controls the New Forum to respond to threats caused by the proliferation of arms and arms-related technologies as well as sensitive dual use items.

We will co-ordinate on preventing the spread of nuclear and other weapons of mass destruction, with particular emphasis on regions and countries of concern.

We will provide support to the Korean Peninsula Energy Development Organisation (KEDO), underscoring our shared desire to resolve important proliferation challenges throughout the world.

II. RESPONDING TO GLOBAL CHALLENGES

We share a common concern to address in an effective manner new global challenges which, without respect for national boundaries, present a serious threat to the quality of life and which neither of us can overcome alone. We pledge our actions and resources to meet together the challenges of international crime, terrorism and drug trafficking, mass migration, degradation of the environment, nuclear safety and disease. Together we can make a difference.

1. Fight Against Organised Crime, Terrorism and Drug Trafficking

We will co-operate in the fight against illegal drug trafficking, money laundering, terrorism, organised crime and illicit trade in nuclear materials.

We will enhance bilateral co-operation and institutional contacts. We will also enhance the capabilities of criminal justice and investigative systems and promote the rule of law through international training programmes at regional institutions such as the International Law Enforcement Academy in Budapest, the Italian Judicial Training Centre, the Middle and East European Police Academy and a similar administration of justice institution for the Western Hemisphere.

We will take steps to establish an information exchange mechanism on co-operation between the US and the EU and its Member States in the law enforcement and criminal justice fields, especially regarding activities in providing training, technical assistance and equipment to other nations.

We will foster the exchange of law enforcement and criminal justice expertise between the US and the EU in three areas:

- scientific and technological developments;
- exchanges of experts and observers between appropriate institutes and agencies;

- the sharing of information such as studies and analyses of emerging trends in international criminal activity.

When mutually agreed, we will jointly prepare reports to include recommended courses of action.

We will discuss the possibility of establishing interim co-operative measures between competent US authorities and the European Drugs Unit and begin implementing the possibilities provided for in the convention on EUROPOL to facilitate relations between EUROPOL and the US Government.

We will examine possibilities for co-operation in support of the UN Drug Control Programme marine interdiction initiatives.

We will co-ordinate alternative development programmes to counter drug production.

We will jointly support the establishment of co-operative links between appropriate EU institutions such as the European Monitoring Centre for Drugs and Drug Addiction and the Comision Interamericana para el Control del Abuso de Drogas.

We will co-ordinate our counter-narcotics assistance programmes and projects in the Caribbean.

We will take action to strengthen the Dublin Group by reinforcing and supporting its members' counter-narcotic measures.

We will work to conclude an agreement in order to exchange, among other things, sensitive information for the preclearance of shipments of essential and precursor chemicals used in the production of illegal drugs and co-operate in joint training programmes in chemical diversion control.

We will co-operate on assessing and responding to terrorist threats.

2.   Immigration and Asylum

We will:

- strengthen information exchanges on illegal immigration and on asylum taking into account, inter alia, the work of the Geneva Intergovernmental Consultative Group;
- co-operate in the fight against the traffic in illegal immigrants;
- co-operate in the fight against the traffic in women;
- exchange information on asylum trends and on successful asylum system reform;
- establish common responses to refugee crisis situations, notably by early warning mechanisms and co-ordination;
- develop a common stance on temporary protection in the United Nations High Commission for Refugees;
- co-ordinate positions on the Conference on Refugees and Migrants in the Commonwealth of Independent States;

   − improve existing arrangements and exchanges of intelligence in areas of mutual concern, for example, forged identity documents and transport carriers' liability;
   − convene seminars in 1996 and compare the results of our respective studies on migration flows both into the US and into the EU.

3.   Legal and Judicial Co-operation

We will:

   − identify means of strengthening international judicial assistance and co-operation in the obtaining of evidence and other relevant information;
   − co-operate on the judicial seizure and forfeiture of assets;
   − identify means to strengthen and improve international mechanisms for extradition, deportation, mutual legal assistance and other co-operative action to ensure that international fugitives have "nowhere to hide";
   − co-operate in promoting the work of the Hague Conference on Private International Law and the International Institute for Unification of Private Law (UNIDROIT).

4.   Preservation of the Environment

We will enhance our exchange of views and co-ordination of negotiating positions on major global issues, with a view to improving the effectiveness of multilateral efforts to protect the global environment.

    We will also strengthen the exchange of information and reporting on global environmental issues such as climate change, biodiversity, ozone layer depletion, persistent organic pollutants, desertification and erosion, water quality and quantity, land-based sources of marine pollution, hazardous wastes and contaminated soils, forest issues and trade and the environment.

    We will work together at the UN Commission on Sustainable Development (CSD) and other relevant bodies, including the Global Environmental Facility, to encourage the world at large in the challenge of caring for the global environment. We will continue working on the successful conclusion of CSD work on the sustainable management of all types of forests.

    We will enhance our bilateral dialogue on regulatory co-operation, including by:

   − extending co-operation on chemicals issues, such as Prior Informed Consent for the trade in hazardous chemicals, harmonisation of classification and labelling, and reduction of risks from hazardous substances, building in particular on our joint call for actions in the OECD to reduce exposure to lead;
   − continuing work on biotechnology issues such as the mutual acceptance of data for assessment and the release of genetically modified organisms;

enhancing work on air pollution, including efforts to decrease emissions from mobile sources and to assess the possibility of developing comparable emission standards.

We will undertake co-ordinated initiatives for the dissemination of environmental technologies, including in developing countries. In this regard, we will use the Climate Technology Initiative and proposals for an international clearinghouse on environmental technologies and practices. Private sector involvement will be a key aspect of this process.

We will engage in a broad and substantive dialogue on ways and means to limit and reduce global emissions of greenhouse gases, including CO_2.

5.   Population Issues

We will co-ordinate to implement the International Conference on Population and Development ("Cairo Conference") Programme of Action. We will work to sustain support for family planning and expand access to reproductive health programmes in the context of a comprehensive approach to population stabilisation and sustainable development.

We will work together to strengthen the effectiveness of bilateral and multilateral population assistance programmes.

6.   Nuclear Safety

We will promote the ratification of the International Convention on Nuclear Safety.

We will co-ordinate positions in the negotiations in the International Convention on Radioactive Residues.

We will improve existing bilateral assistance co-ordination in the field of nuclear safety, extending to onsite and offsite nuclear emergency preparedness, including in the countries of Central and Eastern Europe and the NIS, as well as special G7 Chernobyl assistance. We will co-operate in the preparation of the Moscow Conference on Nuclear Safety.

7.   Health

We will establish an EU-US task force to develop and implement an effective global early warning system and response network for communicable diseases.

We are taking steps to provide for increased training opportunities and professional exchanges in the area of communicable diseases and encourage participation in EU and US programmes by scientists from developing countries.

We will co-ordinate our requests to other nations and to international organisations calling for action against emerging and reemerging communicable diseases. We will encourage the follow-up of recent World Health Organisation (WHO) resolutions dealing with outbreak and reporting responsibilities and strengthened response centres.

We will co-operate, bilaterally and within the framework of the WHO, and other international organisations as appropriate, on respective programmes on health-related matters (AIDS and other communicable diseases, cancer, drug addiction) and identify specific areas for co-operation, especially in the research field.

III. CONTRIBUTING TO THE EXPANSION OF WORLD TRADE AND CLOSER ECONOMIC RELATIONS

We are each other's largest trading and investment partners. Our economic prosperity is inextricably linked. At the same time, our economic and trade relations affect third countries and regions. It is our responsibility to contribute effectively to international economic stability and growth and to broaden our bilateral economic dialogue.

We have a special responsibility to strengthen the multilateral trading system, to support the World Trade Organisation and to lead the way in opening markets for trade and investment.

We will create a New Transatlantic Marketplace by progressively reducing or eliminating barriers that hinder the flow of goods, services and capital between us.

1. Strengthening the Multilateral Trading System

a) Consolidating the WTO

We will promote adherence to multilateral rules and commitments, including the effective functioning of the dispute settlement system, and secure the full implementation of the Uruguay Round Agreements by all WTO members.

We will work to ensure a successful and substantive outcome for the Singapore Ministerial meeting.

We will co-operate on the accession of new members, notably China and Russia.

We will promote the effective management and operation of the WTO.

b) Uruguay Round unfinished business

We will work for the completion of the unfinished business of Marrakech with regard to goods and services. We are committed to the successful conclusion of the current negotiations in all services sectors by the agreed timetables. The most immediate deadlines are 30 April 1996 for telecommunications and 30 June 1996 for maritime services.

c) Financial services

We agree to concert our efforts to promote liberalisation of financial services on a worldwide basis. In particular, we will seek to ensure that the interim agreement concluded in July 1995 is succeeded by a more substantial package of permanent liberalisation commitments from a critica mass of WTO members.

d) Government procurement

We will promote the launching by Ministers in Singapore of negotiations within the WTO aimed at covering substantially all government procurement and WTO members.

e) Intellectual property rights (IPR)

We will co-operate to ensure the full implementation of the TRIPs Agreement and improve the level of IPR protection throughout the world. We will work to develop a comprehensive agenda for future TRIPs negotiations within the WTO.

f) New issues

We will work together in the WTO and/or other appropriate fora. We will give priority to:

(i) Environment: The report to the Singapore Ministerial Meeting should set out clear recommendations for decisions and a process for further work to ensure that trade and environmental measures are mutually supportive.

(ii) Investment: We will work closely together in formulating our respective policies. This co-operation should, in particular, bear fruit in a successful conclusion, as called for in the 1995 OECD Ministerial Declaration, of the negotiations on a Multilateral Agreement on Investment (MAI) espousing strong principles on international investment liberalisation and protection. Meanwhile, we will work to develop discussion of the issue with our partners in the WTO.

(iii) Competition: We will pursue work on the scope for multilateral action in the fields of trade and competition policy. Our competition authorities will co-operate in working with other countries to develop effective antitrust regimes.

(iv) Labour standards: We will join our efforts in the WTO and other fora with a view to dissipating various misunderstandings and preoccupations of trading partners regarding the relationship between trade and internationally recognised labour standards.

g) *Market access: creating additional trading opportunities*

We will co-operate in creating additional trading opportunities, bilaterally and throughout the world, in conformity with our WTO commitments. In view of the importance of the information society, we are launching a specific exercise in order to attempt to conclude an information technology agreement.

In the perspective of the WTO Singapore Ministerial Meeting, we will explore the possibility of agreeing on a mutually satisfactory package of tariff reductions on industrial products, and we will consider which, if any, Uruguay Round obligations on tariffs can be implemented on an accelerated basis.

We will work ambitiously to improve the access we both give to products from the West Bank and the Gaza Strip.

h) *International customs co-operation*

We will work together in the World Customs Organisation and co-operate with the International Chamber of Commerce to develop a comprehensive model of norms and standards for customs procedures throughout the world to promote *inter alia* increased transparency and harmonised approaches to classification, valuation and rules of origin.

i) *Illicit payments*

We will combat corruption and bribery by implementing the 1994 OECD Recommendation on Bribery in International Transactions.

2. The New Transatlantic Marketplace

The creation of the New Transatlantic Marketplace will include the following actions, which also take into consideration the recommendations of the Transatlantic Business Dialogue:

a) *Joint study*

We will carry out a joint study on ways of facilitating trade in goods and services and further reducing or eliminating tariff and non-tariff barriers.

b) *Confidence building*

As part of a confidence-building process, we will reinforce our efforts to resolve bilateral trade issues and disputes.

c) Standards, certification and regulatory issues

We will aim to conclude an agreement on mutual recognition of conformity assessment (which includes certification and testing procedures) for certain sectors as soon as possible. We will continue the ongoing work in several sectors and identify others for further work.

We will co-operate closely in the international standard setting process, drawing on international bodies to achieve the greatest possible use of international standards, and will seek the maximum practical transparency, participation and non-discrimination.

We will devote special attention to co-operatively developing and implementing regulations on vehicle safety requirements and on measures to reduce air and noise emissions. We will build on existing efforts aimed at facilitating international regulatory harmonization, taking account of our respective policies on safety and environmental protection, while recognizing the need to achieve, wherever possible, global regulatory uniformity.

We will strengthen regulatory co-operation, in particular by encouraging regulatory agencies to give a high priority to co-operation with their respective transatlantic counterparts, so as to address technical and other non-tariff barriers to trade resulting from divergent regulatory processes. We will especially encourage a collaborative approach between the EU and the US in testing and certification procedures by promoting greater compatibility of standards and health and safety-related measures. To this end, we will seek to develop pilot co-operative projects.

d) Veterinary and plant health issues

We will conclude an agreement to establish a framework for determining equivalence of veterinary standards and procedures for all live animals and animal products.

We will enhance the established co-operation on plant health issues and in the area of pesticide residues regulation.

e) Government procurement

We will aim to increase substantially in 1996 and beyond the coverage of EU/US bilateral commitments on public procurement under the Government Procurement Agreement and to co-ordinate in developing proposals on information technology under the Agreement.

f) Intellectual property rights (IPR)

With a view to reinvigorating our efforts to solve remaining IPR problems, we will hold a seminar during 1996 addressing current and future IPR issues.

g) *Financial services*

We will expand our ongoing dialogue on financial services to include discussion of the financial and economic aspects of our respective relations with third countries.

h) *Customs co-operation*

We will endeavour to conclude by the end of 1996 a customs co-operation and mutual assistance agreement between the EC and the US. The agreement should cover:

- customs co-operation: simplification of customs procedures, computerisation (information, data exchange, common access to databases etc.), consultation within international organisations, methods of work;
- mutual assistance: exchange of enforcement information, increased investigative co-operation in customs matters, protection of intellectual property rights, commercial fraud, illicit nuclear traffic, trade in severely restricted chemicals;
- programmes for the exchange of officials.

i) *Information Society, information technology and telecommunications*

We will expand and develop the bilateral Information Society Dialogue, in order to further common understanding of global issues implying access to information services through public institutions, regulatory reforms, and technological co-operation, including the continuation of expert-level discussions in the following areas:

- interconnection and inter-operability, including standardisation issues (particularly for interfaces, network terminating equipment, mobile telephones, digital video broadcasting/high definition television);
- universal service;
- pro-competitive interconnection policies and principles;
- access to information and the protection of IPR;
- satellite policy;
- commercial communications;
- privacy and data protection;
- the impact on society, including public services and employment.

The Dialogue will also address those new legislative and regulatory developments which are proposed or are being prepared to achieve progress in these areas, including questions of regulatory transparency.

In the context of enhanced co-operation in science and technology, we will work towards the reduction of obstacles to co-operation in research and development in the field of information and communications. We will jointly support the implementation of the G7 global projects on the Information Society, aiming to spur innovation and ensure interconnection and interoperability. Furthermore, we will exchange information on on-going and future research programmes in the field of information communication technology to foster concrete bilateral co-operation actions in research and development.

We will also discuss regulatory issues relating to online interactive and international service provision, in order to maximise their development, which is essential for the success of the transition towards an Information Society on both sides of the Atlantic.

We will co-operate on the integration of developing countries into the global Information Society, initially through our support for the Information Society Conference in South Africa in 1996 and through our participation in the International Telecommunications Union.

j) Competition

We will pursue, and build on, bilateral co-operation in the immediate term based on the EC-US Agreement of 1991. We will examine the options for deepening co-operation on competition matters, including the possibility of a further agreement.

k) Data protection

We will discuss data protection issues with a view to facilitating information flows, while addressing the risks to privacy.

l) Transport

We will:

- establish a working group for consultations on design and implementation of Global Navigation Satellite Systems;
- improve EU-US co-operation on air traffic management;
- hold consultations on maritime transport safety and crew qualifications.

m) Energy

We will intensify contacts and co-operation on energy-related issues including through contacts in multilateral fora where appropriate such as the environmental implications of energy policy on regulatory frameworks for the energy sector, on technical assistance activities to third countries and on energy technology.

n) Biotechnology

We will encourage regulatory co-operation, including with respect to genetically modified organisms, and expand bilateral co-operation in the preparation of multilateral meetings and negotiations in connection with the UN, FAO, OECD, CODEX Alimentarius and the Biodiversity Convention.

We will continue the activities of the EU-US Biotechnology Task Force, and in this context, will promote joint research efforts in the fields of neuro-informatics and marine biotechnology.

o) Safety and health

We will explore the scope for an agreement for the exchange of information on issues affecting health and safety at work, such as occupational safety and health standards, the development of regulations, high risk activity, carcinogenic substances at the workplace, toxicology, testing programmes, education and information programmes, and the collection of statistics and data.

We will explore the establishment of improved mechanisms for the timely exchange of information related to the general safety of products, including the withdrawal of products from the market.

3. Jobs and Growth

Given the overarching importance of job creation, we pledge to co-operate in the follow-up to the Detroit Jobs Conference and the G7 Summit initiative. We look forward to further co-operation in the run-up to the G7 Jobs Conference in France, at the next G7 Summit in the Summer of 1996 and in other fora such as the OECD and the International Labour Organisation.

We will establish a joint working group on employment and labour-related issues. We will intensify the dialogue, in particular on new forms of labour-management co-operation; increased investment in human resources, including in education and skills training; smoothing the transition from school-to-work and job-to-job; active labour market policies and the relationship between work and welfare; employment and new technologies; and encouraging entrepreneuralism.

We will continue to exchange views on macroeconomic issues in the light of the importance of a sound macroeconomic framework both for the development of an harmonious relationship and for the fostering of non-inflationary growth, the reduction of imbalances and international financial stability.

IV. BUILDING BRIDGES ACROSS THE ATLANTIC

We recognise that the transatlantic relationship can be truly secure in the coming century only if future generations understand its importance as well as their parents and grandparents did. We are committed to fostering an active and vibrant transatlantic community by deepening and broadening the commercial, social, cultural, scientific, and educational ties that bind us.

1.   Transatlantic Business Dialogue

We will support and encourage the development of the Transatlantic Business Dialogue, as an integral part of our wider efforts to strengthen our bilateral relationship. The successful conference of EU and US business leaders which took place in Seville on 10/11 November 1995 was an important step in this direction. We welcome the fact that the participants were able to agree on a series of joint recommendations to build an even stronger framework within which trade, investment, capital and technology can flow across the Atlantic. We commend them for encouraging both business communities to continue to devote attention to possible improvements in the transatlantic commercial relationship.

We have studied carefully the recommendations adopted at Seville, and have already incorporated a number of them into our present Action Plan. Our officials will work closely together with our business leaders on both sides in considering follow-up to the many other suggestions arising from the Seville meeting, and will report at the next EU-US Summit.

2.   Broadening Science and Technology Co-operation

We will negotiate a new, comprehensive EC-US science and technology co-operation agreement by 1997 based on the principle of mutual interest, with a view to achieving a balance of benefits to us both.

We will work to conclude the Agreement on Intelligent Manufacturing Systems (advanced technologies and robotics).

Recognising that scientific and technological advances underlie our ability to meet global challenges and foster economic growth, we will promote co-operative science and technology projects in support of topics identified in this document.

In addition, we will work to identify collaborative projects and exchange information to address crossborder issues such as transportation, health and global climate change. Examples of specific projects include: intermodal transport and fast transhipment techniques; intelligent transportation systems; the study and forecasting of travel behaviour; development of a malaria vaccine; and the study of environmental health and the effects of radiation.

3.   People to People Links

We will:

–   encourage our citizens to increase their contacts in diverse fora, youth, professionals, think tanks etc. with a view to deepening grassroots support for the transatlantic relationship and enriching the flow of ideas for the solution of common problems;

– work for the early creation of the joint consortia and for the implementation of the Fulbright Awards and other activities provided for in our Agreement on Co-operation in Higher Education and Vocational Training;

– co-operate on the reform of higher education in the countries of Central and Eastern Europe, Russia, Ukraine, other NIS and Mongolia by identifying and assessing those projects of the EU's TEMPUS programme which already include US partner universities and exploring possibilities of wider participation of US universities in TEMPUS projects;

– encourage the study of each other's systems of government as well as the histories, cultures and languages of our communities;

– encourage voluntary co-operation and dissemination of information for the mutual recognition of university studies and degrees within the EU Member States and the US;

– examine ways to increase private support for educational exchanges, including scholarships and intern programmes;

– exchange information and co-operate on innovations related to vocational training and intend to convene a conference on vocational training in Spring 1996;

– examine ways new technologies might be employed to link education and training establishments, including schools in the EU with those in the US;

– encourage "sister cities" to promote exchanges.

4. Information and Culture

We will study ways and means of:

– encouraging artistic and cultural co-operation projects, such as exchanges in the field of the visual arts, theatre, ballet, orchestras and musical groups, the co-production of films and TV programmes;

– spreading knowledge of and encouraging literary creativity, including exploring with the private sector the sponsorship of an EU-US prize for literature;

– spreading knowledge of cultural and artistic heritage programmes.

We will use our sites on the INTERNET to provide quick and easy access to the New Transatlantic Agenda, the Joint EU-US Action Plan, information on EU and US studies, descriptions of pertinent library holdings as well as other material relevant to the EU-US relationship.

We will consult and co-operate on the preparation of a medium term communications strategy which will aim to increase public awareness on both sides of the Atlantic of the EU-US dimension.

SELECT BIBLIOGRAPHY

Appleby, John & **Foster,** Edward: *Up in the air. European Union and the transatlantic defence industrial co-operation*, Royal United Services Institute for Defense Studies, London 1993.

Benjamin, Roger, **New,** Richard and **Quigley,** Denise: *Balancing State Intervention: The limits of Transatlantic Markets*, Saint Martin's Press, New York 1995.

Behrens, Peter: *Merger Control: conflicts between the EEC and USA*, in: Kantzenbach, Erhard (ed): *Competition Policy in an interdependent world economy*, Nomos, Baden-Baden 1993, S. 165-184

Bourgeois, Jacques: *Trade Laws of the EC and the US in a Comparative Perspective*, Story-Scientia, Brussels 1992.

Brenner, Michael: *Multilateralism and Western Strategy*, Saint Martin's Press, New York 1995.

Calingaert, Michael: *European Integration Revisited: Progress, Prospects and US Interests*, Westview, Boulder 1996.

Chernoff, Fred: *After Bipolarity: The Vanishing Threat. Theories of Cooperation and the future of the Atlantic Alliance*, University of Michigan Press, Ann Arbor (MI) 1994.

Coffey, Peter: *The European Community and the United States*, Saint Martin's Press, New York 1993.

Cooney, Stephen: *American Industries and the New European Union, National Association of Manufacturers*, Washington 1994.

Duesterberg, Thomas: *Prospects for an EU-NAFTA free trade agreement*, in: The Washington Quarterly 2 (1995), pp. 71–82.

Duignan, Peter and **Gann,** L.H: *The United States and the New Europe*, Blackwell North America, Blackwood (NJ) 1994.

Featherstone, Kevin and **Ginsberg,** Roy Howard: *The United States and The European Union in the 1990's*. Partners in transition, 2nd ed., Macmillan Press, Basingstoke 1994.

Fischer, Thomas: *The Europeanization of America: What Americans need to know about the European Union*, Carolina Academic Press, Durham (NC) 1996.

Frellesen, Thomas and **Ginsberg,** Roy Howard: *EU-US foreign policy* *cooperation in the 1990s: Elements of partnership*, CEPS Paper, Nr. 58, Brussels 1994.

Fröhlich, Stefan: *Möglichkeiten europäisch-amerikanischer Kooperation. Der Aktionsplan zur "transatlantischen Agenda"*, Konrad-Adenauer-Stiftung, Sankt Augustin 1997.

Frost, Ellen L.: *Umgang mit "Schurkenstaaten". US-Sanktionen und die transatlantischen Beziehungen*, in: Internationale Politik, 4 (1997), pp. 1–6.

Gantz, Nanette and **Roper,** John (eds.): *Towards a New Partnership: US-European Relations in the Post Cold War Era*, Institute for Security Studies of the WEU, Paris 1993.

Gebhard, Paul: *The United States and European Security*, Brassey's UK, London 1994.

Gordon, Philip: *Recasting the Atlantic Alliance*, in: Survival 38/1 (1996), pp. 32–57.

Goure, Dan: *From Shadow to Substance: An action plan for Transatlantic Defense Cooperation*, Centre for Strategic and International Studies, Washington (DC) 1995.

Haglund, David (ed.): *From euphoria to hysteria: Western European Security After the Cold War*, Westview Press, Boulder (CO) 1993.

Harris, Scott and **Steinberg,** James: *European Defense and the Future of Transalantic Cooperation*, The Rand Corporation, Santa Monica (CA) 1993.

Hart, Jeffrey: *Rival Capitalists: International Competitiveness in the United States, Japan and Western Europe*, Cornell Universitary Press, Ithaca (NY) 1993.

Hayward, David: *International Trade and Regional Economies: The impact of European Integration on the United States*, Westview Press, Boulder (CO) 1995.

Heuser, Beatrice: *Transatlantic Relations, Sharing ideals and costs*, Pinter (Chatham House Papers), London 1996.

Holbrooke, Richard: *America, a European power*, in: Foreign Affairs, Vol. 74, No. 2, pp. 38–50.

Jackson, Tim: *The next Battleground: Japan, America and the New European Market*, Houghton Miffin Company, Boston (MA) 1993.

Kahler, Miles: *Regional futures and transatlantic economic relations*, Council on Foreign Relations, New York 1995.

Kahler, Miles and **Link,** Werner: *Europa und Amerika nach der Zeitenwende-die Wiederkehr der Geschichte*, Verlag Bertelsmann Stiftung, Gütersloh 1995.

Krenzler, Horst G. and **Schomaker,** Astrid: *A New Transatlantic Agenda*, in: European Foreign Affairs Review, No. 1 (1996), pp. 9–28.

Lundestad, Geir: *"Empire" by Integration. The United States and European Integration, 1945-1997*, Oxford University Press, Oxford 1998.

Mason, David: *Japan, Nafta and the European Community: Trilateral Cooperation or Confrontation?*, Macmillan Press, Basingstoke 1994.

Mey, Holger H.: *A European security and defence identity. What role for the United States?*, in: Comparative Strategy 3 (1995), pp. 311–316.

Nau, Henry: *Europe and America in the 1990s. No time to mothball Atlantic partnership* in: Story, Jonathan (ed.), The new Europe, Blackwell, Oxford 1993.

Nelson, Mark: *Bridging the Atlantic. Domestic Politics and Euro-American Relations*, Centre for European Policy Reform, London 1997.

Nelson, Mark: *Transatlantic travails*, in: Foreign Policy 92 (1993), pp. 75–91

Nomikos, John M.: *The future of the EU-US security relationship*, in: Peace and the Sciences, Vol. 26 (1995), pp. 20–26.

Peterson, John: *Europe and America in the Clinton era*, in: Journal of Common Market Studies 3 (1994), pp. 411–426.

Peterson, John: *Europe and America, The Prospects for Partnership*, Routledge, London 1996.

Pirzio-Biroli, Corrado: *A parting shot on the US-EC relationship*, in: International Economic Insights 1 (1993), pp. 20–23.

Powaski, Ronald: T*he Entangling Alliance: The United States and European Security*, Greenwood Publishing Group, Westport (CT) 1994.

Reinicke, Wolfgang H.: *Deepening the Atlantic-Towards a New Transatlantic Marketplace?*, Verlag Bertelsmann Stiftung, Gütersloh 1995.

Rummel, Reinhardt: *New venues in transatlantic relations*, in: Barry, Charles L. (Ed.): Reforging the transatlantic relationship, Washington DC 1996, pp. 135–152.

Scherpenberg, Jens van: *Transatlantic competition and European defence industries: a new look at the trade-defence link*, in: International Affairs 1 (1997), pp. 99–122.

Siebert, Horst, **Langhammer,** Rolf J., and **Piazolo,** Daniel: *The Transatlantic Free Trade Area. Fuelling trade discrimination or global liberalization?*, in: Journal of World Trade, No. 3 (1996), pp. 37–61.

Smith, Michael: *Clinton and the EC: How much of a new agenda?*, in: The World Today 4 (1993), pp. 70–73.

Smith, Mike and **Hocking,** Brian: *Beyond Forein Economic Policy: United States and the Single European Market*, Pinter, London 1995.

Smith, Michael and **Woolcock,** Stephen: *Learning to cooperate: the Clinton administration and the European Union*, in: International Affairs 3 (1994), pp. 459–476.

Smith, Michael and **Woolcock,** Stephen: *Political Dimensions of the EC-US Relationship*, Pinter, London 1993.

Smith, Michael and **Woolcock,** Stephen: *Redefining the US-EC Relationship*, Council on Foreign Relations, New York 1993.

Smith, Peter: *The Challenge of Integration: Europe and the Americas*, Transaction Publishers, New Brunswick (NJ) 1993.

Steinberg, James: *"An Ever Closer Union": European Integration and its Implications for the Future of US-European Relations*, The Rand Corporation, Santa Monica (CA) 1993.

Steinberg, James and **Harris,** Scott: *European Defense and the Future of Transatlantic Cooperation*, The Rand Corporation, Santa Monica (CA) 1993.

Thiel, Elke: *Die EU und die NAFTA. Egionale Integration und transatlantische Beziehungen*, in: Aussenpolitik, No. 1 (1997), pp. 55–67.

Waldenberger, Franz: *The Political Economy of Trade Conflicts: The Management of Trade Relations in the US-EU-Japan Triad*, Springer-Verlag, New York 1994.

Wallace, William: *Toward transatlantic partnership. A European strategy*, Transatlantic Policy Network, Brussels 1994.

Wallace, William: *European-Atlantic security institutions: Current state and future prospects*, in: The International Spectator 3 (1994), pp. 37–51.

Weidenfeld, Werner: *America and Europe: Is the Break Inevitable?*, Bertelsmann Foundation Publishers, Gütersloh 1996.

Williams, Phil, **Hammond,** Paul and **Brenner,** Michael: *Atlantis lost, paradise regained? The United States and Europe after the Cold War*, in: International Affairs 1 (1993), pp. 1–17.

Woolcock, Stephen: *EU-US Commercial Relations and the Debate on a Transatlantic Free Trade Area*, in: Wiener, J. (Ed.): The Transatlantic Relationship, Macmillan, London 1996, pp. 164–184.

INDEX

Wayne - erudite, forthright

Kranzler - mainly platitudes

Rees - excellent, fluent overview (despite 'the US believes', 'the Americans want' - too little
    appreciation of distinction between Bush & Clinton admins

Hannay - sharp, incisive, perceptive

Haass - short, undigested & simplistic ' ?

Moyar - excellent, clear but short   7 pp.

Cullen - long, over-detailed?   29 pp.   nearly ½ books on JHA Agenda

den Boer - good, interesting - not much on US-EU rels. (repeat helps, p.7)

Haillbroner - interesting + thorough, but very long (½ page) recitals of official EU documents
    tend to glaze the eyes of the non-specialist

Legomsky - short, interesting, descriptive - not much comparison